Media Law and
Human Rights

Media Law and Human Rights

Andrew Nicol QC
Gavin Millar QC
Andrew Sharland

Series Editor: John Wadham

BLACKSTONE
PRESS LIMITED

Published by
Blackstone Press Limited
Aldine Place
London
W12 8AA
United Kingdom

Sales enquiries and orders
Telephone +44-(0)-20-8740-2277
Facsimile +44-(0)-20-8743-2292
e-mail: sales@blackstone.demon.co.uk
website: www.blackstonepress.com

ISBN 1-84174-134-5
© Andrew Nicol, Gavin Millar, Andrew Sharland 2001
First published 2001

The moral rights of the authors have been asserted

British Library Cataloguing in Publication Data
A catalogue record for this book is available from the British Library

Typeset in 10/12pt Times by Montage Studios Limited, Tonbridge, Kent
Printed and bound in Great Britain by Antony Rowe Limited,
Chippenham and Reading

Contents

Acknowledgements

We are very grateful to the many people who helped bring this book to a conclusion. John Wadham at Liberty launched the concept of a *Human Rights* series to coincide with the commencement of the Human Rights Act. Alistair MacQueen at Blackstone's embraced the idea. He and David Stott gently but firmly prodded and encouraged us to complete our contribution with the minimum of slippage on timing. Our delay has at least meant that we have been able to include some significant early decisions by the UK courts on the Act and the Convention. We benefited from the help, advice and suggestions of Rabinder Singh, Murray Hunt, Helen Mountfield, Clive Lewis, Tim Kerr, Michael Beloff QC, Professor Ian Loveland and Alison Steadman. Of course, any errors that remain are ours. We are grateful to Martin Chamberlain for allowing us to use part of a chapter that he and Andrew Sharland wrote on freedom of expression in *A Practitioner's Guide to the Impact of the Human Rights Act 1998*, edited by Rabinder Singh and Murray Hunt (Oxford, Hart Publishing, 2001). We have tried to state the law as at 1 February 2001.

Abbreviations

App. No.	Application Number
BHRC	Butterworths Human Rights Cases
CPR	Civil Procedure Rules
DR	Decisions and Reports (European Commission of Human Rights)
ECHR	European Convention for the Protection of Human Rights and Fundamental Freedoms 1950
EHRLR	European Human Rights Law Review
EHRR	European Human Rights Reports
EHRR CD	European Human Rights Reports (Commission Decisions)
HRA	Human Rights Act 1998
PD	Practice Direction
PPERA	Political Parties, Elections and Referendums Act 2000
RPA	Representation of the People Act 1983
UKHRR	United Kingdom Human Rights Reports

Unless the context shows otherwise, 'the Court' is the European Court and 'the Commission' is the European Commission of Human Rights.

Table of Cases

Table of Primary Legislation

Table of Secondary Legislation

Table of International Instruments

Table of International Rules

Chapter One

Freedom of Expression and Privacy: An Introduction

1.1 INTRODUCTION

This book is aimed at practitioners in the media law field, but it is hoped that it will be of interest to students of media law and of human rights law. It is not intended to be a definitive text on media law; for this see Geoffrey Robertson QC and Andrew Nicol QC, *Media Law*.[1] Neither is it intended to be a comparative academic work; if this is what is required, see Professor Barendt's work entitled *Freedom of Speech*.[2]

The main focus of this book is the jurisprudence of the European Court of Human Rights ('the European Court') and the European Commission of Human Rights ('the Commission'). We hope to give a comprehensive analysis of all relevant case law in the media law field. However, we also intend to draw on jurisprudence from other jurisdictions, particularly the USA and Canada. The US jurisprudence necessarily does not provide all the answers to questions concerning media law, freedom of expression and privacy, but it is by far the most developed in this field and consistently grapples with human rights issues. Additionally, prior to the incorporation of the European Convention on Human Rights (ECHR), English courts have been willing to draw on US case law in the field of freedom of expression (see e.g., *Derbyshire County Council v Times Newspapers Ltd* [1993] AC 534 (HL)) although not the right to respect for privacy. This willingness is likely to increase now that the Human Rights Act 1998 is in force.

---

[1] (4th edn, forthcoming).

[2] (Oxford, OUP, 1992) which examines the protection of freedom of speech in England, Germany, the USA and under the European Convention.

Canadian jurisprudence is useful because, unlike the US First Amendment,[3] the right to freedom of expression contained in Section 2(b) of the Canadian Charter of Rights, guaranteeing everyone the 'fundamental freedom' of 'freedom of thought, belief, opinion and expression, including freedom of the press and other media of communication', is subject to express limitations contained in Section 1 of the Charter which provides that limitations on freedom of expression are permissible if they are 'such reasonable limits prescribed by law as can be demonstrably justified in a free and democratic society'. This approach mirrors that of Article 10 ECHR.

This chapter briefly examines the philosophical justifications underpinning the right to freedom of expression and the right to privacy. While this might seem out of place in a work aimed at practitioners, it is both useful and necessary to understand how the jurisprudence in the media law field has developed in the past and how it is likely to develop in the future. This discussion is followed by a brief outline of English law's treatment of the right to freedom of expression and the right to privacy prior to incorporation of the ECHR.

1.2   FREEDOM OF EXPRESSION THEORY[4]

1.2.1   Mill's argument from truth

The argument from truth is the predominant and most durable of the underlying rationales for the protection of speech. Today it is most commonly associated with John Stuart Mill, who in his book *On Liberty* argued that suppression of opinion was wrong, because it is only by the 'collision of adverse opinions' that truth is discovered or confirmed. This argument had been advanced two centuries earlier by Milton.[5] The rationale was taken up by Justice Holmes in *Abrams* v *US* 250 US 616, 630–1 (1919) who asserted that all truths were relative and that they can only be judged 'in the competition of the market'. Holmes concluded that '[t]he best test of truth is the power of the thought to get itself accepted in the competition of the market' (at 630). This argument for the protection of freedom of expression posits that freedom of expression is not an end in itself but a means of identifying and accepting truth. The argument involves a scepticism both of the state and of accepted beliefs and 'acknowledged truths'. This truth or 'marketplace of ideas' rationale for freedom of expression extends not only to political speech, but also to the ideas of philosophy, history, the social sciences, the natural sciences, other

---

[3] The First Amendment to the Constitution provides: 'Congress shall make no law ... abridging the freedom of speech or of the press.'

[4] For a more learned (and lengthy) discussion of the philosophical underpinnings of the right to freedom of expression, see Schauer, F., *Free Speech: A Philosophical Enquiry* (Cambridge, CUP, 1982).

[5] See Milton, J., 'Areopagitica: A Speech for the Liberty of Unlicenced Printing (1644)' in *Prose Writings* (London, Everyman edn, 1958).

branches of human knowledge and commercial speech. However, it is of little or no application to obscene speech or personal abuse which often contains no factual assertions.

1.2.2　Democratic self-governance[6]

This argument is associated, particularly in the United states, with Alexander Meiklejohn. His view was that the main purpose of protecting freedom of expression was to protect the rights of citizens to understand matters of political concern so as to enable them to participate meaningfully in the democratic process. Meiklejohn stated that:

> The principle of the freedom of speech springs from the necessities of the program of self-government. It is not a Law of Nature or Reason in the abstract. It is a deduction from the basic American agreement that public issues shall be decided by universal suffrage.[7]

This rationale explains the importance placed on political speech by, amongst others, the European Court. However, the disadvantage with the rationale, and the reason why, by itself, it is insufficient to justify the extensive protection of freedom of expression, is that it potentially excludes large areas of expression that are traditionally considered important, such as artistic and literary expression.

1.2.3　Self-fulfilment

While Mill's argument from truth and Meiklejohn's argument from self-governance justify the protection of freedom of expression as a means to an end, freedom of expression can also be an end itself. Under this theory, freedom of expression is protected not just to create a better government and not merely to discover the truth, but to 'enlarge the prospects for individual self-fulfilment' or to allow 'personal growth and self-realisation'. In the words of Justice Thurgood Marshall of the US Supreme Court in *Procunier* v *Martinez* 416 US 396, 427 (1974): '[Freedom of expression] serves not only the needs of the polity but also those of the human spirit — a spirit that demands self-expression.' His rationale is of broadest application, embracing the protection of expression such as obscenity which would not receive protection under either of the two other rationales.

---

[6] See Laws, Sir J., 'Meiklejohn, the First Amendment and Free Speech in English Law' in *Importing the First Amendment, Freedom of Speech and Expression in Britain, Europe and the USA*, Professor I. Loveland ed. (Oxford, Hart Publishing, 1998) for a recent critique of Meiklejohn's theory.

[7] Meiklejohn, A., *Political Freedom: The Constitutional Powers of the People* (Oxford, OUP, 1965) at 27.

1.2.4   The relevance of the rationales for protecting freedom of expression

All three rationales for protecting freedom of expression have been recognised in US and Canadian law (see, e.g., *Irwin Toy* v *Quebec* [1989] 1 SCR 927, at 968–71) and most recently by the House of Lords in *R* v *Secretary of State for the Home Department, ex parte Simms* [2000] AC 115 at 126, where Lord Steyn stated:

> Freedom of expression is, of course, intrinsically important: it is valued for its own sake. But it is well recognised that it is also instrumentally important. It serves a number of broad objectives. First, it promotes the self-fulfilment of individuals in society. Secondly, in the famous words of Holmes J (echoing John Stuart Mill) 'the best test of truth is the power of the thought to get itself accepted in the competition of the market': *Abrams* v *US* (1919) 250 US 616 at p. 630 per Holmes J dissent. Thirdly, freedom of speech is the lifeblood of democracy. The free flow of information and ideas informs political debate. It is a safety valve: people are more ready to accept decisions that go against them if they can in principle seek to influence them. It acts as a brake on the abuse of power by public officials. It facilitates the exposure of errors in the governance and administration of justice of the country: see Stone, Sediman, Sunstein and Tushnett *Constitutional Law* (3rd edn 1996) pp. 1078–86 ...

The European Court has also made reference to the underlying rationales for protecting the right to freedom of expression. In one of the first major judgments on Article 10, the Court stated:

> Freedom of expression constitutes one of the essential foundations of a society, one of the basic conditions for its progress and for the development of every man. Subject to paragraph 2 of Article 10, it is applicable not only to 'information and ideas' that are favourably received or regarded as inoffensive but also to those that offend, shock or disturb the state or any sector of the population. Such are the demands of pluralism, tolerance and broad mindedness without which there is no 'democratic society'.
> (*Handyside* v *UK* (1976) 1 EHRR 737, para. 49)

This quotation encapsulates two of the three main theoretical rationales for the protection of expression: (i) freedom of expression enables citizens to participate effectively in a democracy; and (ii) freedom of expression is an integral aspect of each citizen's right to self-development and fulfilment.[8] The third rationale — namely Mill's argument from truth, which is closely linked to the utilitarian tradition in moral philosophy — has been less influential in the jurisprudence of the European Court than in the US and Canadian Supreme Courts.

---

[8] See, for example, Scanlon, T., 'Freedom of Expression and Categories of Expression' (1979) 40 *U Pittsburgh Law Review* 519.

1.3 PRIVACY THEORY

1.3.1 The right to be left alone: Warren and Brandeis[9]

In arguably one of the most influential academic legal articles ever written, Warren and Brandeis famously discovered the 'right to privacy' implicit in the (predominantly English) common law. The authors drew on case law in the field of defamation, breach of confidence, copyright and trespass to conclude that these cases were merely instances and applications of a general 'right of privacy'. They stated:

> The intensity and complexity of life, attendant upon advancing civilization, having rendered necessary some retreat from the world, and man, under the refining influence of culture, has become more sensitive to publicity, so that solitude and privacy have become more essential to the individual; but modern enterprise and invention have, through invasions upon his privacy, subjected him to mental pain and distress, far greater than could be inflicted by merely bodily injury.[10]

This article had a profound influence on the development of US law[11] with nearly every American state recognising a 'right to privacy'. However, even though the authors relied almost exclusively on English cases, most notably the defamation decision in *Prince Albert* v *Strange* (1849) 2 De G & Sm 652, 64 ER 293; (1849) 1 Mac & G 25, 41 ER 1171, no such development occurred in the more judicially conservative English courts.

1.3.2 Prosser: the four privacy torts[12]

William Prosser classified the tort (or more accurately torts) of breach of privacy in US law as follows:

(a)   intrusion on seclusion, solitude or private affairs;
(b)   publication of embarrassing private (but true) facts;
(c)   publicity which portrays a person in a false light;
(d)   appropriation of a person's name or likeness (now often known as the right of publicity).[13]

Prosser's article, like Warren and Brandeis's, had a profound impact on American law. These four privacy torts have been recognised in most states, although the

---

[9] Warren, S.D. and Brandeis, L.D., 'The Right to Privacy' (1890) 4 Harv L Rev 193, reprinted in Wacks, R., *Privacy and the Law*, vol. II (International Library of Essays in Law and Legal Theory) (London, Dartmouth, 1993; New York, New York University Press, 1993).

[10] Ibid., at 196.

[11] See discussion in Wacks, R., *Privacy and Press Freedom* (London, Blackstone Press, 1995), chap. 1, at 11–12.

[12] Prosser, W., 'Privacy' (1960) 48 Calif L Rev 383, reprinted in Wacks, *op. cit.* n. 9, at 47.

[13] Ibid., at 389.

extent of protection varies from state to state with New York and California leading the way in protecting privacy rights. The second and third privacy torts have given rise to difficulties under the First Amendment — see *Time Inc.* v *Hill* 385 US 374 (1967) (false light privacy) and *Florida Star* v *B.J.F.* 491 US 524 (1989) (disclosure of identity of rape victim) — because they limit the right of the press to publish truthful information. The fourth tort is more concerned with protecting the valuable commercial interests of an individual's name and image rather than the 'right of privacy' as it is commonly understood.

1.4 ENGLISH LAW'S APPROACH TO FREEDOM OF EXPRESSION IN RELATION TO MEDIA LAW PRIOR TO THE INCORPORATION OF THE ECHR

1.4.1 Historical perspective

The absence of any constitutional or statutory provision protecting freedom of expression means that the right to freedom of expression has been largely residual. *Blackstone's Commentaries* do not mention the right to freedom of speech, although there is some discussion of freedom of the press. Dicey wrote that: 'Freedom of discussion is ... in England little else than the right to write or say anything which a jury, consisting of twelve shopkeepers, think it expedient should be said or written.'[14] Thus unpopular or unorthodox expression went unprotected. The suppression of expression critical of the government was viewed as necessary to maintain the reputation of government. Lord Holt, in *R* v *Tuchin* (1704) Holt 424, reasoned:

> If men should not be called to account for possessing the people with an ill opinion of the government, no government can subsist; for it is very necessary for every government, that the people should have a good opinion of it. And nothing can be worse to any government, than to endeavour to produce animosities as to the management of it. This has always been looked upon as a crime, and no government can be safe unless it be punished.

One of the main tools utilised to suppress expression critical of the King or his agents was seditious libel. Truth was not a defence on the grounds that 'the greater the truth, the greater the libel' against the government. Neither was it necessary to prove intent to incite insurrection, because merely intending to publish criticism was unlawful as it found 'fault with his masters and betters'.[15]

---

[14] Dicey, A.V., *Introduction to the Study of the Law of the Constitution* (London, Macmillan, 1959), chap. VI. Such a view is diametrically opposed to the jurisprudence of the European Court, which has repeatedly emphasised the importance of protection of unpopular minority speech.

[15] See Chafee, Z., *Free Speech in the United States* (Cambridge, Mass., Harvard University Press, 1941) at 19.

The second method used to control expression was the elaborate system of licensing, which English writers had to contend with until it was abolished in 1695. All writing had to be licensed prior to publication, otherwise the publication was unlawful. The abolition of the licensing system led to the development of a concept of freedom of the press that prohibited the existence of prior restraints. In 1765, Blackstone wrote that:

> The liberty of the press is indeed essential to the nature of a free state; but this consists in laying no *previous* restraints on publications, and not in freedom from censure for criminal matter when published. Every free man has an undoubted right to lay what sentiments he pleases before the public; to forbid this is to destroy the freedom of the press; but if he publishes what is improper, mischievous or illegal, he must take the consequences of his own temerity.[16]

English courts, while wary of prior restraints, have not adopted the near absolute bar on prior restraints that the US Supreme Court jurisprudence has developed.[17]

1.4.2 Recent developments

More recently, the English judiciary, subject to certain notable exceptions,[18] has consistently failed to give sufficient regard to the right to freedom of expression. Lord Goff, in *Attorney-General* v *Guardian Newspapers Ltd (No. 2)* [1990] 1 AC 109, at 283–4,[19] expressed the opinion that there was no difference in principle between English law on freedom of expression and Article 10 of the Convention (a view reiterated by Lord Keith in *Derbyshire County Council* v *Times Newspapers Ltd* [1993] AC 534). The number of cases in which English law has been held to contravene Article 10 suggests that the protection of freedom of expression afforded by English law is generally less full than that afforded by Article 10. Due in large part to the absence, until now, of a binding code of rights, English law has lacked the developed principles of US and Canadian law. Now

---

[16] Blackstone, W., *Commentaries on the Laws of England*, Book IV, at 151–2 (1765).

[17] Contrast *Near* v *Minnesota* 283 US 697 (1931) and *New York Times* v *US* 403 US 713 (1971) (the *Pentagon Papers* case) with *Attorney-General* v *Times Newspapers Ltd* [1974] AC 273 (concerning an injunction preventing the publication of an article on the dangers of Thalidomide, which was later held, by the European Court of Human Rights, to be a violation of Article 10 ECHR in *Sunday Times* v *United Kingdom* (1979) 2 EHRR 245).

[18] One notable exception is Lord Denning's dissenting judgment in *Schering Chemicals Ltd* v *Falkman* [1982] QB 1. Examples of cases where English courts have failed to give sufficient regard to the right to freedom of expression include *X Ltd* v *Morgan-Grampian (Publishing) Ltd* [1991] 1 AC 1. *Reynolds* v *Times Newspapers* [1999] 3 WLR 1010 has been seen as similarly deficient by the New Zealand Court of Appeal: see 5.6.2 below.

[19] This case concerned publication of extracts from *Spycatcher* by Peter Wright. *Observer and Guardian* v *UK* (1991) 14 EHRR 153, held that the UK was in breach of Article 10 because the injunction restraining the publication of such extracts was not necessary in a democratic society after *Spycatcher* had been published in the USA and was therefore no longer secret.

that the Human Rights Act (HRA) 1998 is in force, the judiciary will have the opportunity, and indeed the obligation, to begin setting out these general principles. The process has already commenced: see, for example, Lord Steyn's speech in *R* v *Secretary of State for the Home Department, ex parte Simms* [2000] AC 115, a case concerning the right of prisoners to communicate with journalists (see 1.2.4 above).

Sedley LJ, in *Redmond-Bate* v *DPP* (1999) 7 BHRC 375, echoing the sentiments of the European Court in *Handyside* v *United Kingdom* (1976) 1 EHRR 737, emphasised the importance of protecting unpopular or offensive speech. Ms Redmond-Bate and her colleagues were Christian fundamentalist preachers who were arrested for breach of the peace after refusing to comply with a police officer's instruction to stop preaching on the steps of Wakefield Cathedral. They were subsequently convicted of obstructing a police officer in the execution of his duty. Sedley LJ, allowing the appeal against conviction, stated:

> Free speech includes not only the inoffensive but the irritating, the contentious, the eccentric, the heretical, the unwelcome and the provocative provided it does not tend to provoke violence. Freedom only to speak inoffensively is not worth having. What Speakers' Corner (where the law applies as fully as anywhere else) demonstrates is the tolerance which is both extended by the law to opinion of every kind and expected by the law in the conduct of those who disagree, even strongly, with what they hear. From the condemnation of Socrates to the persecution of modern writers and journalists, our world has seen too many examples of state control of unofficial ideas. A central purpose of the European Convention on Human Rights has been to set close limits to any such assumed power . . .

These recent judicial pronouncements appear to indicate that some members of the English judiciary, at least, are likely to take a robust approach towards the protection of freedom of expression now that the 1998 Act is in force.

1.5 ENGLISH LAW'S APPROACH TO THE RIGHT TO PRIVACY IN RELATION TO MEDIA LAW PRIOR TO THE INCORPORATION OF THE ECHR

Historically, English law has not recognised a positive 'right to privacy', although the courts have developed the common law, in a number of areas, to protect what today would be described as privacy rights.[20] More recently, the existence of a right to privacy has been the subject of judicial comment. In the notorious case of *Kaye* v *Robertson* [1991] FSR 62, the star of a television series suffered serious head injuries in a car crash. While he was lying in his hospital bed, semi-conscious, a reporter and photographer from the *Sunday Sport* newspaper entered

---

[20] See Warren and Brandeis, *op. cit.* n. 9 and *Prince Albert* v *Strange* at 1.3.1.

his hospital room uninvited and took photographs of him. The Court of Appeal concluded that the newspaper could publish the pictures, provided they did not say that the actor had agreed to be photographed or interviewed. Glidewell LJ stated (at 66):

> It is well-known that in English law there is no right to privacy, and accordingly there is no right of action for breach of a person's privacy. The facts of the present case are a graphic illustration of the desirability of Parliament considering whether and in what circumstances statutory provision can be made to protect the privacy of individuals.

Legatt LJ said (at 71) that the right to privacy 'has so long been disregarded here that it can be recognised only by the legislature'. However, this conservative attitude is by no means accepted by all the judiciary. Laws J (as he then was) stated in *Hellewell* v *Chief Constable of Derbyshire* [1995] 1 WLR 804, at 807H:

> If someone with a telephoto lens were to take from a distance and with no authority a picture of another engaged in some private act, his subsequent disclosure of the photograph would, in my judgement, as surely amount to a breach of confidence as if he had found or stolen a diary in which the act was recounted and proceeded to publish it. In such a case, the law would protect what might reasonably be called a *right of privacy*, although the name accorded to the cause of action would be breach of confidence. (emphasis added)

Laws J's approach reflects the ideas of Warren and Brandeis and Prosser. More recently, Lord Nicholls of Birkenhead, in *R* v *Khan* [1997] AC 558, at 582H–583A (a case concerning the use of covertly gathered evidence) stated: 'I prefer to leave open for another occasion the important question whether the present, piecemeal protection of privacy has now developed to the extent that a more comprehensive principle can be seen to exist.' As we describe in Chapter 6, even in the first few months since the HRA's commencement, Article 8 has stimulated further consideration of the place of privacy law in English law (see 6.7 below).

Chapter Two

Freedom of Expression and the Right to Respect for Private Life and Media Law: General Principles[1]

2.1 INTRODUCTION

This chapter examines the general principles of the ECHR as they are relevant to media law. The main focus of this chapter is Article 10 ECHR, which concerns the right to freedom of expression, but it also briefly discusses Articles 6(1) concerning reporting of judicial proceedings, Article 8 ECHR and the right to respect for privacy, Article 14's prohibition on discrimination in relation to other Convention rights, Article 15's restrictions in the time of war and Article 17 concerning restrictions on activities subversive of Convention rights. First, we outline some general principles applicable to the interpretation of the Convention.

2.2 PRINCIPLES OF INTERPRETATION OF THE ECHR[2]

The ECHR is an international treaty, and therefore it is interpreted in accordance with public international law principles of which the main source is the Vienna Convention on the Law of Treaties 1969. Although the Vienna Convention is not retrospective and therefore does not expressly apply to the 1950 European Convention on Human Rights and Freedoms, it is generally understood to encapsulate the prior principles of public international law on the interpretation of

---

[1] The section of this chapter concerned with Article 10 is based on Sharland, A. and Chamberlain, M., 'Freedom of Expression and Peaceful Assembly' in *A Practitioner's Guide to the Impact of the Human Rights Act 1998*, Singh, R. and Hunt, M. (eds) (Oxford, Hart Publishing, 2001), chap. 17.
[2] See Starmer, K., *European Human Rights Law* (London, Legal Action Group, 1999), chap. 4.

treaties (see *Fothergill* v *Monarch Airlines Ltd* [1981] AC 251, at 282C–D, *per* Lord Diplock). The principles of interpretation developed by the European Court represent a significant departure from common law canons of construction.

2.2.1 The teleological approach

The basic principle of interpretation applied by the European Court is one grounded in a 'teleological approach' which reflects the Vienna Convention. Article 31(1) of the Vienna Convention provides that:

> A treaty shall be interpreted in good faith in accordance with the ordinary meaning to be given to the terms of the treaty in their context and in light of its objects and purpose.[3]

The objects and purpose of the ECHR have been described as 'the protection of human rights' (see *Soering* v *UK* (1989) 11 EHRR 439), and the maintenance and promotion of 'the ideals and values of a democratic society' (see *Kjeldsen, Busk Madsen and Pedersen* v *Denmark* (1976) 1 EHRR 711, at para. 53). The teleological principle permits the meaning of the Convention rights to adapt and change according to the evolving social norms of the member states. The European Court has noted that the Convention is: 'A living instrument which . . . must be interpreted in the light of present day conditions.' (See *Tyrer* v *United Kingdom* (1978) 2 EHRR 1, para. 16.)

This dynamic approach to interpretation means that the older a decision of the Court or Commission, the greater the care that is needed to consider whether changing conditions have undermined its basis. Although there is no formal doctrine of precedent under the Convention, consistency of approach is recognised as desirable in the interests of legal certainty.

2.2.2 The principle of effectiveness

The Court in *Artico* v *Italy* (1980) 3 EHRR 1, at para. 33, asserted that '. . . the Convention is intended to guarantee not rights that are theoretical or illusory but rights that are practical and effective'. So any conditions imposed on the exercise of rights must not 'impair their very essence and deprive them of effectiveness' (*Mathieu-Mohin* v *Belgium* (1987) 10 EHRR 1, at para. 52). Thus the Court must focus on the realities of the situation. This principle of effectiveness has led the European Court to impose positive obligations on states in certain circumstances (see 2.3.2.7 below).

---

[3] The European Court indicated that it will apply the Vienna Convention: see *Golder* v *UK* (1975) 1 EHRR 524, at 532.

2.2.3   Recourse to other human rights instruments

The European Court is increasingly examining other human rights instruments, emanating from both the Council of Europe and other international organisations, to assist in the interpretation of the ECHR. In the media law context, the European Court took into account the Council of Europe's Convention on Transfrontier Television when assessing whether Switzerland's refusal to grant a company a licence to receive and retransmit programmes from a satellite was 'necessary in a democratic society' (see *Autronic AG* v *Switzerland* (1990) 12 EHRR 485). In *Goodwin* v *UK* (1996) 22 EHRR 123 the Court drew on a resolution of the European Parliament. In *Jersild* v *Denmark* (1994) 19 EHRR 1, it examined the International Covenant on the Elimination of All Forms of Racial Discrimination when deciding the extent to which racist speech was afforded protection by Article 10 ECHR (see 7.5 below).

2.3   THE LAW OF THE ECHR: ARTICLE 10 FREEDOM OF EXPRESSION

2.3.1   Introduction

Article 10 of the ECHR provides:

> 1.   Everyone has the right to freedom of expression. This right shall include freedom to hold opinions and to receive and impart information and ideas without interference by public authority and regardless of frontiers. This Article shall not prevent states from requiring the licensing of broadcasting, television or cinema enterprises.
> 2.   The exercise of these freedoms, since it carries with it duties and responsibilities, may be subject to such formalities, conditions, restrictions or penalties as are prescribed by law and are necessary in a democratic society, in the interests of national security, territorial integrity or public safety, for the prevention of disorder or crime, for the protection of health or morals, for the protection of the reputation or rights of others, for preventing the disclosure of information received in confidence, or for maintaining the authority and impartiality of the judiciary.[4]

Article 10(1) sets out the positive freedom, while Article 10(2) sets out the limitations on that freedom. The Court has stated that, when adjudicating on Article 10 cases, the Court is faced:

---

[4] In the period up to 1996, the right to freedom of expression under Article 10 was in issue in approximately 10 per cent of the Court's judgments on the merits of cases. See *The Case-law of the European Court of Human Rights on the Freedom of Expression Guaranteed under the European Convention on Human Rights*, Lecture by Judge Rolv Ryssdal, 13 August 1996 published by the Council of Europe (96) 326.

... not with a choice between two conflicting principles, but with a principle of freedom of expression that is subject to a number of exceptions which must be narrowly interpreted ... It is not sufficient that the interference belongs to that class of the exceptions listed in Article 10(2) which has been invoked; neither is it sufficient that the interference was imposed because its subject-matter fell within a particular category or was caught by a legal rule formulated in general or absolute terms: the Court has to be satisfied that the interference was necessary having regard to the facts and circumstances prevailing in the specific case before it. (*Sunday Times* v *The United Kingdom* (1979) 2 EHRR 245, at p. 281, para. 65)

The importance of freedom of expression has constantly been emphasised. In one of the first major judgments on Article 10, the Court stated:

Freedom of expression constitutes one of the essential foundations of a society, one of the basic conditions for its progress and for the development of every man. Subject to paragraph 2 of Article 10, it is applicable not only to 'information and ideas' that are favourably received or regarded as inoffensive but also to those that offend, shock or disturb the state or any sector of the population. Such are the demands of pluralism, tolerance and broad mindedness without which there is no 'democratic society'. (*Handyside* v *UK* (1976) 1 EHRR 737, at para. 49.)

2.3.2   Article 10(1)

2.3.2.1   Who benefits from the right?
The first sentence of Article 10(1) provides that '*Everyone* has the right to freedom of expression' (emphasis added). Those able to claim the protection of the right include legal as well as natural persons (see, e.g., *Autronic AG* v *Switzerland* (1990) 12 EHRR 485 at para. 47). As far as natural persons are concerned, there is no class of person to which the prima facie right has been held not to apply.[5] Thus, members of the armed forces (e.g., *Engel and Others* v *Netherlands* (1976) 1 EHRR 647), civil servants (e.g., *Vogt* v *Germany* (1995) 21 EHRR 205 and *Ahmed* v *United Kingdom* (1998) 29 EHRR 1) and lawyers (e.g., *Casado Coca* v *Spain* (1994) 18 EHRR 1 and *Schöpfer* v *Switzerland* (App. No. 25405/94, 20 May 1998)) benefit from the protection of Article 10(1), although their status is likely to be relevant in determining whether a restriction is justified under Article 10(2).

---

[5] The only possible exception to this broad statement is 'aliens'. Article 16 provides that 'Nothing in Articles 10, 11 and 14 shall be regarded as preventing the High Contracting Parties from imposing restrictions on the activities of aliens.' See generally Harris, D.J., O'Boyle M. and Warbrick, C., *Law of the European Convention on Human Rights* (London, Butterworths, 1995) at 508–10. There is no Court jurisprudence on this issue. Article 16 is looking increasingly out of place and out of date; see Lester, A. and Pannick, D. (eds), *Human Rights Law and Practice* (London, Butterworths, 2000), 1st Supp. at p. 69.

2.3.2.2   *Which activities are covered by the right?*

The right guaranteed by Article 10 protects more than simply expression in the sense of public communications of opinion. It expressly includes, but is not limited to, the right to hold opinions and to receive information and ideas, as well as the right to impart them.

The European Court has avoided defining exactly which activities are covered by Article 10(1), though the arguments of contracting states that a particular type of activity is not expressive are usually unsuccessful. Governments have unsuccessfully contended that Article 10 was not applicable in *Glasenapp* v *Germany* (1986) 9 EHRR 25 and *Leander* v *Sweden* (1987) 9 EHRR 433. Both of these cases concerned the state's refusal to recruit the applicants to civil service posts because of their extremist political opinions (both right wing and left wing). However, although Article 10 was held to be engaged by the state's refusal to recruit individuals because of their political views, the infringement was held to be justified pursuant to Article 10(2). In *Ahmed* v *United Kingdom* (1998) 29 EHRR 1, where the applicants challenged regulations restricting the political activities of local government officers in 'politically restricted posts', it was common ground that Article 10(1) was engaged; again, however, the Court found that the infringement was justified. More recently, the United Kingdom Government unsuccessfully contended that Article 10 did not apply to non-peaceful protests where the two of the applicants physically impeded the activities of others (see *Steel and others* v *United Kingdom* (1998) 28 EHRR 603). The right to freedom of expression has been held, in certain circumstances, to include the negative right not to speak or to remain silent. (See, e.g., *K* v *Austria* (1993) Series A, No. 255–B, p. 38.)

Furthermore, in *Autronic AG* v *Switzerland* (1990) 12 EHRR 485, at para. 47, the Court said: 'Article 10 applies not only to the content of information but also to the means of transmission or reception since any restriction imposed on the means necessarily interferes with the right to receive or impart information.' In *Cable and Wireless (Dominica) Ltd* v *Marpin Telecommunications and Broadcasting Co. Ltd* (2001) 9 BHRC 486, the Privy Council drew on this authority to find that a state monopoly on the provision of telecommunications interfered with the rights of would-be competitors. As Lord Cooke said: 'Some significant hindrance to a would-be competitor's freedom is normally inherent in any requirement that he provide to his customers certain services only if permitted and on terms laid down by a monopolist.'

2.3.2.3   *The right to receive information*

Article 10 includes the right to receive as well as to impart information. This means that 'victims' who have standing to bring proceedings before the European Court, or in domestic proceedings under the HRA 1998, can potentially include newspaper readers or television viewers (see further 3.5). A good example of the

European Court recognising the right of individuals to receive information is *Open Door Counselling and Dublin Well Woman* v *Ireland* (1992) 15 EHRR 244, where the Court ruled that an injunction, imposed by Irish courts, which effectively restrained staff at the applicants' clinics from imparting information to pregnant women concerning abortion facilities outside Ireland, by way of non-directive counselling, was contrary to Article 10. The Court permitted the applicants contesting the injunction to include two women of child-bearing age (who were not pregnant) as they belonged to a class of women of child-bearing age which might be adversely affected by the injunction because it prevented them from receiving information about abortion services in the United Kingdom.

2.3.2.4 To which types of expression does Article 10 apply?

The right to freedom of expression in Article 10(1) is not limited on the basis of the content of the particular expression at issue. The Court has confirmed that it extends to opinions and ideas that are viewed as offensive by the state, or by a proportion of the state's population (see *Handyside* v *United Kingdom*, quoted at 2.3.1 above). It applies to commercial (*Barthold* v *Germany* (1985) 7 EHRR 383, at para. 42) and artistic (*Müller* v *Switzerland* (1988) 13 EHRR 212, at para. 27) speech as well as to speech the primary purpose of which is political (see 2.3.3.6 below). Expression includes words both spoken and written, the display or dissemination of pictures and images, and also certain forms of conduct (for example, a peaceful march or demonstration, the purpose of which is to communicate a political message: see, e.g., *Steel and others* v *United Kindom*, at 2.3.2.2 above). The Court has held that Article 10(1) applies even where the expression consists of light music and commercials transmitted by cable (*Groppera Radio AG and others* v *Switzerland* (1990) 12 EHRR 321). The protection of Article 10(1) also applies to expression regardless of the medium by which it is conveyed, whether by newspapers, cinema, television, radio or the Internet.

Article 10(1) is likely to extend to symbolic speech or expressive conduct such as flag burning.[6] Its protection has extended to an expulsion order which was specifically intended to restrict the freedom of expression of an individual (see *Piermont* v *France* (1995) 20 EHRR 301). The only potential limit on the type of expression covered by Article 10(1) is expression that is anti-democratic in its sentiment (see, e.g., *Purcell* v *Ireland* (App. No. 15404/89) (1991) 70 DR 262 concerning expression in support of terrorists) or hate speech (an issue which is discussed in depth in Chapter 7).

2.3.2.5 The special position of the media

The European Court has recognised that the press and other media have a special place in a democratic society as 'purveyor of information and public watchdog',

---

[6] See the concurring opinion of Judge Jambrek in *Grigoriades* v *Greece* (1997) 27 EHRR 464, where he drew on the US flag-burning cases including *Texas* v *Johnson* 491 US 397 (1989).

and thus restrictions directed against such organisations tend to be scrutinised very closely. The freedom of expression guaranteed by Article 10 includes centrally freedom of the press (see, e.g., *Observer and Guardian* v *United Kingdom* (1991) 14 EHRR 153). The media receives particularly strong protection under Article 10 because it has a duty to impart, in a manner consistent with its obligations and responsibilities, information and ideas on all matters of public interest (see, e.g., *Jersild* v *Denmark* (1994) 19 EHRR 1, at para. 31). This journalistic freedom allows a degree of exaggeration, or even provocation (see *Prager and Oberschlick* v *Austria* (1995) 21 EHRR 1, at para. 38). Article 10 has also been held to include the protection of informants who provide confidential sources to the press, since without such information the press could not perform its vital role as a 'public watchdog' (see *Goodwin* v *United Kingdom* (1996) 22 EHRR 123, discussed in Chapter 6). This protection is part of the Article 10 rights of both the press and the source. Both parties would be victims of an interference with their right to impart and receive information if disclosure was ordered.

Article 10 requires deference to the media as to the methods of objective and balanced reporting; the Court in *Jersild* v *Denmark* stated that it is not for the courts, whether domestic or European:

> ... to substitute their own views for those of the press as to what technique of reporting should be adopted by journalists. In this context the Court recalls that Article 10 protects not only the substance of the ideas and information expressed, but also the form in which they are conveyed.

2.3.2.6   *'Interference by a public authority'*

In most cases this is not an issue. Interferences with the right to freedom of expression include, in civil proceedings, a damages award (*Tolstoy Miloslavsky* v *United Kingdom* (1995) 20 EHRR 442 and *Bladet Tromso and Stensaas* v *Norway* (1999) 29 EHRR 125, para. 50), the imposition of an injunction (*Open Door Counselling and Dublin Well Woman* v *Ireland* (1992) 15 EHRR 244; *Observer and Guardian* v *United Kingdom* (1991) 14 EHRR 153), an order to disclose a source (*Goodwin* v *United Kingdom* (1996) 22 EHRR 123), and seizure or destruction of material (*Handyside* v *United Kingdom* (1976) 1 EHRR 737). In the criminal field, interferences include convictions (*Prager and Oberschlick* v *Austria* (1995) 21 EHRR 1), fines and the length of a custodial sentence. An expulsion from a country together with a ban on re-entry constitutes an interference (*Piermont* v *France* (1995) 20 EHRR 301).

An 'interference by a public authority' includes restrictions upon freedom of expression which are imposed by a private body which is exercising public law functions. For example, in *Wingrove* v *United Kingdom* (1996) 24 EHRR 1, the British Board of Film Classification refused to grant a certificate for a video, which effectively led to a ban on the distribution of that video. While the Board is a private body, it is designated under s. 4 of the Video Recordings Act 1984 as the authority responsible for the issue of certificates for videos. It was treated by the Court as a public authority.[7] In some circumstances, a state's failure to prevent or control interferences with freedom of expression by *private parties* can give rise to an interference with an applicant's right to freedom of expression by the state because its 'positive obligation' to protect freedom of expression is engaged. It is to this matter which we now turn.

2.3.2.7 *The positive obligation*

Article 10(1) ECHR does not simply prevent states from imposing restrictions on freedom of expression; it imposes a positive obligation on the state to facilitate the exercise of that right. (See, e.g., *Plattform 'Artze für das Leben'* v *Austria* (1988) 13 EHRR 204 (concerning freedom of peaceful assembly, although the reasoning is equally applicable to freedom of expression) and *Informationsverein Lentia and others* v *Austria* (1993) 17 EHRR 93 (concerning a state monopoly broadcaster): see further Chapter 11.) The extent of this positive obligation is at present unclear. The recent case of *Fuentes Bobo* v *Spain* (App. No. 39293/98, 29 February 2000) further develops the concept to ensure the protection of the right to freedom of expression. The applicant was a producer at a state television company (TVE). He was dismissed as a result of voicing offensive and insulting criticism of senior management of TVE in two radio programmes. The applicant complained to the domestic employment tribunals that his dismissal was unfair. On appeal, the Spanish courts held that the applicable employment legislation afforded no remedy. The Spanish Government argued that it could not be held responsible for the applicant's dismissal, as the relationship between the applicant and the employer was governed by private rather than public law. The Court rejected this argument because the state has a positive obligation, in certain circumstances, to protect individuals from interferences with their right to freedom of expression even by private persons. The Court concluded that domestic legislative provisions which had failed to afford a remedy should themselves be regarded as an interference with the applicant's right to freedom of expression, for which the state was responsible.

2.3.2.8 *Access to information*[8]

Article 10 ECHR includes the right to *receive* as well as to impart information. However, the European Court has not interpreted this as requiring a state to provide access to information. In *Leander* v *Sweden* (1987) 9 EHRR 433, at para. 74, the Court held, in relation to the state's refusal to reveal secret information:

---

[7] This treatment accords with the approach taken by the HRA 1998 to 'public authorities'; see 3.4.3.

[8] Other organs of the Council of Europe have encouraged states to protect the right of access to information. See Parliamentary Assembly Resolution 1087 (1996), where, in relation to access to environmental information, it was stated that 'public access to clear and full information ... must be viewed as a basic human right'.

The right to freedom to receive information basically prohibits a Government from restricting a person from receiving information that others wish or may be willing to impart to him. Article 10 does not, in circumstances such as those of the present case, confer on the individual a right of access to a register containing information on his personal position, nor does it embody an obligation on the Government to impart such information to the individual.

The same approach was adopted in *Gaskin* v *United Kingdom* (1989) 12 EHRR 36, where the applicant complained that he had been refused access to a case record relating to him created when he was a minor and held by a local authority. The Court found that there had been no violation of Article 10.[9] However, in both *Leander* and *Gaskin*, the information sought related to a specific individual and its disclosure could not be said to be in the public interest.

The European Commission has recently held that Article 10 places states not only under an obligation to make environmental information accessible to the public, but also under a positive obligation to collect, process and disseminate information which, by its very nature, is not directly accessible and which cannot be known to the public unless the authorities act accordingly. However, the European Court refused to adopt the same approach and concluded that Article 10 was not applicable in the circumstances of the case (*Guerra and others* v *Italy* (1998) 26 EHRR 357). The Court concluded that the failure to supply such information was a violation of the right to respect of family life protected by Article 8.

If, however, the state supports the dissemination of certain materials, it is not permitted to discriminate between types of publication on the basis of the publication's content. This issue was addressed in *Vereinigung Demokratischer Soldaten Österreichs and Gubi* v *Austria* (1994) 20 EHRR 56, where the Court concluded that the failure of the state to distribute *Der Igel* to Austrian soldiers while distributing other magazines for soldiers was a violation of Article 10.

2.3.2.9 *Licensing of broadcasting, television and cinema*
The third sentence of Article 10(1) provides that broadcasting, televison and cinema may be subject to a licensing system. The European Court has stated that the purpose of the third sentence is:

> To make it clear that states are permitted to regulate by a licensing system the way in which broadcasting is organised in their territories, particularly in its technical aspects ... Technical aspects are undeniably important, but the grant or refusal of a licence may also be made conditional on other considerations, including such matters as the nature and objectives of a proposed station, its potential audience at a national, regional or local

---

[9] However, the European Court concluded that the applicant was entitled to the information he sought pursuant to Article 8 because it was essential to his private life.

level, the rights and needs of a specific audience and the obligations deriving from international legal instruments. This may lead to interferences whose aims will be legitimate under the third sentence of paragraph 1, even though they do not correspond to any of the aims set out in paragraph 2. The compatibility of such interferences must nevertheless be assessed in the light of the other requirements of paragraph 2. (*Informationsverein Lentia and others* v *Austria* (1993) 17 EHRR 93, at para. 32)

Therefore, while the state has a considerable degree of autonomy in its licensing system, any restriction must comply with the requirements of Article 10(2) (see 2.3.3 below).

2.3.3   Article 10(2)

2.3.3.1   Introduction
In *Sunday Times* v *United Kingdom* (1979) 2 EHRR 245,[10] the Court set out the issues which arise when considering whether an infringement of the right to freedom of expression meets the Article 10(2) conditions:

(a)   Is the restriction on freedom of expression 'prescribed by law'?
(b)   Does the restriction have a legitimate aim?
(c)   Is the restriction 'necessary in a democratic society'?
(d)   Is the restriction within the state's 'margin of appreciation'?

If any of these questions are answered in the negative, the restriction on freedom of expression is a violation of Article 10. Each substantive chapter in this book will deal with these conditions in detail. However, the general principles are analysed below.

2.3.3.2   'Prescribed by law'
The requirement that a restriction must be 'prescribed by law' ensures that any restriction on the right to freedom of expression must satisfy the requirements of the rule of law. In the British context, a permissible restriction must, as a minimum, be authorised by or pursuant to statute, statutory instrument, by a common law rule or by EU legislation. Restrictions authorised by government circulars, with no statutory underpinning, will lack a sufficient legal basis to be 'prescribed by law' (see *Silver* v *United Kingdom* (1983) 5 EHRR 347). In *R* v *Advertising Standards Authority, ex parte Matthias Rath BV* (2001) *The Times*, 10 January, the Administrative Court held at the permission stage that the British Codes of Advertising and Sales Promotion had sufficient statutory underpinning and were sufficiently clear, precise and accessible for their requirements to be

---

[10] House of Lords decision on contempt of court a violation of Article 10 because not necessary in a democratic society — led to Contempt of Court Act 1981; discussed fully at 9.6.1.

'prescribed by law'. However, a legal basis for a restriction is not in itself sufficient. Restrictions must also be reasonably precise and accessible. The European Court has held that:

> ... the law must be adequately accessible: the citizen must be able to have an indication that is adequate in the circumstances of the legal rules applicable to a given case. [Further], a norm cannot be regarded as a 'law' unless it is formulated with sufficient precision to enable the citizen to regulate his conduct: he must be able — if need be with the appropriate advice — to foresee, to a degree that is reasonable in the circumstances, the consequences which a given action may entail. (*Silver* v *UK*, at para. 49)

The need for foreseeability is of particular importance in relation to Article 10 because vague or imprecise laws have the tendency to 'chill' legitimate expression. In the USA, vague statutes impinging on the right to freedom of speech are invariably struck down as unconstitutional because of their chilling effect on protected speech.[11] In practice, however, the Court has been very reluctant to find that an interference with an applicant's right to freedom of expression is not 'prescribed by law'. It might be thought that common law systems, in which the precise scope of a rule of law may have to be drawn from the *ratios* of several judicial decisions, are more likely than civil law systems to fail to satisfy the requirement of precision. However, in *Steel and others* v *UK* (1998) 28 EHRR 603, at para. 94, the Court concluded that even the notoriously obscure conditions under which a police constable's power of arrest for breach of the peace arises, were defined with sufficient precision at common law to meet the requirements of Article 10(2) even though there was a conflict of judicial authority.

One example where the Court found the domestic law lacking is *Herczegfalvy* v *Austria* (1992) 15 EHRR 437, which concerned interference with the correspondence of mental patients. The person interfering with the correspondence had an unfettered discretion as to whether, and if so when, to do so. The Court concluded from this that the interference was not 'prescribed by law'. More recently, in *Hashman and Harrup* v *UK* (2000) 8 BHRC 104, the Court found that binding over orders requiring persons to be 'of good behaviour' were insufficiently precise to be regarded as 'prescribed by law'.

2.3.3.3   *Legitimate aim*

The requirement that the restriction must have a legitimate aim simply means that the purpose of the interference with the freedom of expression must be one of the

---

[11] See, e.g., *NAACP* v *Button* 371 US 415 (1963), which concerned a Virginia Statute prohibiting attorneys from soliciting prospective clients and had been used against the National Association for the Advancement of Colored People (NAACP) for informing individuals of their rights and referring them to lawyers. See generally, Nowak, J. and Rotunda, R., *Constitutional Law* (5th ed.) (St. Paul, Minn., West Publishing, 1995), at 1001–2 for a discussion of the void for vagueness doctrine.

aims listed in Article 10(2). This long list is intended to be exhaustive. However, a number of the permitted aims, such as 'the prevention of disorder' and the 'protection of the rights of others', are inherently broad. (See, e.g., *Ahmed and others* v *United Kingdom* (1998) 29 EHRR 1, where the Court concluded that ensuring the effectiveness of a system of local political democracy was included in the concept of 'rights of others'.) The Court has, in general, not sought to go behind the purpose for which a particular restriction is said to be imposed. In *Observer and Guardian* v *United Kingdom* (1991) 14 EHRR 153, for example, the Court accepted that the Government had applied for an interlocutory injunction to restrain publication of extracts from *Spycatcher* in order to protect national security. The fact that the book was widely available throughout the world (including the USA and Australia) did not affect the Court's willingness to believe that the restriction had been imposed for a legitimate purpose. The real question was whether the restriction was 'necessary in a democratic society' (see 2.3.3.4 below). The Court concluded that the injunction against the newspapers failed the test of necessity in so far as it prevented publication when the book was widely available elsewhere.

2.3.3.4   *Necessary in a democratic society*

The third, and by far the most important, requirement is that every restriction must be 'necessary in a democratic society'. This means that it must correspond to 'a pressing social need' and be proportionate to meet that need. The European Court has explained that 'necessary' is not synonymous with 'indispensable', but it does not have the flexibility of such expressions as 'useful', 'reasonable' or 'desirable' (*Handyside* v *United Kingdom* (1976) 1 EHRR 737, at para. 48).

The necessity of a restriction must be 'convincingly established' (*Barthold* v *Germany* (1985) 7 EHRR 383, at 403). In the vast majority of cases, the question whether a violation is established depends on whether the restriction imposed is necessary and proportionate. The Court has adopted a number of approaches to the issue of proportionality:[12] if the need could be achieved by less restrictive means, the restriction will fail the test for proportionality; if the measure is unsuitable for achieving the legitimate objective, the measure will fail the test for proportionality. An example of the doctrine of proportionality in operation is the case of *Barthold* v *Germany* (above) which concerned a ban on veterinary surgeons advertising their services. The applicant was prohibited from repeating various remarks he had made in a newspaper interview about the lack of emergency veterinary services as a result of the profession's unwillingness to work unsociable hours. The Court concluded that the ban was disproportionate because it risked '... discouraging members of the liberal professions from

---

[12] See Starmer, K., *European Human Rights Law* (London, Legal Action Group, 1999) at 169–80, for a detailed analysis.

contributing to public debate on topics affecting the life of the community if even there is the slightest likelihood of their utterances being treated as entailing, to some degree, an advertising effect' (at para. 58). The Court recognised that the state had a legitimate aim in protecting the rights of other veterinary surgeons from unfair competition but the restrictions, as drafted, were overbroad as they extended to discussion of matters of public concern. The Court acknowledged the 'chilling effect' of such broad restrictions on veterinary surgeons' speech.

2.3.3.5   Margin of appreciation

The final element of the Court's analysis of restrictions on freedom of expression is the 'margin of appreciation', which refers to the latitude allowed to member states in their observance of the Convention. The Court has held that the 'margin of appreciation':

> goes hand in hand with European supervision, whose extent will vary according to the case. Where ... there has been an interference with the exercise of the rights and freedom guaranteed in paragraph(1) of Article 10, the supervision must be strict, because of the importance of the rights in question; the importance of these rights has been stressed by the Court many times. The necessity for restricting them must be convincingly established. (*Autronic AG* v *Switzerland* (1990) 12 EHRR 485, at para. 61)

The extent of the 'margin of appreciation' varies depending on the subject matter. The margin has tended to be broad in cases concerning obscenity, blasphemy, national security, the protection of morals and commercial speech; whereas in cases of political expression the European Court has applied stricter scrutiny. The Court's use of the margin of appreciation has been described as 'illustrat[ing] a disappointing lack of clarity'.[13] The inapplicability of the doctrine of 'margin of appreciation' in domestic law is discussed at 3.2.2.

2.3.3.6   Factors relevant to the test of necessity in Article 10(2)

Categories of expression   The case law in Strasbourg has tended to deal specifically with three main classes of expression — political, artistic and commercial — with political expression receiving the most protection. However, care should be taken not to apply this threefold classification too rigidly, because the expression at issue may fall within more than one category. One such example of expression that fell into more than one category was *Hertel* v *Switzerland* (1998) 28 EHRR 534, which concerned newspaper articles detailing the alleged dangers of microwave ovens. The manufacturers of microwaves sued under the Unfair Competition Act. The Government sought to argue that the expression in question was commercial in nature, and therefore the state should be afforded a

---

[13] Judge MacDonald, 'The Margin of Appreciation' in *The European System for the Protection of Human Rights*, MacDonald, Matscher and Petzold (eds) at 85.

wide margin of appreciation. The Court rejected this contention as the expression was not purely commercial but was part of a debate affecting the public interest over public health (at para. 47).

(a) *Expression on matters of general public concern* The European Court attaches the highest importance to the protection of political expression, which it has defined expansively to include speech on matters of general public concern. The Court has viewed expression concerning litigation (*Sunday Times* v *United Kingdom* (1979) 2 EHRR 245) alleged police malpractice (*Thorgeirson* v *Iceland* (1992) 14 EHRR 843), the alleged cruelty to seals inflicted by hunters (*Bladet Tromso and Stensaas* v *Norway* (1999) 29 EHRR 125), the practice of cosmetic surgeons (*Bergens Tidende* v *Norway* (App. No. 26132/95, 2 May 2000)), and even comments on the quality of local veterinary services (*Barthold* v *Germany* (1985) 7 EHRR 383) to be expression on matters of public concern worthy of strong protection. In *Lingens* v *Austria* (1986) 8 EHRR 407 (discussed fully in Chapter 5), the applicant was a journalist who had alleged that the then Chancellor of Austria had protected and assisted former Nazis. Mr Lingens was convicted and fined for criminal libel. The Court emphasised the importance of freedom of political debate in a free and democratic society:

> [I]t is incumbent on the press to impart information and ideas on political issues just as those in other areas of public interest. Not only does the press have the task of imparting such ideas: the public also has a right to receive them ... The limits of acceptable criticism are ... wider as regards a politician as such than as regards a private individual: unlike the latter, the former inevitably and knowingly lays himself open to close scrutiny of his every word and deed by both journalists and the public at large, and must consequently display a greater degree of tolerance. (at paras 41–42)

The Court makes clear in the above passage that the limits of permissible criticism depend, to some extent, on the identity of the person being criticised. Restrictions on public criticism will be more closely supervised when those criticised are politicians. Police officers apparently fall into an intermediate category. Though there is a public interest in accurate information about their professional conduct, they do not — unlike politicians — knowingly lay themselves open to close scrutiny of their words and deeds.[14]

---

[14] See *Janowski* v *Poland* (1999) 29 EHRR 705, discussed at 5.4.3 below. Contrast *New York Times* v *Sullivan* 376 US 254 (1964), in which the US Supreme Court held that a public official could not sue for libel except in respect of allegations which he could establish had been made with 'actual malice'. The plaintiff in *Sullivan* was a police officer.

But, although the European Court has said that politicians should not expect to escape criticism, it has also emphasised the importance of not restricting their own freedom of speech. In *Castells* v *Spain* (1992) 14 EHRR 445, at para. 45, the Court drew attention to the importance of the rights of politicians, especially members of opposition parties:

> In [a] democratic system the actions or omissions of the government must be subject to close scrutiny not only of the legislative and judicial authorities but also of the press and public opinion. Furthermore, the dominant position which the government occupies makes it necessary to display restraint in resorting to criminal proceedings, particularly where other means are available for replying to the unjustified attacks and criticisms of its adversaries or the media.

It is particularly important to have a free flow of opinions and information during the run-up to elections (see *Bowman* v *United Kingdom* (1998) 26 EHRR 1). Where, however, the expression is directed at the undermining of democracy and human rights themselves, the state is not required by Article 10 to confer the same protection as it would be obliged to provide in the case of orthodox political expression. This has been applied in particular to expression by extreme left-wing and neo-Nazi groups. (See, e.g., *Glimmerveen and Hagenbeek* v *Netherlands* (App. Nos 8348/78 and 8406/78) (1979) 18 DR 187, see 7.4.1 below; see also the Court's decision in *Jersild* v *Denmark* (1994) 19 EHRR 1, discussed in Chapter 7.) Even in this context, however, the more recent case law from Strasbourg suggests that the collapse of communism in Eastern Europe has meant that it is no longer so necessary to impose restrictions on the speech of communist sympathisers. (See, e.g., *Vogt* v *Germany* (1995) 21 EHRR 205, which concerned dismissal of a teacher on the ground that she was a member of the communist party. This was held to be a violation of the Convention by the Court of Human Rights.)

(b) *Commercial expression*   Though it is now clear that Article 10(1) extends to cover commercial expression, the European Court has frequently invoked the margin of appreciation to justify restrictions on such expression. It has held that consumer protection is a legitimate justification for a ban on false and misleading advertising (*Markt Intern Verlag and Klaus Beermann* v *Germany* (1989) 12 EHRR 161, at para. 26). In *Casado Coca* v *Spain* (1994) 18 EHRR 1, the Court went further and held that a near complete ban on advertising by lawyers, even when truthful and accurate, was permissible in order to maintain confidence in the proper administration of justice and the dignity of the legal profession. In view of the wide divergences of approach to this question between contracting states, national authorities and courts were best placed to determine how to strike the balance between these legitimate purposes and the public right to receive information about the provision of legal services (at para. 55).

The Court's jurisprudence in this area is less developed than that of the US Supreme Court, which provides protection for truthful and accurate commercial speech except in relation to 'sinful' but lawful products or services such as alcohol, tobacco and gambling.[15]

(c) *Artistic expression* Artistic expression has been less well-protected in Strasbourg than either political or commercial expression. Although the Court has consistently held that Article 10 extends to artistic expression, including the public exchange of cultural and social information of all kinds (see *Müller* v *Switzerland*, at 2.3.2.4 above), the protection afforded to this type of expression has been minimal. The Court has permitted states a wide 'margin of appreciation' in this field, particularly in relation to expression which has the potential to offend religious or moral sensibilities.[16] In *Otto-Preminger-Institut* v *Austria* (1994) 19 EHRR 34, the applicants complained about the seizure and confiscation of a film which, in the view of the Austrian authorities, was likely to offend religious feelings. The Court upheld the state's action, even though the film was shown only in private to members of a film club who had been fully informed of its theme and content. Other cases in which interference with expression has been upheld by the Court include *Müller* v *Switzerland* (1988) 13 EHRR 212, which concerned a conviction for obscenity and confiscation of paintings which were shown in an exhibition of contemporary art; and *Handyside* v *United Kingdom* (1976) 1 EHRR 737, which concerned a ban on *The Little Red Schoolbook* in England and Wales even though this book was widely available throughout Continental Europe (and, indeed, in Scotland where a prosecution under Scots obscenity law had failed).

Duties and responsibilities of the applicant Article 10(2) provides that the exercise of the right to freedom of expression carries with it 'duties and responsibilities'. This phrase is occasionally invoked by governments when seeking to limit the right to freedom of expression of a particular class of individuals, such as members of the armed forces (e.g., *Engel and others* v *Netherlands* (1976) 1 EHRR 647) and civil servants (e.g., *Vogt* v *Germany* (1995)

---

[15] The distinction between the jurisprudence can, at least partially, be explained by the difference in the underlying rationales for the protection of freedom of expression by the two legal systems. The jurisprudence of the US, but not of the European Court, has accepted that one of the justifications for the protection of expression is the pursuit of truth (including truth as to the quality of various products or services).

[16] The case law in the area falls short of judicial pronouncements that Article 10 applies to offensive and shocking expression; see *Handyside* v *United Kingdom*, at 2.3.1 above.

21 EHRR 205 and *Ahmed and others* v *United Kingdom* (1998) 29 EHRR 1). It is difficult to define what this phrase adds, as the identity of the applicant is taken into account by the Court when deciding whether a particular restriction is 'necessary in a democratic society' and within the state's 'margin of appreciation'. The 'duties and responsibilities' of certain classes of applicants are enhanced — for example, journalists because of their role as 'public watchdog' (see 2.3.2.5 above). Recently the Court has played down this phrase and has emphasised that regardless of an applicant's particular status, they are still 'individuals' who benefit from the full protection of the Convention (see, e.g., *Vereinigung Demokratischer Soldaten Österreichs and Gubi* v *Austria* (1994) 20 EHRR 56 at para. 36). In *Bladet Tromso and Stensaas* v *Norway* (1999) 29 EHRR 125 at para. 65, the Court interpreted the phrase 'duties and responsibilities' as meaning that the freedom of expression of journalists was subject to the proviso that they were acting in good faith in order to provide accurate and reliable information in accordance with the ethics of journalism.

The medium of the expression   The European Court has considered the medium of the expression when deciding whether a given restriction is legitimate. For example, in relation to television and radio, which have a very wide potential audience, the state is likely to find it easier to justify a restriction than with a medium with a small potential audience, such as a film show in a licensed sex shop (see *Scherer* v *Switzerland* (App. No. 17116/90, 14 January 1993). The Court has taken into account the difficulty of controlling the circulation of videos once they have been put into circulation when deciding on Draconian restrictions on the blasphemous video, *Visions of Ecstasy* (*Wingrove* v *United Kingdom* (1996) 24 EHRR 1).

Prior restraint or ex post facto sanction?   The Court has made clear that Article 10 is engaged whether the restriction imposed is a prior restraint or a sanction imposed after publication. However, it will be more difficult to justify prior restraints (e.g., injunctions)[17] than subsequent punishment (e.g., committal for contempt of court) or civil liability (e.g., damages for defamation).[18] In *Observer and Guardian* v *United Kingdom*, the Court held:

> The dangers inherent in prior restraints are such that they call for the most careful scrutiny on the part of the Court. This is especially so as far as the press is

---

[17] See generally, Barendt, E., *Freedom of Speech* (Oxford, OUP, 1992), chap. IV.

[18] This distinction is already to some extent recognised in English law, e.g., in the rule that an interlocutory injunction will not generally issue in proceedings for defamation where the defence of justification has been raised (*Bonnard* v *Perryman* [1891] 2 Ch 269); see also the rule that interim relief will not normally be granted to prevent publication of an adjudication by a public regulatory authority (*R* v *Advertising Standards Authority, ex parte Vernon Pools Organisation Ltd* [1992] 1 WLR 1289).

concerned, for news is a perishable commodity and to delay its publication for even a short period may well deprive it of all its value and interests. ((1991) 14 EHRR 153, at para. 60)

In his dissenting judgment in *Wingrove* v *United Kingdom* (1996) 24 EHRR 1, at 36, Judge de Meyer went further, taking the view that all prior restraints are unacceptable interferences in the field of freedom of expression. This view has never commanded majority support from the Court.[19]

2.4   OTHER CONVENTION RIGHTS OF PARTICULAR IMPORTANCE TO MEDIA LAW

There are a number of other Convention Articles that may be relevant in deciding whether restrictions on freedom of expression are permissible.

2.4.1   Article 6(1): Reporting of judicial proceedings

(See generally Chapter 9 for a more detailed analysis of this area.) Article 6(1) is concerned with the right to a fair trial. The starting position is that a fair trial requires a public trial because a public trial, 'protects litigants from the administration of justice in secret' (*Pretto* v *Italy* (1983) 6 EHRR 182) and it maintains public confidence in the judicial system (*Diennet* v *France* (1995) 21 EHRR 554, at para. 33). However, the right to a public hearing is not unqualified; Article 6(1) expressly permits some restrictions on the reporting of judicial proceedings:

> In the determination of his civil rights and obligations or of any criminal charge against him, everyone is entitled to a fair and public hearing within a reasonable time by an independent and impartial tribunal established by law. *Judgment shall be pronounced publicly but the press and public may be excluded from all or part of the trial in the interests of morals, public order or national security in a democratic society, where the interests of juveniles or the protection of the private life of the parties so require, or to the extent strictly necessary in the opinion of the court in special circumstances where publicity would prejudice the interests of justice.* (emphasis added)

The scope of Article 6(1) has given rise to a great deal of case law.[20] It applies to all criminal proceedings, and to all ordinary civil litigation between private parties including tort, contract, restitution, family law and employment law. Article 6(1) also applies to most licensing decisions (see *X* v *Belgium* (1980) 23 DR 237

---

[19] A near absolute ban on prior restraints exists in the USA: see, e.g., *New York Times* v *United States; Washington Post* v *United States* 403 US 713 (1971).

[20] See Starmer, K., *European Human Rights Law* (London, Legal Action Group, 1999), chaps 6, 11, and 12.

(licence to run a public house terminated as a result of the appliant's conviction for keeping a brothel)) and professional disciplinary tribunals (see *Guchez* v *Belgium* (App. No. 10027/82) (1984) 40 DR 100 (concerning suspension of the applicant by the disciplinary board of the Architects' Association for canvassing custom)). The Court has held that prison disciplinary proceedings, although within the ambit of Article 6(1), can be conducted inside a prison without public or media access for 'reasons of public order and security' (*Campbell and Fell* v *United Kingdom* (1984) 7 EHRR 165). However, such an exclusion is not permissible in ordinary criminal proceedings (at para. 87). While Article 6(1), unlike Article 10, does not require that any restriction or interference be 'necessary in a democratic society', the Court in *Campbell and Fell* considered the restrictions under a similar proportionality analysis.

A litigant may waive his or her right to a public hearing, provided this waiver does not run counter to any important public interest (*Schuler-Zgraggen* v *Switzerland* (1993) 16 EHRR 405). The media have unsuccessfully asserted their right to attend a criminal hearing. In *Atkinson, Crook and The Independent* v *UK* (App. No. 13366/87) (1990) 67 DR 244, the Commission rejected an application under Article 10 brought by two journalists complaining about the decision of a trial judge to hold sentencing proceedings in camera. The Commission rejected the applicant's argument that the state could not restrict a person from receiving information that others wish to impart to him, because the rights of the defendant and the interests of justice also had to be taken into account.

2.4.2   Article 8: The right to respect for private life[21]

Article 8 concerns various privacy rights, of which the right to respect for private life is relevant to media law. An individual's right to respect for private life can potentially conflict with the media's right to freedom of expression under Article 10.

Article 8 provides:

> 1.   Everyone has the right to respect for his private and family life, his home and his correspondence.
>
> 2.   There shall be no interference by a public authority with the exercise of this right except such as is in accordance with the law and is necessary in a democratic society in the interests of national security, public safety or the economic well-being of the country, for the prevention of disorder or crime, for the protection of health or morals, or for the protection of the rights and freedoms of others.

As with Article 10, the first paragraph of Article 8 asserts the positive right, namely the right to respect for private life, while the second paragraph sets out

---

[21] See Chapter 6 for a detailed discussion of the issues relating to privacy and the media.

how and when restrictions on that positive right can be justified. The methodology of Article 8 is the same as Article 10, and therefore the first stage is to identify an interference with the right. If such an interference exists, first, it must be 'in accordance with the law', which is identical in meaning to the Article 10 requirement that the interference is 'prescribed by law' (see *Sunday Times* v *United Kingdom*, at 2.3.3 above); secondly, the interference must achieve a legitimate aim; and, thirdly, the interference must be 'necessary in a democratic society' and within the state's 'margin of appreciation'.

In the media law context, invasions of privacy are likely to be perpetrated by private bodies such as newspapers and television stations rather than by the state.[22] However, as discussed at 2.3.2.7 above in relation to Article 10, states have a positive obligation to ensure the effective protection of the right to respect for private life. The concept of a positive obligation in relation to protection of this right is more developed than the Article 10 jurisprudence. The Court has stated that the positive obligation will extend to requiring action to protect an individual from the acts of other private parties:

> The Court recalls that although the object of Article 8 is essentially that of protecting the individual against arbitrary interference by the public authorities, it does not merely compel the state to abstain from such interference: in addition to this primarily negative obligation, there may be positive obligations inherent in an effective respect for private or family life. These obligations may involve the adoption of measures designed to secure respect for private life even in the sphere of the relations of individuals between themselves. (*X and Y* v *Netherlands* (1985) 8 EHRR 235, at para. 23)

The European Court has yet to apply the concept of positive obligations under Article 8 in the media law context, where it will need to balance the effective protection of the right to respect to private life with the media's conflicting right to impart information and the right of the public to receive such information. The European Commission has considered the issue on a number of occasions but has side-stepped it each time. (See *Winer* v *United Kingdom* (App. No. 10871/84) (1986) 48 DR 154; *Earl Spencer* v *United Kingdom* (App. Nos 28851/95 and 28852/95) (1998) 25 EHRR CD 105; *N* v *Sweden* (App. No. 11366/85) (1986) 50 DR 173, discussed in detail in Chapter 6.)

2.4.3 Article 14: The right not to be discriminated against[23]

The ECHR's discrimination provision is not freestanding but is limited to those rights embodied in the Convention and the Protocols. To invoke Article 14, it is

---

[22] But some television stations such as the BBC are likely to be public authorities under the Human Rights Act and therefore an individual will be able to rely directly on Article 8, see Chapter 3 at section 3.4.3.

[23] See Chapter 7 for a further discussion of the issues relating to discrimination. See also Starmer, *op. cit.* n. 20, chap. 29.

necessary to show that the facts in question fall 'within the ambit' of one or more of the Convention rights. Article 14 ECHR provides:

> The enjoyment of the rights and freedoms set forth in this Convention shall be secured without discrimination on any ground such as sex, race, colour, language, religion, political or other opinion, national or social origin, association with a national minority, property, birth or other status.

Article 14 sets out a number of categories of prohibited discrimination, but it is clear from the use of words 'such as' and 'other status' that these categories are not closed.

Article 14 does not prohibit all kinds of differential treatment, merely differential treatment which has 'no reasonable justification'. The existence of such justification depends on the aim and effect of the measure in question, and whether the measure is proportionate to the aim that is sought to be realised (*Belgian Linguistic Case (No. 2)* (1968) 1 EHRR 252). One example of discrimination in the media law field where one would have expected the European Court to have recourse to Article 14, is *Vereinigung Demokratischer Soldaten Österreichs and Gubi* v *Austria* (1994) 20 EHRR 56, which concerned the failure of the state to distribute *Der Igel* to Austrian soldiers while distributing other magazines for soldiers. The Court concluded that there was a violation of Article 10, because the state was not permitted to discriminate between types of publication on the basis of the publication's content. However, the Court reached this conclusion without recourse to Article 14.

Other areas of media law where Article 14 may be relevant include the criminal law of blasphemy, which explicitly discriminates against non-Christian religions. See generally Chapter 8.

2.4.4   Article 15: Restrictions in time of war or other public emergency threatening the life of the nation

Article 15 permits the suspension of various Convention rights in times of war and other public emergencies threatening the life of the nation. Article 15 provides:

> 1.   In time of war or other public emergency threatening the life of the nation any High Contracting Party may take measures derogating from its obligations under this Convention to the extent strictly required by the exigencies of the situation, provided that such measures are not inconsistent with its other obligations under international law.
> 2.   No derogation from Article 2, except in respect of deaths resulting from lawful acts of war, or from Articles 3, 4 (paragraph 1) and 7 shall be made under this provision.
> 3.   Any High Contracting Party availing itself of this right of derogation shall keep the Secretary-General of the Council of Europe fully informed of the measures which it

has taken and the reasons therefor. It shall also inform the Secretary-General of the Council of Europe when such measures have ceased to operate and the provisions of the Convention are again being fully executed.

This Article may be relevant to reporting on wars and, arguably, the Northern Ireland conflict. Despite the language of Article 15(1) restricting it to measures that are 'strictly required', the Court has recognised a margin of appreciation for the contracting state in assessing whether such an emergency exists and, if so, what steps are necessary to overcome it (see *Ireland* v *United Kingdom* (1978) 2 EHRR 25, at paras 91–92). Van Dijk and van Hoof,[24] contend, correctly in our view, that the exceptions provided for in Article 15 can never be applicable to the 'freedom to hold opinions' contained in Article 10, since an exception to that right can in no circumstances be 'strictly required' in the sense of Article 15(1).

2.4.5   Article 17: Restrictions on activities subversive of Convention rights — the problem of hate speech

(See Chapter 7.) Article 17 permits restrictions on those who seek to destroy the Convention rights of others and has been invoked in relation to prosecutions for hate speech (see, e.g., *Glimmerveen and Hagenbeek* v *Netherlands* (App. Nos 8348/78 and 8406/78) (1979) 18 DR 187). Article 17 ECHR provides:

> Nothing in this Convention may be interpreted as implying for any state, group or person any right to engage in any activity or perform any act aimed at the destruction of any of the rights and freedoms set forth herein or at their limitation to a greater extent than is provided for in the Convention.

Any measures taken pursuant to Article 17 must be proportionate to the threat to the rights of others (*De Becker* v *Belgium* (1960) 2 YB 215, para. 279).

---

[24] *Theory and Practice of the European Convention on Human Rights*, 3rd ed. (Kluwer Law International, 1998) at p. 585.

Chapter Three

The Human Rights Act 1998

3.1 INTRODUCTION

The long title to the Human Rights Act (HRA) 1998 declares its purpose to 'give further effect to rights and freedoms guaranteed under the European Convention on Human Rights'. As Chapter 1 showed, even before the HRA 1998, the ECHR was referred to with increasing regularity in cases concerning freedom of expression. The House of Lords declared on several occasions that it could see no difference between Article 10 and the common law's approach to the right of freedom of speech (*Derbyshire County Council* v *Times Newspapers Ltd* [1993] AC 534; *Attorney-General* v *Guardian Newspapers Ltd (No. 2)* [1990] 1 AC 109; *Reynolds* v *Times Newspapers Ltd* [1999] 3 WLR 1010). The number of occasions on which the European Court found the UK media law decisions to be in violation of Article 10 suggests that this rosy outlook was not always justified in practice. However, it has meant that Article 10 and its jurisprudence have been referred to in connection with appropriate developments for the common law (e.g., *Reynolds* v *Times Newspapers Ltd*), the interpretation of legislation which is ambiguous or which was passed to bring UK law into line with the Convention (notably the Contempt of Court Act 1981) and in connection with the exercise of judicial discretion (*Derbyshire County Council* v *Times Newspapers Ltd* [1992] 1 QB 770 (CA), *per* Balcombe LJ at 812).

Nevertheless, the 1998 Act has the capacity to affect even this area of law. In particular:

(a) It puts an obligation on courts to interpret legislation 'so far as it is possible to do so' compatibly with the Convention. This gives wider scope to read UK legislation in conformity with the Convention than the traditional common law approach to statutory interpretation would allow.

(b) It puts an obligation on all public authorities (including the courts) to act in conformity with the Convention. This is new and gives new scope for invoking respect for freedom of expression.

(c) It provides new remedies where a public authority has violated a Convention right.

(d) It contains special provisions concerning freedom of expression (s. 12). Some of these are familiar features of current practice, but others will require an adjustment of the way in which courts approach their task.

(e) It supports those trends that can be detected in the common law in favour of freedom of expression.

3.2 'CONVENTION RIGHTS'

3.2.1 Omitted rights

It is convenient shorthand to refer to the HRA 1998 as 'incorporating the Convention into UK' law, but it is not completely accurate. In the first place, it is not the whole of the Convention and its Protocols which is referred to when the Act speaks of 'Convention rights'. Unsurprisingly, they do not include those Protocols to which the UK is not a party, or situations where the UK has entered a reservation to the Convention or a Protocol (see HRA 1998, Schedule 3). Schedule 1 to the Act sets out those parts of the Convention and Protocols which *are* included in the term 'Convention rights'.

There are two provisions of the Convention which are not included in Schedule 1 even though the UK has agreed to be bound by them — Article 1 and Article 13. Article 1 provides:

Article 1   Obligation to respect human rights
The High Contracting Parties shall secure to everyone within their jurisdiction the rights and freedoms set out in Section I of this Convention.

Article 13 provides:

Article 13   Right to an effective remedy
Everyone whose rights and freedoms as set forth in this Convention are violated shall have an effective remedy before a national authority notwithstanding that the violation has been committed by persons acting in an official capacity.

The Government explained these omissions by saying that the 1998 Act itself was the means by which the Convention rights were to be secured, and the HRA itself ensured that there would be an effective remedy. To the extent that the HRA 1998 did not provide a complete remedy (in particular, where primary legislation was indisputably in conflict with the Convention), this reflected deliberate Government policy that the Act should leave untouched Parliament's ultimate power to legislate, even in a manner which conflicted with human rights.

It remains to be seen whether the omission of Articles 1 and 13 from Schedule 1 has any other effects. There are occasions when the reasoning of the European Court or the Commission has depended in part on these two provisions. Notably, the concept of 'positive obligations' has relied on the duty on contracting states under Article 1 to 'secure' the rights and freedoms set out in the Convention. In some contexts it is possible to envisage the courts relying (in part at least) on this omission as a reason for leaving it to Parliament to take necessary steps to comply with a positive obligation. In others, it may be possible to discharge the UK's positive obligation by developing the common law. Here, it is less obvious that the omission to include Article 1 will inhibit the courts.

Section 7 of the Act (which provides for remedies) is the domestic equivalent of Article 13. It will be unreal to expect the UK courts to disregard entirely the case law which Strasbourg has built up as to what is required of an 'effective remedy'.

3.2.2   Strasbourg case law

At a European level, 'Convention rights' mean more than the plain text of the Convention and its Protocols. As Chapter 2 showed in the context of the provisions that most affect the media, a considerable body of case law has grown up which explains and to some extent amplifies the meaning which is to be given to the treaties themselves. Section 2 of the Act requires this case law to be taken into account whenever any question has to be determined in connection with a Convention right.

The obligation, though, is only to 'take into account' the European case law. This choice of phrase was deliberate. Clearly, where the European Court has established principles in relation to the Convention rights, the UK courts will have to follow them. Similarly, the application of those principles to the facts of the particular cases will illustrate how the European Court regards those principles as having to be applied in practice. Yet there are some respects in which the role of the European Court is different from that of the domestic courts. This can be seen most strikingly in the Court's concept of the 'margin of appreciation'. This is a jurisprudential tool which the Court has adopted because of its position as an international court. It reflects the Court's sensitivity to the fact that it is composed of international judges and does not have the same contact with, or experience of, the legal system and culture of a particular contracting state as do the domestic courts of that state. In any case, the function of the European Court is not to act as a further tier of appeal within the domestic judicial scheme. Many of the decisions of the Court reflect on the one hand the pull towards restraint which the concept of the margin of appreciation implies, and on the other hand the opposite pull of the need to maintain European supervision. These concepts and the struggle between them are not material for domestic courts, tribunals or other decision-makers. So, when 'taking account' of the case law, courts will have to assess how much they need to make allowance for a concern which they need not share. Similarly, the Convention rights are intended to establish a floor of rights, not a ceiling: s. 11 of the HRA 1998 makes clear that the Act is intended to add to, not detract from, existing rights.

There are already signs that while the 'margin of appreciation' is an immaterial concept for a domestic court, some discretionary area of judgment may still be left to the legislature and the Government (*R* v *DPP, ex parte Kebilene* [1999] 3 WLR 972, at 993F–994E; *Stott (Procurator Fiscal, Dunfermline)* v *Brown*, 5 December 2000 (PC)). This is a controversial area. Its working out may vary according to the rights in issue and the nature of the act of the public authority in question.

Courts take judicial notice of the case law of UK courts. In practice, they have also taken judicial notice of the case law of the Strasbourg organs. However, strictly speaking, this is a matter of evidence, and the Act gives the Lord Chancellor the power to prescribe by Rules the manner of proving it (HRA 1998, s. 2(2) and (3)). Instead of Rules, a Practice Direction has been adopted which requires the citation of 'an authoritative and complete report' and for copies to be provided to the court and other parties not less than three days before the hearing. Printouts from the European Court's database (HUDOC) can be used. (See Practice Direction to CPR Part 39, para. 8.1.)

3.3 INTERPRETING LEGISLATION CONSISTENTLY WITH CONVENTION RIGHTS

3.3.1 Introduction

(1) So far as it is possible to do so, primary legislation and subordinate legislation must be read and given effect in a way which is compatible with Convention rights. (HRA 1998, s. 3(1))

This provision is one of the cornerstones of the 1998 Act. Thus recourse to the Convention is no longer confined to situations where the legislation is ambiguous. Nor are the courts merely to take account of the requirements of the Convention. On the contrary, they must, so far as possible, achieve an interpretation of domestic legislation which is compatible with Convention rights.

This new obligation carries the qualification 'so far as it is possible to do so'. The phrase deliberately echoes the way in which the courts of member states of the EU are required to interpret their domestic legislation compatibly with EU legislation so far as it is possible to do so (*Marleasing SA* v *La Commercial*

Internacional de Alimentacion SA (case C-106/89) [1992] CMLR 305). This means that where more than one interpretation of the legislation is possible, the court must choose that which is consistent with the Convention right. Lord Cooke has described it as 'a strong adjuration', and suggested that a provision in a criminal statute which appeared to put the legal burden of proof on a defendant might be interpreted as no more than an evidential burden (*R* v *DPP, ex parte Kebilene*, 3.2.2 above, at 987C). In the same case, Lord Hope drew an analogy between issues under the HRA 1998 and the approach of the Privy Council to constitutional protections for individual rights. Both called for a generous and purposive construction.

The interpretative obligation under s. 3 is a different approach to statutory construction than that which the courts normally employ. It means, for instance, that the intention of the legislator is not a reliable guide to meaning. It cannot be, because the new interpretative obligation applies whenever the legislation was enacted, even if this was before the passage of the 1998 Act (HRA 1998, s. 3(2)(a)). It also follows that pre-HRA judicial decisions as to the meaning of legislation will have to be re-examined if their conclusions conflict with Convention rights. Since the post-HRA court would be following a different legislative mandate, the pre-HRA decision would not be binding even if given by a court which was superior in the judicial hierarchy. It is different once the higher courts have themselves considered and ruled upon the effect for English law of the relevant Strasbourg decisions (*R* v *Central Criminal Court, ex parte The Guardian, The Observer and Martin Bright* [2000] UKHRR 796 (QBD) at pp. 817 and 828).

Although this new obligation gives the courts much more latitude to arrive at a conclusion which is compatible with the Convention, it is not limitless. In the context of EU law, the courts have cautioned that domestic legislation must not be distorted in the process (*Duke* v *G.E.C. Reliance Systems Ltd* [1988] AC 618, at 639–40). As the House of Lords recently recalled, the exercise is still one of construction and must not exceed the limits of what is reasonable (*Clarke* v *General Accident Fire and Life Assurance Corp. plc* [1998] 1 WLR 1647, at 1656).

3.3.2 Primary and secondary legislation

The obligation applies to primary and secondary legislation. The HRA 1998 makes clear, though, that primary legislation remains valid if, even when adopting this new method of interpretation, it is incompatible with the Convention and the legislation's continuing operation or enforcement is not affected (HRA 1998, s. 3(2)(b)). 'Primary legislation' is defined as meaning: a public general act; a local and personal act; a private act; a Church Assembly Measure; a Measure of the General Synod of the Church of England; an Order in Council made under the

Royal Prerogative; an Order in Council made under s. 38(1)(a) of the Northern Ireland Act 1973 or the corresponding provision of the Northern Ireland Act 1998; or an Order in Council amending a public, private or local Act. 'Primary legislation' also includes an order or other instrument under primary legislation bringing the legislation into force or amending primary legislation. However, this later category does not include an order or instrument by the National Assembly of Wales, a member of the Scottish Executive, a Northern Ireland Minister or a member of a Northern Ireland department (HRA 1998, s. 21(1)).

With subordinate legislation (as defined by HRA 1998, s. 21(1)), there are two elements to the inquiry: (i) the meaning of the subordinate legislation; and (ii) the power under the primary legislation to make subordinate legislation. The courts must interpret the subordinate legislation so far as it is possible to do so compatibly with the Convention, and they will likewise try to interpret the enabling primary legislation as conferring power to act in accordance with the Convention. However, this may not be possible. If (disregarding any possibility of revocation) primary legislation prevents removal of the incompatibility, the validity of both the primary legislation and its subordinate offshoot are valid and the continuing operation and enforcement of the incompatible subordinate legislation are unaffected (HRA 1998, s. 3(2)(c)).

3.3.3 Declarations of incompatibility

While primary legislation and this restricted class of subordinate legislation remain valid and effective even if it is impossible to read them compatibly with Convention rights, the courts are not completely powerless. Any court or tribunal can, of course, express its view as part of its decision. The cogency of its arguments may have the force of persuasion that amending legislation is necessary. However, the High Court (and the higher appellate courts) can go further and formally make a 'declaration of incompatibility' (HRA 1998, s. 4). Once again, the declaration does not affect the validity, continuing operation or enforcement of the provision (HRA 1998, s. 4(6)), but it does give the government the power to amend the legislation by an expedited procedure (HRA 1998, s. 10 and Schedule 2).

The courts which can make declarations of incompatibility do not include magistrates' courts or the Crown Court, even though the judges of the latter include High Court judges. Where a criminal case raises such an issue, the matter must therefore reach (in England or Wales) the Court of Appeal or, if the case proceeds by way of judicial review or an appeal by case stated, the High Court, before a declaration can be made. County courts cannot make declarations of incompatibility. A case can be transferred from the county court to the High Court if there is a real prospect that a declaration of incompatibility will be made (see CPR Part 30, r. 30.3(2)(g)). Within the High Court declarations of incompatibility can only be made by High Court judges, and a deputy High Court judge, master or district judge cannot try a case where a claim is made for such a declaration or in respect of a judicial act under the HRA (CPR, PD 2B, para. 7A).

If a court is considering whether to make a declaration of incompatibility, the Crown is entitled to 21 days' notice and to be joined as a party to the proceedings (CPR Part 19, r. 19A; the court can specify an alternative period of notice).

A declaration of incompatibility does not affect the validity, continuing operation or enforcement of the provision as a matter of law (HRA 1998, s. 4(6)(a)). However, in practice, the government would be under considerable political pressure to bring UK law into conformity with what our courts have said the Convention requires. If the government thought that the UK courts had misunderstood the Convention's obligations, it could conceivably refuse to pass the necessary legislation and contest the inevitable complaint to the European Court. The Act makes clear that the decision of the UK courts is not binding on the parties to the proceedings (HRA 1998, s. 4(6)(b)) so that as a matter of UK law there would be no formal obstacle to the Government taking such an obdurate stance.

3.3.4   Matters covered by European law

Although generally speaking the courts can make a declaration of incompatibility only if primary legislation is unavoidably in conflict with Convention rights, their powers are greater if the legislation in question concerns a matter covered by European Community law. The European Court of Justice has declared on numerous occasions that it will be guided by general principles of law common to the member states, including their shared commitment to the protection of fundamental human rights. The ECHR is a valuable source for determining the content of those rights.

Consequently, Community measures will be assessed in the light of the obligations in the ECHR. Correspondingly, domestic implementation of those measures must also accord with the principles of the Convention. If domestic law — even primary legislation — cannot be reconciled with the Convention's requirements, it must give way. This is not a result of the HRA 1998 but of the European Communities Act 1972.

An example of the potential influence of the ECHR in the European context is considered in Chapter 12 in the context of restrictions on tobacco advertising.

3.4   PUBLIC AUTHORITIES' DUTY TO COMPLY WITH CONVENTION RIGHTS

3.4.1   Introduction

(1)   It is unlawful for a public authority to act in a way which is incompatible with a Convention right. (HRA 1998, s. 6(1))

This is the second major innovation of the 1998 Act. In the past, the courts were reluctant to impose even the attenuated duty to have regard to the ECHR in the exercise of statutory powers (*R v Secretary of State for the Home Department, ex parte Brind* [1991] 1 AC 696). This provision goes further. It is not sufficient for authorities to take account of the Convention or to have regard to it; they must not act in a way which is incompatible with a Convention right.

3.4.2 Incompatible primary legislation

Once again, the duty is qualified in the case of primary legislation which requires incompatible behaviour so that the 'authority could not have acted differently' (HRA 1998, s. 6(2)(a)), or where the authority was acting so as to give effect to or to enforce primary legislation provisions which 'cannot be read or given effect in a way which is compatible with the Convention rights' (HRA 1998, s. 6(2)(b)). The strength of this language is a reminder of how keenly Parliament wishes the courts to strive in carrying out their interpretative duty to find a reading of even primary legislation which is compatible with Convention rights.

3.4.3 Meaning of 'public authority'

The Act does not try to list 'public authorities'. It expressly *includes* courts and tribunals (HRA 1998, s. 6(3)(a); 'tribunal' means any tribunal in which legal proceedings may be brought (s. 21(1)): (see 3.6.4 below). It expressly *excludes* either House of Parliament (except the House of Lords in its judicial capacity) or a person exercising functions in connection with proceedings in Parliament (HRA 1998, s. 6(3) and (4)). This exclusion is intended to continue the immunity which proceedings in Parliament have from judicial scrutiny as a result of the Bill of Rights. The immunity, though, does not extend to Strasbourg, where the UK will remain liable for any breaches of Convention rights as a result of Parliamentary proceedings or the acts of Parliamentary officials (see, e.g., *Demicoli* v *Malta* (1991) 14 EHRR 47).

Departments of central government, local authorities and the police are all obvious examples of what is meant by 'public authorities', but the term is meant to extend beyond these easy examples. This is clear from the further partial definition that includes 'any person certain of whose functions are functions of a public nature' (HRA 1998, s. 6(3)(b)). This hybrid category would, for instance, include Railtrack, which has statutory functions relating to safety (in which connection it would be a public authority) and private functions (e.g., in connection with property development). In the case of a hybrid body, the duty under s. 6 does not apply if the nature of the particular act in question was private (HRA 1998, s. 6(5)). This focus on the particular function in question reflects UK case law as to the types of decisions which are amenable to judicial review. But the analogy may need to be treated with care. The courts have found that matters of employment and commercial contracts are outside the scope of judicial review because they are the exclusive concern of private law (see, e.g., *R* v *Derbyshire County Council, ex parte Noble* [1990] ICR 808; *R* v *BBC, ex parte Lavelle* [1983] 1 WLR 23). That will still be the case with hybrid bodies. It might be argued that any public body must be a hybrid if any of its functions are of a private nature. However, during the House of Lords debate on the Human Rights Bill, the Lord Chancellor thought that where a body was clearly a public authority without the need to have recourse to s. 6(3)(b), there would be no exemption from the duty to abide by the Convention for private acts.[1] There is support for this in a close reading of s. 6.[2]

An important influence on the Government in casting the 'public authority' definition widely was the attitude of the European Court to a state's obligation under Article 1 of the ECHR to 'secure' Convention rights.[3] The Court has certainly treated a state as responsible for the decisions of its courts even though (as the Convention requires) courts are independent of the government. Likewise, it is responsible if it has delegated obligations to private individuals or bodies (see, e.g., *Costello-Roberts* v *UK* (1993) 19 EHRR 112).

In the media context this still leaves considerable uncertainty. The statutory regulators (such as the ITC, the Radio Authority, the BSC) will clearly be public authorities. The Advertising Standards Authority (ASA) is a company limited by guarantee. It operates on a voluntary basis, but it does so within a framework of Community law[4] and the power of the Director-General to obtain an injunction to control misleading advertisements.[5] The ASA is subject to judicial review[6] and will be a public authority for the purpose of the HRA 1998. The British Board of Film Classification (BBFC) is another example of a private body which has been brought within a statutory system of regulation. It has been designated by the Home Secretary for the purpose of operating the system of classifying videos which the Video Recordings Act 1984 requires. It would therefore be a 'public authority' when discharging these duties. So, too, would the Video Appeals Committee which hears appeals from decisions of the BBFC (see *R* v *Video Appeals Committee, ex parte BBFC* (2000) *The Times*, 7 June).

---

[1] H, Debs, col. 811, 24 November 1997.

[2] Section 6(3) does not pretend to be an exhaustive definition of 'public authority' and in some cases it will be possible to identify a body as a public authority without recourse to s. 6(3). In that case s. 6(5) would be inapplicable since the person would not be a public authority 'by virtue *only* of subsection (3)(b)' (emphasis added). For further discussion of 'public authority', see Grosz, S. et al. *Human Rights* (London, Sweet & Maxwell, 2000), paras 4-02–4-20; Lester, A. and Pannick, D., *Human Rights Law and Practice* (London, Butterworths, 1999), para. 2.6.3.

[3] See Home Secretary, HC Debs, col. 775, 16 February 1998.

[4] Directive 84/450.

[5] Control of Misleading Advertisement Regulations 1988 (SI 1988 No. 915).

[6] See *R* v *Advertising Standards Authority Ltd, ex parte Insurance Service plc* (1990) 2 Admin LR 77; *R* v *Advertising Standards Authority Ltd, ex parte Vernon Organisation Ltd* [1992] 1 WLR 1298; *R* v *Advertising Standards Authority, ex parte City Trading Ltd* [1997] COD 202; *R* v *Advertising Standards Authority Ltd, ex parte Direct Line Financial Services Ltd* [1998] COD 20.

The Press Complaints Commission (PCC), on the other hand, is a private body and an example of voluntary self-regulation. It does not exercise statutory powers and has no statutory power to enforce its rulings. It has had no statutory underpinning, although both the HRA 1998 and the Data Protection Act 1998 have the potential to make use of its Code of Conduct. It may also be said that the Commission is an example of a self-regulatory body set up by the press in the shadow of implicit (and sometimes express) threats to impose governmental regulation if self-regulation cannot be made to work. In the context of public law, this has sometimes been sufficient to make the industry's own regulator amenable to judicial review. Indeed, the PCC itself has faced judicial review proceedings, although it has never been necessary for a court to rule definitively on the matter (*R* v *Press Complaints Commission, ex parte Stewart-Brady* [1997] EMLR 185).[7] The Government said in the course of the HRA debates that it considered that the PCC undertook public functions but the press did not.[8]

Newspapers, themselves, are clearly private bodies which will not owe the duty under s. 6 even though they operate in the public domain and fulfil a public service (*Venables and Thompson* v *News Group Newspapers Ltd*, 8 January 2001, Butler-Sloss P, para. D1).

For the broadcast media, the position is again unclear. Channel 4 is a statutory corporation with statutory duties. The BBC is set up under a Royal Charter. By its Agreement with the Government it has accepted a duty to treat controversial subjects with due impartiality, an obligation which mirrors that of the ITC in the Broadcasting Act 1990, s. 6(1). The ITC is clearly subject to judicial review and it would be anomalous if the BBC was not also. The courts have avoided giving a direct answer on several occasions, but the trend seems to be in favour of recognising that for at least some of its functions the BBC is subject to judicial review (see *R* v *BBC, ex parte Referendum Party* [1997] EMLR 605 (QBD); *R* v *BBC, ex parte McAliskey* [1994] COD 498 (QBD); *R* v *BBC, ex parte Pro-Life Alliance Party* [1997] COD 457 (QBD), distinguishing *Lynch* v *BBC* [1983] NI 193). Corresponding reasoning is likely to lead the courts to treat the BBC as a 'public authority' for the purposes of the HRA 1998, at least in relation to the BBC's regulatory functions or discharge of its duties under the Charter, Licence and Agreement. In the House of Lords debates, Lord Williams of Mostyn said that the Government anticipated that the BBC would be a public authority and that Channel 4 might well be, but he emphasised that these were ultimately matters for the courts.[9] It is likely, though, that if they are public authorities, both the BBC

---

[7] Stewart-Brady's subsequent complaint to the Commission under Article 8 was dismissed as inadmissible (App. No. 36908/97, 21 October 1998)) — see Chapter 6.

[8] Hansard HC Debs, 6th ser., col. 414. On the position of the Press Complaints Commission see further Lewis, C., *Judicial Remedies in Public Law*, 2nd edn, (London, Sweet & Maxwell, 2000) at para. 2–069.

[9] HL Debs, vol. 583, coll. 1309–1310, 3 November 1997.

and Channel 4 will be so because certain of their functions are of a public nature.[10] Consequently, in their functions which are of private nature, they will not be obliged to comply with Convention rights.

3.4.4   Omissions to act

The prohibition in s. 6 against 'acting' in a way which is incompatible with a Convention right also applies to failing to act. There is a qualification for failure to introduce legislation or to make any primary legislation or remedial order (HRA 1998, s. 6(6)).

3.5   ENFORCEMENT OF CONVENTION RIGHTS: STANDING

The third key element in the HRA 1998 is its provision for the enforcement of Convention rights. They can be relied upon in the course of proceedings which have some independent purpose, or in proceedings brought specifically to enforce the Convention right. They can be raised in an appeal or on judicial review (HRA 1998, ss. 7–9).

However, a Convention right can only be enforced by a person who has been or would be a 'victim' of the violation (or potential violation) of the right (HRA 1998, s. 7(1)). The concept of 'victim' comes from the Convention itself, which allows any 'person, non-governmental organisation or group of individuals claiming to be the victim of a violation by one of the High Contracting Parties of the rights set forth in Convention or the Protocols' to make an application to the European Court of Human Rights (Article 34 ECHR). This right of individual petition to the Court was a major step forward in the growth of international human rights law. Initially, it was not an integral part of the Convention but an optional extra. Thus, although the UK was one of the original signatories to the Convention, it did not allow the right of individual petition until 1966. It then did so for renewable periods of five years. However, the right of individual access has now come to be seen as an indispensable part of the Convention's structure and is no longer optional. The UK's agreement to the right of individual petition is thus now indefinite. It is important to note that despite the HRA, those who believe that their Convention rights have been violated will still be able to make a complaint in Strasbourg (see Chapter 4). Because of the much higher profile which has been given to the Convention by the debates around the 1998 Act, and because lawyers have had to become more aware of the Convention and its jurisprudence, the legislation may have the ironic consequence that more, not fewer, cases are taken to the European Court. Decisions of the UK courts which directly address

---

[10] Note that the Commission left open the question of whether the UK Government was responsible for security vetting undertaken by the BBC in *Hilton* v *UK* (App. No. 12015/86) (1988) 57 DR 108, at 117–18. See further below at 3.5.2.

Convention issues are likely to be treated with greater respect by the Court, but there are plenty of instances where the Court has found violations from countries which have incorporated the Convention's requirements into their domestic laws.

A 'victim' must be directly affected by the violation or prospective violation of the Convention. In most cases concerning freedom of expression, this has not given rise to any problems — it has been relatively easy to identify whether the applicant has been directly affected. Applications have been accepted from publishers, printers, and individual journalists. The reach of Article 10 is even wider because it protects the right to *receive* as well as the right to *impart* information and ideas. Thus women of child-bearing age could be considered to be victims of an Irish Supreme Court injunction prohibiting the publication of information about abortion facilities provided outside Ireland (*Open Door Counselling and Dublin Well Woman* v *Ireland* (1992) 15 EHRR 244). Nonetheless, it is important to observe some of the comments which the Court and Commission have made in developing the autonomous meaning of the concept of victim.

The Irish case illustrates another proposition — that complaints can be made in advance by those who would be directly affected. The Court accepted that women of child-bearing age were potentially affected by the injunction and so were able to come within the category of 'victims' even if they were not actually pregnant. It is not easy to predict precisely when the Court will regard the potential future application of a general measure as sufficient to make a person a victim. In *Times Newspapers Ltd* v *UK* (App. No. 14631/89) (1990) 65 DR 307, it found that a newspaper publisher could in principle claim to be a victim of defamation laws that were too vague, but that on the facts of the case Times Newspapers failed because it could not point to any particular jury award which had inhibited any particular article. The Commission also rejected the complaint of a journalist to whom discovered documents had been shown by a solicitor after the documents had been read out in court. The solicitor had been treated as in contempt of court and she was therefore a victim, but no action had been taken against the journalist and the alleged chilling effect of the court's ruling against the solicitor was not sufficient to constitute him a victim (*Leigh, Guardian Newspapers Ltd and Observer Ltd* v *UK* (App. No. 10039/82) (1984) 38 DR 74). In *Bowman* v *UK* (1998) 26 EHRR 1, an anti-abortionist was able to complain of restrictions on election campaign spending even though criminal proceedings against her had been unsuccessful. She had succeeded on a technicality (the charge, which was a summary one, had not been laid within the requisite time limit). The Court accepted that the risk of further prosecutions in future campaigns was sufficiently real to mean that she could still claim to be a victim.

In many cases involving Article 10 and the media it will be all too obvious that a restriction on freedom of expression has been imposed. That will not always be the case with breaches of other Convention rights. The rights to private life and security of correspondence in Article 8, for instance, may be violated by secret surveillance. The test which the Commission used is that there must be a reasonable likelihood that some such measure had been taken against the complainant (*Hilton* v *UK* (1988) 57 DR 108).

In principle a company can claim to be a victim of a violation of Convention rights. Article 10 has frequently been invoked by companies in Strasbourg applications (e.g., *Observer and Guardian* v *UK* (1991) 14 EHRR 153; *Autronic AG* v *Switzerland* (1990) 12 EHRR 485). However, not all the Convention rights are capable of applying or are intended to apply to artificial persons. In particular, the right to a private life under Article 8 may well be essentially a right which can only be claimed by individuals. The issue was raised but not decided in a challenge by the BBC to a decision of the Broadcasting Standards Commission (BSC) upholding a complaint by the company which owned Dixons stores. The Court of Appeal held that on the proper interpretation of the Broadcasting Act 1990, the BSC could receive a complaint that a company had suffered an unwarranted infringement of its privacy. It did so expressly on the basis that the statutory jurisdiction of the BSC was not necessarily the same as the meaning of 'private life' in Article 8 (*R* v *Broadcasting Standards Commission, ex parte BBC* [2000] 3 All ER 989 (CA)). A further right under Article 8 is a right to respect for 'correspondence'. This may include business as well as personal communications (see, for instance, *Niemietz* v *Germany* (1992) 16 EHRR 97) and it may well be that the restrictions on state surveillance or intrusion protect corporate as well as individual communications.

It seems clear from Article 34 that an organ of the state cannot be a victim since it is only *non-governmental* organisations who can bring applications. Thus the Commission rejected as incompetent a complaint by a Spanish local authority (*Ayuntamiento* v *Spain* (App. No. 15090/89) (1991) 68 DR 209). On several occasions the Commission has left open the question as to whether the BBC can be a 'victim', presumably because the same question arises (see *BBC* v *UK* (App. No. 25798/94, 18 January 1996); *BBC Scotland* v *UK* (App. No. 34324/96) (1997) 25 EHRR CD 179). The UK courts may well treat the test of 'public authority' as setting appropriate limits on this exclusion (see 3.4.3 above). In particular, this model would allow the courts to avoid a crude categorisation of hybrid bodies. Whether they should be able to rely on a Convention right would depend on whether the activity in question was within their public functions (in which case they would not) or their private functions (when their position would be the same as any other company). The possibility that the BBC as a 'public authority' may be precluded from relying on Convention rights shows the continuing importance of the UK courts' new-found enthusiasm for common law principles of freedom of expression. If these are fed or underpinned by principles developed in the context of the Convention, the disadvantage of not being able to claim the status of 'victim' will be mitigated.

Strasbourg has set its face against allowing individuals or groups to bring complaints on behalf of those affected (e.g., *Klass* v *Germany* (1978) 2 EHRR 214). The *actio popularis* is not recognised by Article 34 ECHR. This means that the concept of 'victim' has a narrower meaning than the qualification for bringing an application for judicial review. The test in that context is whether the applicant has a 'sufficient interest' (see Supreme Court Act 1981, s. 31(3)), and this has been liberally interpreted to allow public interest groups (especially those with an established reputation) to test the legality of the decisions of public authorities (e.g., *R* v *Secretary of State for Social Services, ex parte Child Poverty Action Group* [1990] 2 QB 540).[11] Despite pressure to adopt the same approach to rights under the HRA 1998, the Government remained firm in its view that challenges under the Act would have to satisfy the 'victim' criterion. This is now reflected in s. 7(3), which says that: 'If the proceedings are brought on an application for judicial review, the applicant is to be taken to have a sufficient interest in relation to the unlawful act only if he is, or would be, a victim of that act.' Strasbourg has on occasions allowed interest groups to present argument as 'intervenors' (Rules of Procedure of the European Court of Human Rights, r. 61). Groups apply to the President of the Chamber who, if permission is granted, will normally restrict it to written observations. As human rights litigation develops in the UK, there may be an increasing willingness to allow similar interventions in domestic proceedings.

The position is different where the organisation represents the interests of those who are or will be directly affected. Strasbourg has accepted that professional bodies, trade unions and non-governmental organisations can represent members in this way, but they must be prepared to identify the affected members and establish that they do in fact have authority to act on their behalf (*Confédération des Syndicats Médicaux Français* v *France* (1986) 47 DR 225 and *Ahmed* v *UK* (1995) 20 EHRR CD 72). In these circumstances, the individuals become the applicants (a matter which may have profound consequences in terms of costs of unsuccessful proceedings). In judicial review, trade unions have sufficient standing to represent the interests of affected members (see *R* v *Horsham Justices, ex parte Farquharson* [1982] QB 762, holding that the National Union of Journalists had sufficient standing to challenge an order of magistrates postponing reporting of committal proceedings, and *Royal College of Nursing* v *Department of Health and Social Security* [1982] AC 800.

Of course, an organisation may on occasions allege that it is itself a victim of a violation of a Convention right (e.g., *Council of Civil Service Unions* v *UK* (1987) 50 DR 228; *Christians against Racism and Fascism* v *UK* (App. No. 8440/78) (1980) 21 DR 138). So, for instance, the refusal to allow a pressure group to advertise on the television or radio may lead to a claim by the group that its own right to freedom of expression has been violated.

---

[11] See Lewis, *op. cit.* n. 8, at para. 10-024.

3.6   ENFORCEMENT OF CONVENTION RIGHTS: WHICH COURT?

3.6.1   Introduction

Assuming that the complainant satisfies the test of 'victim' (see 3.5 above), there are essentially two ways in which Convention rights can be enforced:

    (a)   in proceedings brought specifically to enforce the Convention right;
    (b)   in the course of other legal proceedings (HRA 1998, s. 7(1)).

The Act makes clear that these procedures are intended to be additional to any other rights which the person might have under domestic law and are not intended to restrict his or her right to make any other claim or bring any other proceedings apart from these new remedies under the 1998 Act (HRA 1998, s. 11).

3.6.2   Independent proceedings to enforce Convention rights

A new right to bring proceedings specifically to enforce Convention rights is created by s. 7(1)(a) the Act.[12] The proceedings must be brought in the 'appropriate court or tribunal' (HRA 1998, s. 7(2)). These are defined by rules, which presently only stipulate that a claim under s. 7(1)(a) in respect of a judicial act must be brought in the High Court. Other claims under s. 7(1)(a) may be brought in any court (CPR Part 7, r. 7.11).

3.6.3   Limitation period

There is a one-year time limit for bringing independent proceedings. The court has a power to extend this limit if it considers that it would be equitable to do so having regard to all the circumstances. However, if the procedure which is adopted sets a stricter time limit, that will prevail (HRA 1998, s. 7(5)). Thus, where the challenge is made by judicial review, claimants will still have to observe the requirement to apply promptly, and in any event within three months of the act complained of (but with the court having power to extend time: Supreme Court Act 1981, s. 31(4)).

3.6.4   Human rights claims in other proceedings

The second alternative is for the Convention claim to be made in proceedings which have an independent life (HRA 1998, s. 7(1)(b)). This includes legal proceedings which are brought by or at the instigation of a public authority (HRA 1998, s. 7(6)(a)). This provision will have particular importance in the early days of the implementation of the Act. Ordinarily it will not be possible to enforce

---

[12] These will be civil proceedings. The Act does not create any new criminal offences: s. 7(8).

Convention rights by any of the methods established by s. 7 if the act complained of took place before that section came into force (2 October 2000). However, an exception is made where the Convention right is sought to be enforced in legal proceedings brought by or at the instigation of a public authority. In that case, a Convention right can be enforced whenever the act in question took place (HRA 1998, s. 22(4)).

We have seen that courts and tribunals are included in the category of 'public authority' (3.4.3 above). It follows that they have their own duty to act compatibly with Convention rights. A complaint that a lower court or tribunal has failed in this duty cannot be the subject of independent proceedings; it can be raised only by exercising a right of appeal or making an application for judicial review (HRA 1998, s. 9(1)). This does not derogate from any rule of law which prevents a court from being the subject of judicial review (HRA 1998, s. 9(2)). Thus the prohibition in the Supreme Court Act 1981, s. 29(3), which prevents judicial review of matters relating to trial on indictment, remains.

Because courts are public authorities, any orders which they make which would have the effect of restricting freedom of expression will have to satisfy the Convention right under Article 10. Thus the possibility of raising Convention issues in proceedings which have an independent existence is not confined to proceedings which are brought by or at the instigation of a public authority. Ordinary libel litigation, actions for breach of confidence, actions for copyright infringement, or indeed any of the media torts could potentially raise issues under Article 10 ECHR. This conclusion is reinforced by the special measures required by s. 12 of the HRA, discussed at 3.8 below (*Douglas* v *Hello!* (2001) *The Times*, 16 January, Sedley LJ at para. 134 and *Venables and Thompson* v *News Group Ltd*, 8 January 2001, para. D2–3).

3.7 ENFORCEMENT OF CONVENTION RIGHTS: REMEDIES

3.7.1 Introduction

If a court finds that an act of a public authority is or would be unlawful because of a conflict with a Convention right, it can grant such relief or remedy or make such order within its powers as it considers just and appropriate (HRA 1998, s. 8(1) and (6)).

These are broad words, and the Government intended that through the scheme of remedies established by the Act it would have complied with its obligation under Article 13 ECHR to provide effective remedies for alleged breaches of Convention rights.[13] It is likely, therefore, that the courts will have regard to the Convention case law on Article 13 for this purpose, even though that part

---

[13] HL Debs, col. 475, 18 November 1997.

of the ECHR is not included among the Convention rights set out in Schedule 1 to the Act (see 3.2.1 above).

3.7.2 Damages

The remedy can include damages, but there are three important restrictions:

(a) the court or tribunal must have the power to award damages or order the payment of compensation in civil proceedings (HRA 1998, s. 8(2));

(b) the court must be satisfied that damages are necessary to afford 'just satisfaction' having regard to any other remedy that is granted and the consequences of any decision in respect of the challenged act (HRA 1998, s. 8(3));[14]

(c) the court must be guided, in deciding whether to award damages and the amount of any damages which it does give, by the principles of the European Court in awarding compensation (HRA 1998, s. 8(4)).[15]

The Strasbourg approach to damages is generally parsimonious. There are three headings under which it will consider loss: pecuniary; non-pecuniary; costs and expenses. Understandably, there must be a causal link between the violation and the pecuniary loss which is alleged, and the loss must actually have occurred. Journalists fined in situations where the Court has found a violation of Article 10 have been awarded the amount of the fine (e.g., *Lingens* v *Austria* (1986) 8 EHRR 407, where the Court also awarded a sum to represent lost opportunity). That will not be necessary in the domestic context if (as would be likely) the court considering the allegation of Article 10 infringement would be able to quash the fine. Otherwise the establishment of pecuniary loss to the satisfaction of the European Court has been rare.[16] So far as non-pecuniary loss is concerned, the court has tended to hold that the finding of a violation amounts to just satisfaction.[17]

---

[14] The phrase 'just satisfaction' is taken from Article 41 ECHR, which requires the Court if necessary after finding a violation to 'afford just satisfaction to the injured party'.

[15] This refers expressly to Article 41 of the Convention. Prior to the adoption of the Eleventh Protocol, remedies were granted by the European Court of Human Rights under Article 50. The UK courts are likely to look at decisions under both provisions which are not materially different.

[16] Unusual examples were the *Open Door* case (see 3.5 above) where the pregnancy counselling service was awarded £25,000 Ir for pecuniary loss and *Bergens Tidende*, where the Norwegian government had to pay over £400,000 to compensate the applicants for their pecuniary loss (see further below at 5.5.3).

[17] See Reid, K., *A Practitioner's Guide to the European Convention of Human Rights* (London, Sweet & Maxwell, 1998), Part III, who sets out tables of cases where the Court has made awards. The table is reproduced and updated in Simor, J. and Emmerson, B. (eds), *Human Rights Practice* (London, Sweet & Maxwell, 2000 — loose-leaf).

3.7.3 Damages for judicial acts

Special restrictions apply where a 'judicial act' is found to be unlawful because it violates a Convention right. 'Judicial act' means a judicial act of a court, and includes an act done on the instructions of or on behalf of a 'judge'. For these purposes, 'judge' includes a member of a tribunal, a magistrate and a clerk or other officer entitled to exercise the jurisdiction of a court (HRA 1998, s. 9(5)). Damages cannot be awarded in respect of a judicial act unless it is to compensate for unlawful detention (see Article 5(5) ECHR) or the act was not done in good faith (HRA 1998, s. 9(3)). In these special cases, the award of damages is against the Crown, but the Minster responsible for the court concerned, or a person or government department nominated by him, must first be joined to the proceedings (HRA 1998, s. 9(4)).

3.8 SPECIAL PROVISIONS CONCERNING FREEDOM OF EXPRESSION

3.8.1 Criminal proceedings

Section 12 of the HRA 1998 makes several specific provisions relating to freedom of expression. They apply whenever a court (or tribunal) is considering whether to grant relief which, if granted, might affect the exercise of the Convention right to freedom of expression (HRA 1998, s. 12(1)). 'Relief' is defined to include any remedy or order 'other than in criminal proceedings' (HRA 1998, s. 12(5)). The qualification means that the specific provisions in s. 12 cannot be invoked when a criminal court is, for instance, considering an application for reporting restrictions. However, s. 12 does not derogate from the interpretative obligation in s. 3 or the duty on all courts (including criminal courts) as public authorities to act compatibly with Convention rights in s. 6.[18] These obligations would anyway require the courts to have regard to the extent to which the material is or is about to become available to the public, or to the public interest in the material being published (see s. 12(4)(a)). Neither does s. 12 affect s. 11, which makes clear that the new obligations are cumulative and do not restrict any pre-existing rights. The exclusion of criminal courts from s. 12 should not therefore affect the case law which has already accumulated as to the principles to be applied in dealing with applications for reporting restrictions of criminal proceedings.

3.8.2 Restrictions on *ex parte* relief

Where s. 12 does apply it restricts the grant of relief which is given without notice to the respondent and which would affect Convention rights concerning freedom

---

[18] As the Home Secretary said in the House of Commons Committee: Hansard, vol. 315, col. 540 (2 July 1998).

of expression. The court must be satisfied that the applicant has taken all practicable steps to notify the respondent, or that there are compelling reasons why the respondent should not be notified (HRA 1998, s. 12(2)). These requirements are not significantly different from the practice which prevails in any event (see CPR Part 25, r. 25.2(1)), but the requirement is now peremptory and statutory. Future applications for *ex parte* injunctions will have to address specifically these matters as to which the court must be satisfied.

3.8.3   Restrictions on pre-trial injunctions

Section 12(3) makes new provision for pre-trial injunctions (whether or not notice of the application was given to the respondent):

> (3)   No such relief [19] is to be granted so as to restrain publication before trial unless the court is satisfied that the applicant is likely to establish that publication should not be allowed.

This should make clear that courts cannot in freedom of expression cases simply apply the test in *American Cyanamid Co.* v *Ethicon Ltd* [1975] AC 396, of deciding whether the claimant has shown an arguable case and then determining whether or not to grant an injunction on the balance of convenience. In cases concerning breach of confidence, in particular, *American Cyanamid* has led the courts to be ready to grant pre-trial injunctions in order to preserve the *status quo*. That will no longer be a proper approach. Difficult as it may be in the rushed circumstances in which applications are often heard, and with the evidence then only in an incomplete state, the court will have to determine the likelihood of the claimant succeeding at trial. The onus is on the claimant, who will, presumably, have to address and dispose of any likely defences which the defendant might advance at trial.

The effect of s. 12(3) was considered by the Court of Appeal in *Douglas* v *Hello!* (2001) *The Times*, 16 January (especially Keene LJ at paras 150–153 with whom Brooke LJ, para. 54, and Sedley LJ, para. 136, agreed). It recognised that the subsection did not give automatic priority to freedom of expression, but required the court to attempt to look ahead to the final trial and decide whether any balancing exercise between competing rights would come down in favour of the claimant. Even if the answer was in the affirmative, the court retained a discretion — a discretion which ultimately led to the claimants failing to obtain their injunction (see further Chapter 6).

The test of likely success at trial is probably rather lower than the test which is presently applied in libel cases. A claimant will not succeed in obtaining a pre-trial injunction to restrain a defamatory publication if the defendant states that he is prepared to justify the truth of the publication at trial (or defend it as fair

---

[19] That is relief which might affect the exercise of the Convention right to freedom of expression.

comment or a publication on a privileged occasion) (see *Bonnard* v *Perryman* [1891] 2 Ch 269 (justification); *Quartz Hill Consolidated Mining Company* v *Beal* [1882] 20 ChD 501 (privilege); *Fraser* v *Evans* [1969] 1 QB 349 (fair comment). Here it is not enough for the claimant to show that he will be likely to succeed at trial. In exceptional cases, if the claimant could show that the libel was plainly untrue or (in the case of fair comment or qualified privilege) plainly malicious he might succeed despite the defendant's intention to defend, but it is an extremely difficult hurdle for the claimant to overcome. Section 12(3) ought not to affect the operation of these principles. As already noted, s. 11(a) makes clear that the purpose of the Act is to give further protections for human rights, not to detract from those which already exist.

3.8.4   Prior publicity, public interest and privacy

In dealing with matters which might affect freedom of expression, the court is required to have 'particular regard to the importance of the Convention right to freedom of expression' (HRA 1998, s. 12(4)). This is harmonious with the approach of the European Court, which on several occasions has spoken of the special importance of freedom of expression in a democracy (e.g., *Lingens* v *Austria* (1986) 8 EHRR 407, at 418–9). Although in applying this principle, the courts will need to consider the qualifications on that right in Article 10(2) (*Douglas* v *Hello!* above at para. 137).

Section 12(4) gives more specific direction where the proceedings relate to material which the respondent claims, or which appears to the court, to be journalistic, literary or artistic material (or to conduct connected with such material). In these cases, the court must have particular regard to:

    (a)   the extent to which—
       (i)   the material has, or is about to, become available to the public; or
       (ii) it is, or would be, in the public interest for the material to be published;
    (b)   any relevant privacy code.

Paragraph (a) represents considerations which the court would presently take into account in any event, at least in connection with breach of confidence claims. In copyright claims, the Court of Appeal has recently rejected the idea that there is a general 'public interest' defence to claims for infringement of copyright (*Hyde Park Residence Ltd* v *Yelland* [2000] 3 WLR 215 (CA)). In *Ashdown* v *Telegraph Group Ltd*, 11 January 2001, the Vice-Chancellor rejected an argument that this decision and the pre-HRA interpretations of the defences to infringement claims and the Copyright, Designs and Patents Act 1988 defence of fair dealing for the purposes of reporting current events or for criticism and review needed to be reconsidered in the light of the HRA 1998. He considered that the balance between freedom of expression and the rights of a copyright owner were already struck by the 1988 Act. He did, however, give the defendant leave to appeal to the Court of Appeal.

The reference to a relevant privacy code is not further defined. This contrasts with the Data Protection Act 1998, which allows the Government to specify a relevant code by subordinate legislation (see s. 32(3) of that Act). The obvious candidates include the codes of the ITC, the Radio Authority, the BSC and the Press Complaints Commission.[20] However, because the court can have regard to *any* relevant privacy code, there is the possibility that other codes (such as codes adopted within a particular media organisation) may also be examined by the court.

Some have seen the reference to privacy codes as a signal that Parliament intends the courts to develop a tort of privacy infringement. We discuss this more generally in Chapter 6. It would be odd, though, if s. 12 did have this effect. Its whole tenor and purpose is to make special provision for freedom of expression. Section 12(4) itself begins with an injunction to the courts to have particular regard to the importance of freedom of expression. Section 12(4)(a) sets out matters which would militate in favour of freedom of expression. Compliance with a privacy code would do so as well. However, like the factors in para. (a), this would be material for the media in constructing a defence to a cause of action (or ground for interference with freedom of expression) which independently exists. Neither can it be said that para. (b) assumes the existence or future development of a tort of privacy. There are many other contexts in which a court may presently be faced with claims which would impinge on freedom of expression and where a privacy code might be relevant. They include breach of confidence actions, the decisions of the regulators of the broadcasting media and the data protection provisions. It has been strenuously argued that, if the PCC is a public authority which is required to comply with the Convention, the courts should be even more reluctant to develop a new tort.[21]

---

[20] These were all examples given by the Home Secretary in the House of Commons: Hansard, vol. 315, coll. 538–539, 2 July 1998. He also suggested that an internal code of a newspaper or a broadcaster might be relevant: see Chapter 6 for the website addresses where these codes can be viewed.

[21] Lester and Pannick, *op. cit.* n. 2, at para. 2.12.

Chapter Four

When Rights Have Not Been Brought Home: Taking a Case to Strasbourg

4.1 INTRODUCTION

By Article 1 ECHR, contracting states assume two fundamental obligations. First, they must ensure that 'their domestic body of law is compatible with the Convention, and if need be to make any necessary adjustments to this end';[1] secondly, they must remedy any breach if and when it occurs. Although the Convention leaves it to each contracting state to decide how to secure the enforcement of the rights enshrined in it through its domestic law, Article 13 requires an effective remedy before a national authority where a violation has occurred. The substance of a complaint to the European Court of Human Rights is that a state which is a party to the Convention has failed to honour its obligations, and thereby to 'secure' one or more of the Convention rights and freedoms 'to everyone within their jurisdiction'.

The HRA 1998 seeks to ensure that the United Kingdom honours these obligations by introducing the Convention into the existing legal system. However, there will still be cases where complainants will have to go to the Strasbourg Court for their remedy. The most obvious examples are where the domestic courts cannot remedy a breach because of primary legislation which cannot be interpreted compatibly with Convention rights and which the Government will not amend, or because of the lack of specific legislation where the common law or interpretation of more general legislation cannot be used to provide the remedy. Cases will also still be brought where the domestic courts fail to recognise a breach of the ECHR. Although Article 33 permits one contracting state

---

[1] 214/56 Yearbook 234.

to bring another before the Court, this is done very rarely. This chapter is therefore concerned only with complaints by victims whose rights have been infringed, whether about the law, acts of government bodies or decisions of domestic courts.

4.2   THE STRASBOURG COURT

4.2.1   The permanent Court

Section II of the ECHR deals with the Court. Before 1 November 1998, two organs were involved: the European Commission and the European Court of Human Rights. On that date Protocol 11 came into force. This brought about a radical change in the procedures for enforcement. Both existing institutions were abolished. For the first time individuals were given direct access to a newly constituted European Court of Human Rights. Whereas previously the Court had sat only part-time, now under Article 19 the new Court functions on a permanent basis to 'ensure the observance' of the obligations of contracting states. States must not 'hinder in any way the effective enforcement of this right' by obstructing the applicant's communications with the Court or exerting pressure to withdraw or modify the complaint. (See Article 34 for the right of individual petition and *Akdivar* v *Turkey* (1996) 23 EHRR 143, at para. 105.) Protocol 11 also revised the role of the Committee of Ministers of the Council of Europe in the Convention process. Its only important remaining function is to receive final judgments of the Court and ensure compliance by the relevant member state (see Article 46 ECHR).

The Court consists of 40 judges, each elected by the Parliamentary Assembly of the Council of Europe from a list of nominees put forward by each ratifying state. The full plenary Court is convened only for administrative decisions. A President and Vice-President, responsible for the administration of the Court, are elected each three years by the plenary Court. In outline, the Court receives complaints, considers whether they are 'admissible' and, if they are, decides whether the Convention has been violated. Under Article 41, it may order the state to pay compensation and costs to the successful applicant. The current rules of the Court were adopted at its inception on 1 November 1998.

4.2.2   The judicial structures of the Court

All complaints are initially referred to a single judge known as a 'rapporteur', who reports to either one of the Chambers set up by the plenary Court or to a Committee of three judges on the question of admissibility.[2] Each Chamber constitutes its own Committees. When deciding cases Chambers consist of seven

---

[2] Rules of Procedure of the European Court of Human Rights, r. 49(1) and (2)(b). See also 4.5.4 below. Throughout this chapter, references to rules are to the Rules of Procedure of the ECHR, unless specified otherwise.

judges, one of whom sits as President, plus at least one judge from, or chosen by, the state against whom the complaint is made (r. 26(1)(a)). The highest judicial body within the Court structure is the Grand Chamber, consisting of 17 judges. This may determine complex and serious cases 'relinquished' to it by a Chamber with the agreement of the parties (Article 30 ECHR and r. 72) and may hear appeals from Chambers' judgments on the merits (Article 43 ECHR and r. 73). Permission for such an appeal is required from a screening panel of five judges, but will be given if 'the case raises a serious question affecting the interpretation of the Convention ... or a serious issue of general importance'. There is no appeal against Committee or admissibility decisions.

4.2.3   The Registry

This consists of lawyers (known as 'legal secretaries') and support staff, and carries out most of the day-to-day administration of the Court. It is headed by a Registrar and two Deputies appointed by the plenary Court (rr. 15 and 16). The Registry lawyer assigned to the case will be the applicant's point of contact with the Court. For this reason, he or she will usually be a national of the state concerned.

4.3   LEGAL AID

At present our domestic legal aid scheme does not cover the bringing of a complaint to the Court. However, lawyers may enter into conditional fee agreements to pursue cases to Strasbourg.[3] Limited legal aid may be granted by the Court towards the end of the examination of a complaint's admissibility (r. 91). It will be granted, if necessary for the proper conduct of the case, where the applicant has insufficient means to meet all or part of the costs (r. 92). The contracting party is asked to submit its comments on the question of 'sufficient means'. In practice the United Kingdom authorities respond by indicating whether the applicant meets the standards of financial eligibility for civil legal aid. If so, the Court will invariably grant legal aid. In most cases this involves the payment of set amounts for specified pieces of work, such as drafting the application or the reply to the government's response, and representing the applicant at hearings. The amounts are not generous and would not correspond to normal professional fees for domestic work. The Court will meet the representation costs of one lawyer only, and these may not extend much beyond travelling and hotel costs. A successful complainant may be awarded costs, though again these are not generous.

---

[3] See the Courts and Legal Services Act 1990, ss. 58 and 58A, as amended by the Access to Justice Act 1999, s. 27 and the Conditional Fees Order 2000 (SI 2000 No. 823). As with all conditional fees, the maximum success fee is 100% of the normal fee — see Article 4 of the Order.

4.4   MAKING A COMPLAINT

The procedure for making a complaint is relatively straightforward but moves slowly. The majority of cases are rejected as inadmissible without a hearing. It is therefore vital that complaints explain why the admissibility criteria are met (see 4.5 below) and set out in full the facts, domestic law and the arguments of Convention law as to why the grievance amounts to a violation.

4.4.1   The time limit for submitting complaints

Under Article 35(1) ECHR, a complaint may be considered only if it is made 'within a period of six months from the date on which the final decision was taken'. The decision is the final effective domestic remedy. This rule is applied strictly, save that time is taken to run from the date upon which the applicant receives the reasons for the decision (*Worm* v *Austria* (1997) 25 EHRR 454, at para. 33) or becomes aware of the violation (*Isabel Hilton* v *UK* (App. No. 12015/86) (1988) 57 DR 108, at 113). However, where the complaint is about the continuing operation of a law and the complainant is a potential, rather than an actual, victim of the law (see 4.5.2 below), or is about a continuing state of affairs, such as a ban on particular publications, where there is no effective domestic remedy time does not begin to run at all until the law is repealed or the situation ends. Where a domestic remedy is pursued but may, in the end, prove to be ineffective (for example, because leave to appeal is refused), an applicant must protect his or her position by submitting an appeal within six months of the previous decision. A claim is submitted as at the date of the initial written communication, which may be a letter or fax to the Court, provided it sets out basic details of the complaint (*Khan* v *UK* (1995) 21 EHRR CD 67).

4.4.2   The application form

There is a standard application form. If this has not been used as the initial communication, the Court will reply by sending one. Once this has been returned completed, the complaint will be registered. The form requires:

(a)   the applicant's name, age, address, nationality, sex and occupation;

(b)   the name, occupation and address of any representative;

(c)   the name of the respondent country;

(d)   a clear statement of the relevant facts, including dates;

(e)   identification of the Articles of the Convention said to have been violated and the arguments (with reference to case law) to support these allegations;

(f)   a clear statement as to why the admissibility criteria (see 4.5 below) are met. The six-month rule and the requirement to exhaust domestic remedies must be addressed;

(g)   information as to the overall object of the complaint (for example, repeal of legislation) and any 'just satisfaction' including compensation sought under Article 41 ECHR (see 4.7 below);

(h) copies of relevant documents, including decisions;
(i) an indication of what, if any, other international procedures have been used to remedy the grievance.

If the form is lacking in detail or unclear, the complainant runs the risk that the rapporteur who considers it will be unable to identify a proper Convention point and will make a recommendation for rejection of the complaint through the Committee procedure.

4.5 ADMISSIBILITY

4.5.1 Initial inadmissibility

Complaints will fall at the first hurdle if they do not comply with the following requirements of Article 35(2) and (3) ECHR:

(a) The complainant must have been identified. The Court will not consider anonymous applications. Although the applicant may ask to be identified only to the respondent state, such a request will be granted only in exceptional and duly justified cases.[4]
(b) The complaint must not be substantially the same as one already examined by the Court or some other international body, and must not be 'incompatible with the Convention . . ., manifestly ill-founded, or an abuse of the right of application'.

The more detailed grounds for rejection, beyond these, are dealt with at 4.5.2 and 4.5.3 below.

A complaint is 'incompatible' if it is clearly outside the scope of the Convention altogether, for example because it does not concern a right protected by the ECHR or is about the acts or omissions of private persons rather than the failure of the state to protect such a right. However, the Court appears increasingly willing to use the concept of 'positive obligation' to uphold complaints arising out of disputes between private persons, particularly in the context of Article 10 ECHR. In the recent case of *Fuentes Bobo* v *Spain* (App. No. 39293/98, 29 February 2000), the applicant had been dismissed by the state television company for speaking out publicly against management in a labour dispute. The Spanish High Court had found the dismissal to be lawful in employment law, and the Constitutional Court had dismissed a subsequent appeal by the applicant based on his right to freedom of expression. A majority of the European Court, however,

---

[4] Since this is a departure from the principle in Article 40(2) ECHR that all documents deposited at the Registry are public, where confidentiality is requested the application must contain a statement of reasons: r. 47(3).

held that the dismissal amounted to a violation of his Article 10 right, emphasising that Article 10 ECHR applies to relations between an employer and employee governed by private law and that a state has a positive obligation in some such cases to protect freedom of expression.

The violation must occur within the jurisdiction of the state concerned, but not necessarily within its territory. The question is whether the state has *de facto* control over the events in issue. (See, for example, *Loizidou* v *Turkey* (1996) 23 EHRR 513, at para. 52, where it was held that Turkey exercised sufficient control over the administration in Northern Cyprus.) Thus although a state has no control over standards of justice in other countries, it may be liable if it expels a person knowing that he or she will face detention and trial involving a 'flagrant denial of justice' (*M.A.R.* v *UK* (App. No. 28038/95, 16 January 1996)). Complaints cannot be brought in respect of protocols which the contracting state has not yet ratified. However, Protocol 11 now precludes a state ratifying a protocol but refusing to accept that there is a right of individual petition in connection with it.

The cases do not establish any clear or consistent approach to the application of the 'manifestly ill-founded' ground of rejection. The best that can be said is that it represents a threshold merits test. If a complaint is prima facie within the scope of the Convention and the Court considers that a full examination of its merits is justified, it will pass the threshold test.

4.5.2   The applicant must be a 'victim'

A complaint may be brought only by a person, non-governmental organisation (such as a commercial company, voluntary organisation or political party) or a group of individuals 'claiming to be the victim of a violation' (Article 34 ECHR). In 1990, Times Newspapers tried to challenge the use of juries with unrestricted powers to award damages to try libel actions. The applicant complained of the 'chilling effect' on journalistic freedom of expression of a series of recent large awards in the High Court. The Commission found the application to be manifestly ill-founded because Times Newspapers could not be regarded as a victim. Rather, it was simply trying to challenge 'the general state of the law relating to jury trial in defamation actions' (*Times Newspapers* v *UK* (App. No. 14631/89) (1990) 65 DR 307, at 312). However, there is no requirement that the complainant be a citizen of, or in some way physically present in, the state concerned, or indeed any state of the Council of Europe. Thus an American magazine or newspaper could complain if its freedom to circulate in a contracting state was interfered with by the government. Where the victim is incapacitated, an authorised representative may make the complaint on his or her behalf. A child may complain through a parent, guardian or other authorised representative, including a lawyer (*PP and T* v *UK* (1996) 22 EHRR CD 148).

The Court recognises three types of victim. An 'actual victim' must already have been personally affected by the violation. Such a victim does not have to show that damage or detriment has been suffered, though whether it has been will be relevant to the nature of just satisfaction under Article 41 (see 4.6.2). In the Times Newspapers admissibility decision, the Commission observed that the applicant could have been regarded as a victim if it had identified a particular article or allegation which it had decided not to publish because of the risk of high damages award (at 312). The complaint raised by Times Newspapers was eventually considered by the Court in *Tolstoy Miloslavsky* v *UK* (1995) 20 EHRR 442, where the applicant was 'personally affected' as a defendant against whom a massive damages award had actually been made. This case is discussed in detail in Chapter 5.

Victim status can be lost if the government provides sufficient redress to the applicant in the teeth of the challenge. However, the redress must be effective and the national authority must acknowledge that there has been a breach of the Convention. In *Dalban* v *Romania* (2000) 8 BHRC 91, the applicant was a journalist who had been convicted and ordered to pay damages in criminal libel proceedings. After the Commission had ruled in his favour he died, and his widow continued the proceedings. Before the case reached the Court the applicant's conviction was quashed by the Romanian Supreme Court. The government argued that this removed his status, and therefore that of his widow, as a 'victim'. This argument was rejected. The Court noted that the Supreme Court had quashed his conviction on one of the charges only because of his death, a decision which did not involve any acknowledgement of breach of the Convention. It also doubted whether the widow could obtain compensation for the financial losses through civil proceedings easily or, indeed, at all. This case is also discussed in more detail in Chapter 5.

A 'potential victim' is at risk of being personally affected. In one case the Court accepted that a group of German lawyers could challenge laws permitting secret phone tapping even though there was no evidence of a particular risk that their lines would be tapped. The fact that any tapping would be secretive was regarded as an important factor by the Court in treating them as potential victims (*Klass* v *Germany* (1978) 2 EHRR 214, at para. 34). An 'indirect victim' is one who is immediately affected by the direct violation of the rights of another person — for example, the family of a prisoner.

4.5.3 Exhaustion of all effective domestic remedies

Article 35(1) ECHR specifies that the jurisdiction of the Court can be invoked only 'after all domestic remedies have been exhausted'. Only then can it be said that the contracting state's own institutions have conclusively failed to protect the substantive Convention rights in issue. As the Court has put it, applicants must provide the national courts with a full opportunity 'of preventing or putting right the violations' before going to Strasbourg (*Cardot* v *France* (1991) 13 EHRR 853, para. 36). This is one of the key procedural rules under the Convention, but one which is often misunderstood or misapplied by applicants and their lawyers, with the result that many complaints are ruled inadmissible.

The application should set out why the applicant believes that all domestic remedies have been exhausted. The onus is then on the state to show why this is not the case. In seeking to do this the state can rely on any effective and available remedy which has some prospect of success. Because of this, if there is more than one effective possible remedy, they should all be pursued by the applicant before turning to Strasbourg. In *Earl Spencer v United Kingdom* (App. Nos 28851/95 and 28852/95) (1998) 92 DR 56 (see further Chapter 6), Earl Spencer and his wife complained under Article 8 ECHR about the failure of domestic law to protect them against unwanted tabloid intrusions into their private lives. Although they had complained to the Press Complaints Commission, their applications to Strasbourg were ruled inadmissible because they had failed to sue the papers concerned and had settled breach of confidence proceedings against two friends suspected of being the source of the stories.[5] If in doubt, claimants should always try to pursue the remedy, or obtain the opinion of a senior lawyer specialising in the relevant area of law that it would be futile to do so. Provided this is fully reasoned and its conclusion cannot be conclusively challenged by the Government (for example, because it has failed to take into account a determinative piece of case law), it will normally be accepted by the Court. (In *Wingrove v UK* (1996) 24 EHRR 1, a complaint about a decision of the British Board of Film Censors was admitted on the basis of leading counsel's advice that judicial review was futile; this case is discussed fully in Chapter 8.) In the past the Government has sometimes agreed that further appeals would be pointless where the domestic law is sufficiently clear, although this may not happen so often in the years following the implementation of the HRA 1998. Similarly, where legal aid has been sought to pursue the remedy but refused on the merits, the Court is usually prepared to treat the remedy as exhausted. If it has been refused on grounds of financial ineligibility, however, the claimant must either instruct a lawyer privately, or exercise his or her rights to litigate in person.

If the state identifies a possible avenue which has not been pursued, the applicant must show why it would have been ineffective, or that there were special reasons for not pursuing it. A remedy may be ineffective because it is discretionary, particularly if the discretion lies with a public authority rather than a court. An appeal may be ineffective because it is bound to fail because of binding legal precedent or a statutory provision. In due course the Court will have to decide whether the procedure for seeking a declaration of incompatibility under the HRA 1998 affords an effective remedy. This remedy is discussed in detail at

---

[5] See also *Chappell v UK* (1989) 12 EHRR 1, where documents had been wrongly seized under an *Anton Piller* order. Contempt proceedings, a damages claim and an application for return of the documents all had to be pursued.

Chapter 3. In principle it is difficult to see how this procedure (which is not a full constitutional challenge to overturn the law) could be regarded as effective to remedy the *applicant's* complaint. The Court has considered the effectiveness of judicial review proceedings under Article 13 ECHR, which guarantees an effective remedy for the enforcement of substantive Convention rights, in the context of decisions to expel and deport. It has accepted that the High Court's power to quash such decisions where there is a serious risk to life (Article 2) or of inhuman or degrading treatment (Article 3) means that there is an effective remedy (*Soering* v *United Kingdom* (1989) 11 EHRR 439; *D* v *United Kingdom* (1997) 24 EHRR 423). However, this was not the case where the factual basis for the decision to expel could not be reviewed because of national security considerations (*Chahal* v *United Kingdom* (1996) 23 EHRR 413), or when the decision under challenge was a government policy and where the domestic court could not properly measure the policy against Convention rights (*Smith and Grady* v *UK* (1999) 29 EHRR 493). The implementation of the HRA 1998 requires the High Court to scrutinise cases involving infringements of Convention rights even more closely. It therefore increases the effectiveness of the judicial review remedy, in particular through the s. 6 requirement that public authorities act compatibly with Convention rights and the Court's consideration of whether infringements are 'necessary in a democratic society' (see further Chapter 3).

The remedy must be effective in all respects. For example, a challenge to an extradition order which is said to expose the individual to serious mistreatment will not be effective unless the order is stayed pending the outcome. If the state wishes to argue that there is an effective remedy, it must do so at the admissibility stage and cannot take a different position on 'availability' to that which it took in the national courts (*Bricmont* v *Belgium* (1989) 12 EHRR 217, at para. 73). The exhaustion must have occurred by the time admissibility is considered, which may take some time. It is therefore possible to get a 'flying start' by submitting an anticipatory application to the Court as the conclusion of the final stage approaches, in the expectation that the remedy will not be obtained.

4.5.4 Procedure for determining admissibility

The rapporteur writes a report to the Committee or Chamber to which the complaint is referred. Where the rapporteur considers that it is inadmissible on its face (perhaps after clarification has been sought from the applicant), it will simply be referred to a Committee which (if unanimous) may declare it inadmissible without further formality (Article 28 ECHR and r. 53(3)). Where the case is referred to a Chamber, whether by the rapporteur or because the Committee cannot agree unanimously upon inadmissibility (r. 53(4)), the Chamber decides how to deal with the case under r. 54. It may also declare the case inadmissible without taking any further steps (r. 54(2)). If it does not, it may investigate further with the complainant and will formally 'communicate' the complaint to the state asking it to give its observations on the issues concerning the Court by way of a response (r. 54(3)). This will address the merits of the complaint and any admissibility points the Government takes. The applicant replies to this. The Chamber may then convene a short oral admissibility hearing before giving its decision, particularly if the complainant asks for one (r. 54(4)). In rare cases it may combine this with the final merits hearing (Article 29(3) ECHR). The decision may be reached by a majority and will be given in writing (r. 56). While it is considering a case, the Chamber, or its President, may indicate to the parties an 'interim measure' which it considers should be adopted in the interests of the parties or the proper conduct of the proceedings (r. 39; for example, to prevent destruction of an artistic work held to be obscene, though usually the state will postpone irreversible action once it is aware of a complaint to the Court).

4.6   CONSIDERATION OF THE COMPLAINT

Once the Court has decided that a case is admissible it considers the merits of the complaint. It may invite the parties to submit further evidence and submissions in writing (r. 59(1)). The Chamber can decide to hold an oral hearing on the merits. If it does not, and there was no oral hearing on the merits at the admissibility stage, one of the parties can request a hearing post-admissibility. However, the parties do not have the right to insist on an oral hearing: the Chamber may 'exceptionally decide that the discharging of its functions under Article 38(1)(a) does not require a hearing to be held' (r. 59(2)). After admissibility, the Chamber will try to reach a negotiated agreement, known as a 'friendly settlement', between the applicant and the state 'on the basis of respect for human rights as defined in the Convention' (Article 38 ECHR and r. 62). This gives the state an opportunity to avoid the political embarrassment of a decision involving censure by the Court. Settlements have become more common as the jurisprudence of the Court has developed, enabling states to predict more accurately when they may lose a case. However, the Court must be satisfied that any settlement takes account of the general interest. It may therefore require changes in the law, or the convening of an inquiry or commissioning of an independent report, in addition to compensation and other redress for the complainant. In *Harman* v *UK* (App. No. 10038/82) (1984) 38 DR 53, the applicant challenged contempt proceedings brought against her for showing a journalist documents disclosed to her in court proceedings as the solicitor to one of the parties, notwithstanding that the documents had actually been read out in open court. The Government accepted the admissibility ruling of the Commission and entered into a friendly settlement which required amendment of the discovery rules of the Supreme Court. This case is discussed more fully in Chapter 9. In *Hodgson and Channel 4* v *UK* (App. Nos 11553/85 and 11658/85) (1988) 56 DR 156, the television company had been prohibited from using actors to read out daily transcripts of the Clive Ponting official secrets trial in nightly broadcasts. There was no right of challenge to the order of the criminal trial court. The Government again entered into a friendly settlement of the applicant's complaint as to the lack of a remedy. This time legislation was introduced granting the media a special right of challenge before the Court of Appeal when excluded or gagged by order of a Crown Court (see s. 159, Criminal Justice Act 1988).

If there is no settlement the President may permit any third party, whether a legal person, a government or an interested organisation, such as Liberty, to intervene and make written submissions if it is 'in the interests of the proper administration of justice' (Article 36 ECHR and r. 61). The final oral hearing is held in public (Article 40(1) ECHR) and is short, being usually no more than half a day with time limited arguments. Judgments are given at short notice, and printed copies are faxed to the parties and their representatives to avoid the need to attend. As indicated at 4.2.2 above, in important cases the Grand Chamber may hear an appeal on the merits against a Chambers judgment. The Defamation Act 1996, Schedule 1, paras 2 and 16(3)(b), gives a qualified privilege to fair and accurate reports of Court judgments. There is immunity in respect of statements made by participants in proceedings before the Court.[6]

4.7   JUST SATISFACTION

Where a complaint is upheld the Court must consider whether the applicant is entitled to compensation or an award of costs (Article 41 ECHR). As with the grant of legal aid, any award of costs by the Court will not be generous. The complainant is asked for details of any compensation claim within two months of the admissibility decision. Compensation is intended to place the victim in the same position as if the violation had never happened, and may therefore be substantial if there have been large pecuniary losses (see *Bergens Tidende* v *Norway* (App. No. 26132/95, 2 May 2000), discussed in Chapter 5, where some £411,000 was awarded to cover the damages and costs paid out by a newspaper in a defamation case). The Court has no power to make any other orders against a state. Though binding, the Court's judgment does not have any legal effect in the United Kingdom, save as relevant authority in later domestic cases (HRA 1998, s. 2).

---

[6] See European Court of Human Rights (Immunities and Privileges) Order 2000 (SI 2000 No. 1817) which will allow the UK to give effect to the Sixth Protocol to the General Agreement on Privileges and Immunities of the Council of Europe (Cm 4727) and the European Agreement Relating to Persons Participating in Proceedings of the European Court of Human Rights (Cm 4728).

Chapter Five

Defamation

5.1 INTRODUCTION

Every first-year law student is acquainted with the 'ordinary reader' sitting next to the 'man on the Clapham omnibus' and can recite the basic tests for a defamatory meaning in English law. Does the statement complained of, in the circumstances of the publication, carry a meaning 'lowering the Plaintiff in the estimation of right-thinking members of society generally' (*Sim* v *Stretch* (1936) 52 TLR 669, *per* Lord Atkin at 671), or 'exposing him to hatred ridicule or contempt' (*Parmeter* v *Copeland* (1840) 6 M & W 105, *per* Parke B at 108) or which causes him to be 'shunned or avoided' (*Youssoupoff* v *MGM* (1934) TLR 581 at 587, *per* Slesser LJ)?

At the same time, every journalist and media lawyer knows that beneath these unobjectionable sounding principles lies the biggest single inhibitor of freedom of speech in this country. The fear that material might contain falsehoods which damage the reputation of a claimant with the means and inclination to sue, causes much of what we read, view and hear to be trimmed before it reaches us. Those exposed to damages awards and legal costs as 'publishers' in our libel law often want to side-step the financial risks altogether by deleting material or 'spiking' it. Investigative and polemic writing or broadcasting are the primary victims. Truth, or 'justification', is an absolute defence in libel. But the law presumes that the statement is false unless the defendant proves otherwise. And the demands of constructing a watertight defence case that will persuade a High Court jury, do not sit easily with the need to meet a print deadline or fill a slot on television or radio when news is a perishable commodity. To make matters worse, the other main defences of honest (or fair) comment on a matter of public interest and privilege (absolute or qualified) are limited and complicated.

The law must strike a balance between protecting reputations and encouraging free speech and legitimate criticism. This is reflected in Article 10(2) ECHR, which recognises that the exercise of the right to freedom of expression 'carries with it duties and responsibilities' and that it may be limited or penalised 'for the protection of the reputation or rights of others'. In this chapter we consider, first, how this difficult balancing act has been performed under Article 10 of the Convention. We then consider what the future may hold for the common law.

5.2 WHO MAY COMPLAIN

Applications may be made by natural persons, as well as by corporations, voluntary organisations and interest groups. Many of the defamation cases before the Court have been brought by journalists. However, any legal person who is a 'publisher' at common law is in principle able to complain of a violation of Article 10 rights. Thus editors, proprietors, media organisations, printers and distributors whose rights have been interfered with by defamation proceedings or the threat of proceedings can complain.

The applicant must *be* a 'victim' of a violation in the sense recognised by the Court. This concept is dealt with in Chapters 3 and 4. An application cannot be made in the abstract (see, for example, *Times Newspapers* v *UK* (1990) 65 DR 307) or on behalf of others who are 'victims'. However, the applicant does not have to be a citizen of a contracting state of the Council of Europe, so a publication based outside these territories could complain because of restrictions operating on its circulation within a contracting state.

5.3 'WITHOUT INTERFERENCE BY PUBLIC AUTHORITY'

In defamation cases, prior restraint is rare both for practical and legal reasons. It has long been established in this country that an injunction will not be granted where the defendant states an intention to put forward a defence of justification, fair comment or privilege.[1] However, the protection offered to the media by Article 10 ECHR applies to pre-publication censorship in the form of anticipatory injunctions, or threats of criminal proceedings, or threats of civil proceedings by a public authority. Any such interference is particularly closely scrutinised by the Court because it inhibits or prevents the dissemination of ideas and information altogether (*Observer and Guardian* v *UK* (1991) 14 EHRR 153, at para. 60). Sanctions in criminal proceedings, awards of damages, final injunctions and other orders following judgment are also 'interferences' and, unless they satisfy Article 10(2), will violate Article 10 rights. As described below, the Court has also recognised the 'chilling effect' of high levels of damages on freedom of speech.

---

[1] See further at 3.7.3 above, where pre-trial injunctions are discussed in the context of the special provision concerning freedom of expression in s. 12 of the HRA 1998.

Times Newspapers Ltd v *United Kingdom* (App. No. 31811/96) [1997] EHRLR 430, however, is an interesting example of the Commission declining to find an interference in the defamation context. The *Sunday Times* had published an article suggesting plagiarism by the author of a novel who was purportedly identified by his photograph. In fact the photograph was of a property developer with the same name as the author. The newspaper apologised to the developer for 'suggesting that he had plagiarised' the novel, and then found itself sued by the author in respect of the apology as well as the original article. After it had failed to persuade the domestic courts that its honest apology had been published on an occasion of qualified privilege, the paper complained that the denial of this defence interfered with its Article 10 rights. The Commission disagreed, noting in particular that there was no evidence that the newspaper was discouraged from publishing apologies because of the absence of a qualified privilege defence.

5.3.1   Criminal libel

A number of the decisions of the Court have involved the conviction and punishment of journalists for offences of criminal libel. In the landmark case of *Lingens* v *Austria* (1986) 8 EHRR 407, the Court rejected an argument that such proceedings did not 'strictly speaking prevent [the convicted journalist] from expressing himself', observing that the penalty imposed:

> ... nonetheless amounted to a kind of censure, which would be likely to discourage him from making criticisms of this kind again in future ... In the context of political debate such a sentence would be likely to deter journalists from contributing to public discussion of issues affecting the life of the community. By the same token a sanction such as this is liable to hamper the press in performing its task as purveyor of information and public watchdog ... (at para. 44)

5.3.2   Orders to publish

In *De Haes & Gijsels* v *Belgium* (1997) 25 EHRR 1, the applicants had been successfully sued by a number of Antwerp judges over articles alleging bias in their handling of a high-profile child custody case in which accusations of abuse had been raised against the father, a Belgian notary. They were ordered to publish the judgment in favour of the judges in their magazine. The Court found that there had been an unnecessary interference with their freedom of expression. The Court also upheld their complaint that there had not been 'equality of arms' in the proceedings (Article 6(1)). In publishing the articles they had relied upon the fact that expert reports had been submitted in the custody case supporting the accusations of abuse. They were denied these documents even though the judgments in that case, in which the judges rejected the reports, were in evidence in the libel trial.

In *Ediciones Tiempo SA* v *Spain* (App. No. 13010/87) (1989) 62 DR 247, at 253, the applicant magazine published an article alleging irregularities in the management of a public company. A Spanish court, applying statutory provisions for a right of reply, ordered it to publish an article in response by one of the managers of the company who had been attacked. The Commission accepted that the order amounted to an interference with the magazine's freedom of expression. The complaint was, however, declared inadmissible on its facts (see 5.5 below).

5.3.3 Damages awards and final injunctions

In *Tolstoy Miloslavsky* v *United Kingdom* (1995) 20 EHRR 442, the Court considered the record award of libel damages of one and a half million pounds made by a High Court jury against the applicant and in favour of Lord Aldington. The award was three times more than had ever been awarded before in a defamation case. The High Court also granted an injunction restraining further publication of the defamatory statements. The applicant had written a pamphlet alleging that, while a British army officer in 1945, Aldington had 'arranged the perpetration of a major war crime' by handing over Cossacks to the Soviets and Yugoslavs. Many of these were said to have been massacred or placed in labour camps. The pamphlet was distributed to people connected with Winchester College where Aldington was by then the Warden.

The applicant complained that the common law prescribed no upper or lower limits on the amount, did not impose a requirement that the award be proportionate to the aim of repairing the damage to the claimant's reputation and allowed only limited guidance to be given by the judge to the jury. Because of this, he said, he could not reasonably foresee the amount awarded against him and it was not prescribed by law. The case reached the Court after s. 8 of the Courts and Legal Services Act 1990 had come into force, giving the Court of Appeal the power to substitute its own award for an excessive jury award. However, at the time of the judgment against the applicant it was not in force and the Court of Appeal had only limited power to overturn the award on grounds of irrationality or bad faith. The European Court did not accept that the applicant was entitled to anticipate the amount of the award with a 'degree of certainty' and found that the interference represented by the award was 'in accordance with law'. It observed that a 'high degree of flexibility' could be justified in the law of defamation damages. The well-established matters a jury were required to take into account (such as injury to feelings, the anxiety caused by having to litigate, the absence of an apology and so on) were sufficient to ensure that the award was 'prescribed by law'. The fact that these did not include the principle of proportionality was not fatal (at paras 41 and 42).

But the Court ruled unanimously that the sheer amount of the award gave rise to a violation of Article 10 ECHR because it did not bear the required 'reasonable relationship of proportionality to the injury to reputation suffered'. Referring back to its first finding, it commented that 'An award of the present size must be particularly open to question where the substantive national law applicable at the time fails itself to provide a requirement of proportionality' (at para. 49). The Court noted that the Court of Appeal itself had already accepted in *Rantzen* v *Mirror Group Newspapers (1986) Ltd* [1994] QB 670, that the wide discretion of High Court juries to award damages was an unsatisfactory method of ensuring proportionality for the purposes of Article 10. By contrast, the injunction was not a disproportionate interference, given that it was a 'logical consequence' of the jury's finding and was 'framed precisely to prevent the applicant from repeating the libellous allegations' and nothing more (at para. 54).

In *Tolstoy Miloslavsky* the interference complained of was the *size* of the damages since the complainant had no justifiable complaint under Article 10 as to the finding of liability to pay compensation for defaming Lord Aldington. But the award of damages, even if not disproportionate, may amount to an 'interference' so that the imposition of liability must be justified in accordance with the principles of Article 10(2) (*Bladet Tromso and Stensaas* v *Norway* (1999) 29 EHRR 125, para. 50, where the Norwegian government did not contest the point).

In *Skrine and Co. (a firm) and others* v *Euromoney Publications plc and others* (2000) *The Times*, 10 November, the claimants had compromised Malaysian libel proceedings based on statements attributed to them in the defendants' magazine criticizing the Malaysian judiciary. The High Court accepted that the amount of any order for a 'just and equitable' contribution to the settlement sum under the Civil Liability (Contribution) Act 1978 should be determined taking into account the defendants' Article 10 rights and the 'chilling effect' of damages awards. However, it considered that this protection was already built into the Court of Appeal guidance on damages awards in *John* v *MGN Limited* [1997] QB 591.

5.4 LEGITIMATE AIM

In all of the defamation cases that have come before the European Court, the contracting state has been able to show that the interference complained of was in pursuit of a legitimate aim. This has invariably been the need to protect the reputation of others. In principle it is a legitimate aim to protect the reputation of 'others', even though they have not been named or somehow identified in the defamatory material. In *Thorgeirson* v *Iceland* (1992) 14 EHRR 843, at para. 59, the applicant had written newspaper articles describing unspecified members of the Reykjavik police as 'beasts in uniform' and 'police brutes'. Although his conviction and sentence for criminal defamation was found to be in violation of Article 10 ECHR, the Court accepted that it was aimed at protecting the reputations of officers.

5.4.1 Protecting the reputations of private individuals

In *Bladet Tromso and Stensaas* v *Norway* (1999) 29 EHRR 125, the applicant's newspaper articles had accused seal hunters of cruelty to animals and offences against seal hunting regulations. The crew members had successfully sued for damages. The Court accepted that the interference pursued the legitimate aim of protecting their reputations, but nonetheless found a violation. Another example is *Bergens Tidende* v *Norway* (App. No. 26132/95, 2 May 2000), involving an award of 4.7 million Norwegian kroner in damages and costs to a plastic surgeon who had been accused of professional malpractice in a series of newspaper articles. Again, however, the Court found a violation (see 5.5.3 below).

5.4.2 Politicians

The reputation concerned does not have to be that of a private individual. However, there are a number of decisions in which the Court has distinguished between private and public reputations and ruled that the extent to which the latter may be protected is more limited, particularly where the press is acting as 'watchdog' on matters of public interest. The leading case is *Lingens* v *Austria* (1986) 8 EHRR 407. The applicant had published two articles accusing the Austrian Chancellor, Bruno Kreisky, of protecting and helping former Nazi SS officers for political reasons. Kreisky successfully prosecuted the applicant for an offence of criminal defamation. The Court accepted that the protection of his reputation as a politician was a legitimate aim. However, it emphasised that 'the limits of acceptable criticism' of a politician in his public life are wider than those applying to private individuals. The Court stressed that:

> ... a politician ... inevitably and knowingly lays himself open to close scrutiny of his every word and deed by both journalists and the public at large, and he must consequently display a greater degree of tolerance. No doubt Article 10(2) enables the reputation of ... all individuals — to be protected, and this protection extends to politicians too, even when they are not acting in their private capacity; but in such cases the requirements of such protection have to be weighed in relation to the interests of the open discussion of political issues. (at para. 42)

This important principle was reiterated in *Oberschlick* v *Austria (No. 2)* (1997) 25 EHRR 357, in which an editor had run an article reporting a speech of Jorg Heider, leader of the Austrian Liberal Party, under the headline 'P.S.: "Idiot" instead of Nazi', which went on to state that this is how he would describe Heider. The speech had praised the Austrian 'soldiers' of the Second World War, including those in the SS or Wehrmacht, for their role as founders of the contemporary, prosperous Austrian democratic state. The applicant was convicted of 'insult' contrary to the Austrian Criminal Code in a private prosecution brought by

Heider. In finding a violation, the Court rejected the suggestion that in describing the politician as an 'idiot' he had overstepped the mark required for orderly discussion of matters of public interest in a democracy.

5.4.3 Judges and other public servants

Judges, like police officers, are entitled to have their reputations protected. In *Barfod* v *Denmark* (1989) 13 EHRR 493, the applicant had been convicted of defaming two lay judges employed by the local government in Greenland. He had written an article accusing them of bias in finding for the authority in a tax case. The Court accepted that the prosecution had been pursued for the legitimate aim of protecting the judges' reputations. Indeed, judges are entitled to a greater degree of protection than politicians. In *Prager and Oberschlick* v *Austria* (1995) 21 EHRR 1, at para. 34, two journalists had engaged in a wide-ranging attack on the judiciary and criticised a number of particular judges in strident terms. While the Court accepted that 'The press is one of the means by which politicians and public opinion can verify that judges are discharging their heavy responsibilities in a manner which is in conformity with the [democratic] aim which is the basis of the task entrusted to them', it also recognised that judges:

> ... must enjoy public confidence. They must accordingly be protected from destructive attacks that are unfounded, especially in view of the fact that judges are subject to a duty of discretion that precludes them from replying to criticism ...

This observation was repeated in *De Haes & Gijsels* v *Belgium* (1997) 25 EHRR 1, at para. 37. Criticism of the judiciary in the context of court reporting is dealt with in Chapter 9.

The Court stated in *Janowski* v *Poland* (1999) 29 EHRR 705, that other public servants must 'enjoy public confidence in conditions free of perturbation if they are to be successful in performing their tasks', rejecting the contention that the limits of acceptable criticism should be extended as with politicians. However, the case was a rather unusual one. The applicant had been convicted for orally abusing two municipal guards during heated exchanges in a public square. The guards had removed some unlicensed traders from the area and had therefore been pursuing their law enforcement duties. The applicant was a journalist but clearly acting in his private capacity. As the Court itself observed, the case did not therefore require it to balance the need to protect such officials against the freedom of the press (at para. 33). In a more recent case, *Dalban* v *Romania* (2000) 8 BHRC 91, however, the conviction of a journalist for a criminal defamation of the Chief Executive of a state-owned agricultural company (in the form of allegations of serious frauds which were under police investigation) was unanimously held to be in violation of Article 10 ECHR. The Court's observations in *Janowski* v *Poland* must therefore be read in the light of the Court's own caveat and, as we indicate below, the media must have greater freedom to attack public servants who abuse their positions as part of their 'watchdog' role.

5.4.4 Other legitimate aims: the prevention of disorder

In *Castells* v *Spain* (1992) 14 EHRR 445, the applicant was a Senator of the opposition political grouping, Herri Batasun, which supported independence for the Basque Country. In 1979 he had published an article suggesting that the Government had been behind the killings of pro-separatist dissidents. He was convicted of an offence of insulting the Government under the Spanish Criminal Code following the withdrawal of his Parliamentary immunity. The article had been published shortly after the adoption of the Constitution, as the Government put it during '... a sensitive, indeed critical, period for Spain ... when groups of differing political persuasions were resorting to violence'. The Court accepted that 'in the circumstances obtaining in Spain in 1979' the criminal proceedings had been instituted for the 'prevention of disorder' as well as to protect the reputations of others (at paras 39 and 41). It would be difficult to envisage such an argument succeeding, however, other than in similarly extreme circumstances of political instability. This potential danger was recognised, but not made out on the facts, in *Piermont* v *France* (1995) 20 EHRR 301, at para. 77, in which the expulsion of an MEP and anti-nuclear campaigner from New Caledonia was found to have breached Article 10.

5.5 RESTRICTIONS 'NECESSARY IN A DEMOCRATIC SOCIETY'

The Court has observed, in the context of defamation, that:

> ... perceptions as to what would be an appropriate response by society to speech which does not ... enjoy the protection of Article 10 ... may differ greatly from one state to another ...

so that contracting states enjoy a wide margin of appreciation in determining the appropriate responses (*Tolstoy Miloslavsky* v *UK* (1995) 20 EHRR 442, at para. 48). These may include measures allowing the courts to enforce a 'right of reply'. In *Ediciones Tiempo SA* v *Spain* (App. No. 13010/87) (1989) 62 DR 247, the Commission emphasised that 'in a democratic society the right of reply is a guarantee of the pluralism of information which must be respected'. The applicant magazine had complained about a court order requiring it to publish a reply by a businessman it had accused of mismanaging a company. The Commission dismissed the application as manifestly ill-founded and found that the measure was proportionate to the aim pursued, in particular since the magazine was not required to change the original allegations and was free to repeat its own version of the facts when it published the reply. The Court observed that:

> ... the purpose of the regulations governing the right of reply [was] to safeguard the interest of the public in receiving information from a variety of sources and thereby to guarantee the fullest possible access to information ... (at 253–4)

However, the Court has also consistently referred to the theoretical basis for the protection of freedom of expression articulated in *Handyside* v *UK* (1976) 1 EHRR 737, in the context of restrictions and penalties in the law of defamation, namely that:

> ... freedom of expression, as secured in paragraph 1 of Article 10, constitutes one of the essential foundations of a democratic society and one of the basic conditions for its progress and for each individual's self-fulfillment. Subject to paragraph 2, it is applicable not only to 'information' or 'ideas' that are favourably received or regarded as inoffensive or a matter of indifference, but also those that offend, shock or disturb. Such are the demands of that pluralism, tolerance and broadmindedness without which there is no 'democratic society' ... (*Lingens* v *Austria* (1986) 8 EHRR 407, at para. 41)

Because of this the 'necessity for any restrictions [to] be convincingly established' has been restated a number of times in the context of defamation (see, for example, *Thorgeirson* v *Iceland* (1992) 14 EHRR 843, at para. 63 applying *Observer and Guardian* v *UK* (1991) 14 EHRR 153, at para. 59).

5.5.1   The unique position of the press as a 'watchdog'

The Court has also consistently acknowledged that the press has a unique position under Article 10 ECHR. It has ruled that the press has not only a right but a duty to impart information and ideas on all matters of political and public interest, which the public has a corresponding right to receive. This extends to interpretation of the facts which is not simply to be left to the reader (*Sunday Times* v *United Kingdom* (1979) 2 EHRR 245, para. 65 and *Lingens* v *Austria*, at para. 41). The role of the press as public watchdog is 'essential ... in a democratic society' (*De Haes & Gijsels* v *Belgium* (1997) 25 EHRR 1, at para. 37). Indeed 'journalistic freedom covers possible recourse to a degree of exaggeration, or even provocation' (*De Haes & Gijsels* v *Belgium*, at para. 46 and, recently, *Dalban* v *Romania* (2000) 8 BHRC 91, at para. 49 and *Lopes Gomes Da Silva* v *Portugal* (App. No. 37698/97, 28 September 2000).

5.5.2 The form of the expression

It is well established that Article 10 ECHR protects not only the substance of the ideas and information expressed, but also their form (see, for example, *Jersild* v *Denmark* (1994) 19 EHRR 1, at para. 31 and *De Haes & Gijsels* v *Belgium*, at para. 48). The Court has therefore emphasised that journalists have considerable latitude in the methods they use to convey their ideas or information. It will not substitute its own views for those of the press as to what methods of reporting or presentation should be used to get a story across. This is a matter for the journalist. Indeed, the Court recognises that news reporting based on interviews may deserve special protection because of its value in imparting information effectively on matters of public interest (see *Jersild* v *Denmark*, at para. 35, which is discussed at length in Chapter 7; see also *Bergens Tidende* v *Norway*, referred to at 5.5.3 below). Neither will it impose its own views as to how a view or an allegation should be counter-balanced, provided balance is present when needed (*Jersild* v *Denmark*, at para. 31).

The Court has also emphasised that a 'careful distinction' must be drawn between expression in the form of statements of fact and the expression of value judgments. This is because 'the existence of facts can be demonstrated, whereas the truth of value judgments is not susceptible of proof'. This makes it difficult, or sometimes impossible, for a journalist to defend himself if this is the test of legality (*Lingens* v *Austria*, at para. 46). The cases show that a penalty imposed for expressing an honest 'value judgment' is likely to involve a violation of Article 10 rights.

This principle was applied in *Schwabe* v *Austria*, 28 August 1992, Series A, No. 242-B. The applicant had issued a press release comparing a 1966 road traffic accident caused by another politician, Fruhbauer, to a recent, more serious incident in which a local mayor had been convicted for abandoning the victim of a road accident while under the influence of alcohol. The applicant had based his press release on a newspaper account of Fruhbauer's conviction. This made clear that although he had been tested for blood alcohol close to the level at which the law could presume impairment by intoxication, the conviction had been for negligent driving only. Fruhbauer successfully prosecuted the applicant for criminal defamation. The European Court found a violation of Article 10 ECHR, holding that even though there were differences between the two offences, the comparison essentially amounted to a value judgment made in good faith which had not exceeded the limits of freedom of expression (at para. 34). Although the classification of the statement as fact or opinion is a matter which comes within the margin of appreciation (*Prager & Oberschlick* v *Austria* (1995) 21 EHRR 1, at para. 36), the Court has decided cases on its own classification of the material. Where the statement is considered to be fact, the journalist must be permitted to call relevant evidence to try to prove truth (*Castells* v *Spain* (1992) 14 EHRR 445, at para. 48).

This does not mean that Article 10(2) ECHR can never be successfully invoked where there has been a defamatory comment which damages a person's reputation. There must still be some established or undisputed factual basis for the expression of the opinion, which must be made in good faith (*Lingens* v *Austria*, at para. 46 and *De Haes & Gijsels* v *Belgium*, at para. 47). In *Prager & Oberschlick* v *Austria*, the Court was satisfied that the journalists had overstepped the mark by reason of the width of their accusations which lacked a 'sufficient factual basis' (at para. 37). The interference in the form of convictions for criminal defamation was not, in this case, considered disproportionate. However, there is undoubtedly more scope for a journalist to attack through the expression of opinion.

5.5.3 Political controversy and issues of public interest

Freedom of 'political debate is at the very core of the concept of a democratic society which prevails throughout the Convention' (*Lingens* v *Austria*, at para. 42). The scope for attack on politicians in the media will be greater in a highly charged political climate. The articles in the *Lingens* case (see 5.4.2 above) had been published in such a climate. The President of the Austrian Liberal Party, Mr Friedrich Peter, had been identified as a former SS officer by the Jewish Documentation Centre a few days after a general election. The next day, only hours after ruling out a coalition with the Liberals, Mr Kreisky (the Austrian Chancellor) had likened the Centre to the 'mafia' in a television interview. In finding that the interference was disproportionate, the Court emphasised that the political circumstances in which the words had been written 'must not be overlooked'. On the facts it felt that, in the 'struggle' represented by the post-election controversy as to the revelations about Mr Peter's past, 'each used the weapons at his disposal; and these were in no way unusual in the hard-fought tussles of politics' (at para. 43). In making the same finding in *Oberschlick* v *Austria (No. 1)* (1991) 19 EHRR 389, the Court relied on the fact that the provocative opinions expressed about the politician concerned were a reaction to his own 'shocking' views (that the state should discriminate against immigrant families in the payment of benefit) made in the course of an election campaign.

There is, similarly, greater scope for hard-hitting criticism of public officials in matters of public interest. In *Thorgeirson* v *Iceland* (at para. 64), the Court found 'no warrant in its case law for distinguishing ... between political discussion and discussion of matters of public concern' such as police brutality. In finding the interference disproportionate, the Court took into account the fact that the journalist's principal purpose in launching the attack was to secure the establishment of an independent body to investigate complaints of police misconduct (at para. 66). In *De Haes & Gijsels* v *Belgium*, it was prepared to find that the journalistic polemical attack on the judges was not 'excessive' in the light of the public concern about the 'the fate of young children and the functioning of the system of justice in Antwerp' at the time (at paras 39 and 47). In *Dalban* v *Romania* (see 5.4.3 above), the applicant's articles had alleged fraud by the Chief Executive of the state-owned company and had also criticised one of its directors, a Senator, who received a large salary and a car from the company. In finding a violation, the Court stressed that the articles 'concerned a matter of public interest: the management of state assets and the manner in which politicians fulfill their mandate' (at para. 48).

However, the attack does not have to be on a public figure for the issues of public concern to come into play. In *Bladet Tromso and Stensaas* v *Norway* (1999) 29 EHRR 125 (see 5.4.1 above), the applicant was the local newspaper in the town of Tromso. In its majority finding of a breach of Article 10 ECHR, the Court stressed that 'the contents of the impugned articles cannot be looked at in isolation of the controversy that seal hunting represented at the time in Norway and in Tromso, the centre of the trade in Norway' (at para. 62). The majority also noted that the material complained about formed only part of a series of serious articles in the local paper which had built upon concerns expressed in an official report and which aimed at improving the reputation of seal hunting. In these circumstances, even the failure of the journalist to seek the sealers' comments on the allegations before publishing these particular allegations was not fatal (at paras 63 and 60). In *Nilsen and Johnsen* v *Norway* (1999) 30 EHRR 878, the applicants were representatives of the Police Association. They had made statements in the press attacking a writer who had published a book entitled *Police Brutality*. These included an allegation that he had deliberately lied and a series of statements of opinion as to his motives. The writer had brought defamation proceedings, obtaining damages and a declaration that the statements were 'null and void'. The background was a long-running and heated debate about police violence, in particular in Bergen where one of the applicants worked. A Grand Chamber held by 12 votes to 5 that the judgments of the Norwegian Court, in so far as they related to the statements of opinion, interfered with the applicants' freedom of expression and were disproportionate to the legitimate aim of protecting the writer's reputation. The majority were satisfied that there was some factual basis for the criticisms, which were made in the context of a heated and continuing public debate. It also found that the applicants had some entitlement to 'hit back in the same way' at the writer on behalf of their members as part of this ongoing debate (at para. 52).

The decision of the Court in *Bergens Tidende* v *Norway* (App. No. 26132/95, 2 May 2000), is another important example of this principle. The applicants were a large regional newspaper and two of its journalists. The paper had run a series of articles reporting the complaints of women who had experienced unsatisfactory cosmetic surgery on their breasts. The surgeon who had carried out the operations was awarded a substantial sum in defamation proceedings, after the Norwegian Supreme Court had found that, though not stated in terms, the articles created an 'impression' that he had been reckless in his conduct of the surgery. The European Court found that the articles raised matters of 'consumer protection of direct concern to the local and national public'. It was satisfied that the reporting was balanced, not 'excessive or misleading' and that the interviews with the women gave a factually accurate account of their experiences. It repeated the principle that 'news reporting based on interviews constitutes one of the most important means whereby the press is able to play its vital role of "public watchdog" ...' Critically, it found that the 'common sting' of the articles was the true allegation that the doctor had failed to provide proper post-surgical treatment to remedy the results of unsuccessful operations, and that this allegation in itself would inevitably have caused damage to the doctor's professional reputation (at paras 56 and 57). In the light of these considerations the Court could not find that:

> ... the undoubted interest of Dr R in protecting his professional reputation was sufficient to outweigh the important public interest in the freedom of the press to impart information of legitimate public concern ...

The interference with the applicants' freedom of expression represented by the large monetary award was not therefore necessary in a democratic society (at para. 60). The Norwegian Government was ordered to pay over £400,000 to compensate the applicants for the pecuniary losses resulting from the judgment of the Supreme Court (at paras 62–64).[2]

5.6   THE COMPATIBILITY OF DOMESTIC DEFAMATION LAW WITH THE CONVENTION

5.6.1   Criminal libel

There has not been a public prosecution of the media for the ancient offence of criminal libel for many years, although there are very rare examples of private prosecutions. The Law Commission has long since recommended abolition of the offence altogether.[3] It enables an extremely serious libel to be punished as a crime triable on indictment. Leave of a High Court judge is required before a newspaper or periodical can be prosecuted (Law of Libel Amendment Act 1888, s. 8). However, justification is a defence only if the defendant can persuade the jury that the publication was for the 'public benefit' (Libel Act 1843, s. 6), and it is not even certain that fair comment is a defence.

Although the European Court has accepted that criminal prosecutions for defamation do not necessarily involve a violation of Article 10 ECHR, any

---

[2] The applicants did not seek compensation for non-pecuniary damage, accepting, as the Court would no doubt have ruled, that the judgment itself was just satisfaction under this head.
[3] Law Commission, *Criminal Law: Report on Criminal Libel* (Law Com. No 149, Cm. 9618, 1985).

conviction in this country of a journalist writing in good faith on a matter of public interest, would almost certainly do so. It is clear from the European cases referred to above that there must be an unrestricted defence of truth and that the law must guarantee a wide freedom to engage in value judgments on such matters. In the leading House of Lords case, *Gleaves* v *Deakin* [1980] AC 477 (HL), at 483, Lord Diplock suggested that the offence as presently formulated would be difficult to reconcile with Article 10.

5.6.2 The civil law of defamation

The effect of the HRA 1998 on the development of the civil law is more difficult to predict. In recent years the domestic courts have stressed that the common law of defamation is consistent with Article 10 ECHR.[4] The fundamentals of the two bodies of law are comparable. The competing interests of free speech and reputation, broadly speaking, are respected and balanced on a case-by-case basis. There is a common emphasis on the need for a factual foundation and for honesty if a person's reputation is to be attacked. The effect may therefore be limited, at any rate in the early years. It may be that the two bodies of law will evolve side by side in the longer term.

5.6.2.1 A general protection for political speech?
In the landmark case of *New York Times Co.* v *Sullivan* 376 US 254 (1964), the US Supreme Court held that the First Amendment, prohibiting any law 'abridging the freedom of speech or the press', prevents a public official defamed in his public life from suing in defamation, unless he can establish that the defendant knew the allegation was false or was reckless as to its truth or falsity. This principle has evolved into a wider 'public figure' defence in America (*Gertz* v *Welch* 418 US 323 (1974)) with no distinction between false statements of fact and opinions (*Hustler Magazine and Flynt* v *Falwell* (1988) 485 US 46). Commonwealth jurisdictions have taken different approaches on this issue. In a case that did not involve political speech, *Hill* v *Church of Scientology of Toronto* (1995) 126 DLR (4th) 129 (SCC), the Canadian Supreme Court declined to incorporate the *Sullivan* defence into Canadian law. Although slightly different tests apply, in Australia and New Zealand communications to the public about government and the conduct of Parliamentarians in matters of legitimate public concern are protected by qualified privilege.[5] A similar approach has been adopted in India (*Raja Gopal* v *State of Tamil Nadu AIR* 1995 SC 264).

---

[4] See *Attorney-General* v *Guardian Newspapers Ltd (No. 2)* [1990] 1 AC 109, *per* Lord Goff of Chieveley at 283–4; *Derbyshire County Council* v *Times Newspapers Ltd* [1993] AC 534, *per* Lord Keith of Kinkel at 551G; *R* v *Secretary of State for the Home Department, ex parte Simms* [2000] 2 AC 115 at 126E, *per* Lord Steyn.

[5] See in Australia *Lange* v *Australian Broadcasting Corporation* (1997) 189 CLR 520 and in New Zealand *Lange* v *Atkinson* [1998] 3 NZLR 424; and see below for a further decision by the NZCA in this litigation.

In the recent case of *Reynolds* v *Times Newspapers Ltd* [1999] 3 WLR 1010 (HL), the House of Lords considered whether English law should develop a new, subject-matter category of qualified privilege for political speech along these lines. The claimant was the former Irish Prime Minister, Albert Reynolds, who had sued the *Sunday Times* over an article in its British mainland edition alleging that he had lied to the lower house of the Irish Parliament. The jury found in his favour but awarded only one penny in damages. The Court of Appeal then ordered a retrial because of misdirections by the judge, but refused the newspaper the opportunity to argue qualified privilege at the retrial (*Reynolds* v *Times Newspapers Ltd* [1998] 3 WLR 862 (CA), at 911–12). The newspaper appealed against this refusal. In the leading speech, Lord Nicholls acknowledged that 'Without freedom of expression by the media, freedom of expression would be a hollow concept' (at 1023C), and commented:

> ... The press discharges vital functions as a bloodhound as well as a watchdog. The Court should be slow to conclude that a publication was not in the public interest and, therefore, that the public had a right to know, especially when the information is in the field of political discussion. Any lingering doubts should be resolved in favour of publication ... (at 1027H)

However, their Lordships declined to develop a generic qualified privilege test protecting political speech or information. Instead they made clear that the traditional two-fold test for qualified privilege (a legal, social or moral duty to make the statement and a corresponding interest in the recipient in receiving it) may be met in circumstances where newspapers and broadcasters are imparting information to the public on matters of 'serious public concern' (at 1027B), provided they do so through careful, balanced and responsible investigative journalism.

The decision in *Reynolds* v *Times Newspapers Ltd* is an example of the common law being formulated consistently with the European jurisprudence, to the extent that neither seeks to protect any particular category of expression on a hard and fast basis. Whether it will bring about any significant thaw in the chilling effect of our defamation law on discussion of matters of public interest is another matter. Journalists, editors and media lawyers will have to make difficult judgments about how a court might apply the *Reynolds* 'circumstantial test' before deciding whether to publish. They will probably continue to err on the side of caution in most cases. Only time will tell whether the courts will apply the *Reynolds* principles bearing in mind the European Court's recent robust recognition of the need to safeguard journalists where 'matters of legitimate public concern' are under discussion (see, for example, *Bergens Tidende* v *Norway*, 5.5.3 above, at para. 53). There have already been High Court decisions both for and against newspapers seeking to make out the *Reynolds* defence. (See, for an example of the latter, *Saad Al-Fagih* v *HH Saudi Research & Marketing (UK) Ltd* (unreported) 28 July 2000 (QBD, Smith J).)

The House of Lords decision on the facts in *Reynolds* was not an encouraging start. Their Lordships upheld the decision of the Court of Appeal under appeal, albeit by a majority of only 3:2. The majority, like the Court of Appeal, considered it a 'telling criticism of the article' that the reporter had failed to mention Mr Reynolds's explanation to the Dail of the events in question, simply because he did not believe it, in circumstances where the explanation had been included in a longer article published in the Irish edition of the newspaper and Mr Reynolds had issued a press statement indicating that it would be his only statement in answer to various allegations against him (*per* Lord Nicholls at 1028C). However, in *Turkington and others* v *Times Newspapers Ltd* [2000] 3 WLR 1670, the House of Lords has since re-emphasised the importance of the press as both a watchdog and a channel of communication on matters of public importance. The case raised the issue of whether a press conference discussing matters of public concern, namely the conviction of Private Lee Clegg as a possible miscarriage of justice, was a 'public meeting' within the meaning of s. 7 of and para. 9 of the Schedule to the Defamation Act 1955 of Northern Ireland.[6] The House of Lords held that it was, with the result that a fair and accurate press report of it would attract qualified privilege. All of their Lordships agreed with Lord Bingham of Cornhill that: '... A meeting is public if those who organise it ... by issuing a general invitation to the press, manifest an intention that the proceedings of the meeting should be communicated to a wider public. Press representatives may be regarded ... as the eyes and ears of the public to whom they report ...' Although the case did not concern the *Reynolds* principles, and the decision as to the ambit of the statutory defence was reached without resort to the HRA 1998,[7] this re-emphasis of the importance of the press can only assist future argument in favour of a robust application of the *Reynolds* defence.

On the day of the speeches in the *Reynolds* case, the same Law Lords, sitting as the Privy Council, allowed an appeal against the decision of the New Zealand Court of Appeal in *Lange* v *Atkinson* [1998] 3 NZLR 424 and remitted the case. The New Zealand Court has since reconsidered its judgment in the light of *Reynolds*, but has declined the invitation to 'strike the balance differently to the way it was struck in 1998', opining that *Reynolds* 'only adds to the uncertainty and chilling effect almost inevitably present in this area of the law' and expressing concern that the *Reynolds* approach blurs the distinction between the *occasion* of qualified privilege and its *misuse* ([2000] 3 NZLR 385 at 399). It may yet be that, in time, the European Court's emphasis on freedom of journalistic expression in matters of genuine public concern will lead both Convention and domestic law to

---

[6] Corresponding to s. 15 of, and para. 12 of the Schedule to, the Defamation Act 1996.

[7] But rather by using 'ordinary principles of reasonably liberal and purposive contemporary interpretation', as Lord Cooke of Thorndon put it at p. 1687H.

recognise a qualified privilege for political speech comparable to that which exists in Australia and New Zealand.

5.6.2.2 'Value judgments', 'journalistic ... exaggeration', 'comments' and 'public interest'

English judges often equate 'comment' to 'pure' statements of evaluative opinion, representing a personal view on something which cannot be meaningfully verified. This can limit the availability of the fair comment defence. The European case law, however, suggests a rather wider freedom to engage in 'value judgments' on matters of public interest. Some of the cases in which the European Court has classified the expression as a value judgment could probably be defended in this country only through a defence of justification. The best example may be *Schwabe* v *Austria*, 28 August 1992, Series A, No. 242-B (discussed in detail at 5.5.2 above), where the applicant was not even a journalist. The applicant had suggested that Mr Fruhbauer had caused the 1966 accident while under the influence of alcohol. Yet he had not been convicted of this and the relevant Austrian criminal law did not lead automatically to this conclusion. Notwithstanding this, the Court decided the case on the footing that the applicant was free to engage in a broad, comparative 'value judgment' as to the nature of the two convictions, and the implications for the political debate surrounding the more recent conviction of the local mayor. It may be that a broader view of comment may evolve in domestic cases where a journalist was referring to matters of public interest. The European case law also suggests that a broad view should be taken of what is a matter of public interest. This may assist the media in making out a qualified privilege defence in accordance with *Reynolds* v *Times Newspapers Ltd* (see 5.6.2.1).

5.6.2.3 Other possible developments

There may be scope to argue that some aspects of our damages law, in particular awards of exemplary damages, are 'disproportionate'. Many journalists are angered by the rule that an unsuccessful attempt to justify a defamatory meaning, even in good faith, can aggravate damages. The 'chilling effect' that this rule has upon freedom of expression was raised by the applicant in *Tolstoy Miloslavsky* v *UK* (1995) 20 EHRR 442, at para. 46, but the Court did not refer to it specifically in its reasons. Another possible target for challenge is the rule in *Plato Films* v *Speidel* [1961] AC 1090. This prevents defendants from raising evidence of particular acts of misconduct by the claimant in order to show bad character and thereby mitigate damage. The abolition of this long-standing rule would bring our law closer to that in America. Abolition has been proposed in the past,[8] but

---

[8] See the *Report on Practice and Procedure in Defamation* of the Supreme Court Procedure Committee (1991).

Parliament has declined to legislate for fear of creating a 'muckrakers' charter'[9] of the sort that is often said to exist in the US. The rule can enable claimants to protect reputations they do not deserve, at the expense of journalists and publishers. Again, it must be questionable whether such a rule is 'necessary in a democratic society' and whether the recovery of damages for an undeserved reputation can be proportionate.

There may also be scope to challenge the principle that repetition of a defamatory statement renders a journalist liable in defamation as a 'publisher'. The most obvious challenge would be in a case where a journalist is held liable for, or inhibited from, publishing a defamatory statement in an interview on a matter of public importance (see 5.5.2 above). The issue of 'reportage' is likely to be considered soon by the European Court (in *Thoma* v *Luxembourg* (App. No. 38432/97, 25 May 2000)) declared admissible on Article 10 grounds. Another candidate for challenge is the rule that innocent distributors and vendors must prove that they have not been careless in disseminating defamatory material if they are to avoid liability. This may be a difficult burden to discharge in some cases, and may lead to small investigative or polemical publications being unable to find a distributor.

At the time of writing at least one case is before the Court challenging the unavailability of legal aid for defendants in defamation cases as contrary to Articles 6(1) and 10 ECHR.[10] As the Court's case law develops, it may be difficult for the Government to justify its continuing refusal to grant legal aid to deserving defendants if called upon to do so.[11] The fact that claimants can now employ lawyers under conditional fee agreements makes justification more difficult. However, the availability of conditional fee agreement has not resulted in a flood of libel claims, probably because the claimant remains at risk of paying the defendant's costs, a risk which is not easy to cover by insurance in libel claims.

---

[9] Hansard HC, vol. 280, col.133.

[10] See *McVicar* v *UK* (App. No. 46311/99) which has been communicated to the Government; though in *Steel and Morris* v *UK* (1993) 18 EHRR CD 172, the Commission ruled that a similar complaint by the defendants in the McDonald's libel case was inadmissible.

[11] As from 1 April 2000, the Lord Chancellor has powers under s. 6 of and Schedule 2, para. 1 to the Access to Justice Act 1999 to provide funding for defamation cases by reference to categories, or in individual cases, through the Community Legal Services Fund (the successor to the Legal Aid Fund). See Legal Service Commission Funding Code, Part 3C for the Lord Chancellor's Direction and the Lord Chancellor's guidance on the funding of the classes of case and individual cases within the categories presumptively excluded by the Access to Justice Act 1999.

Chapter Six

Privacy and Confidential Information

6.1 INTRODUCTION

'Will the Human Rights Act lead to the courts creating a new right of privacy?' ought to be a straightforward question, but it raises some of the more difficult issues which will flow from incorporation of Convention rights. The question is a natural one to ask since Article 8(1) ECHR provides that 'Everyone has the right to respect for his private and family life, his home and his correspondence.' Furthermore, Article 10(2) includes in its list of objectives which may legitimately give rise to restrictions on freedom of expression 'the protection of the . . . rights of others' and 'preventing the disclosure of information received in confidence'. But it is too simplistic to conclude from the juxtaposition of these two provisions that the Convention necessarily requires the courts to balance the competing interests of privacy and freedom of expression by creating a new right of privacy.

In this chapter we will examine the extent to which the European Court has considered issues of privacy and confidence as grounds for restricting freedom of expression. We examine the ways in which the English law of breach of confidence has already grown in recent years. We consider the Court's recognition of the importance of allowing journalists to protect the anonymity of their sources in the context of Article 10 ECHR. We then look at Article 8. Its core application is to limit and restrict interferences by public bodies on privacy and confidentiality. We consider how this aspect protects the media, but also how it might place new obligations on those parts of the media which might be said to be 'public authorities'. Lastly, we return to the issue of whether and how Article 8 ECHR might impose positive obligations to create or extend the current laws of privacy so as to give protections against intrusions by the media, which are not 'public authorities' under the HRA 1998. The impact of the HRA will be considered throughout the chapter.

6.2 BREACH OF CONFIDENCE

The Article 10 ECHR principles to be applied when a claimant seeks an injunction, or damages or some other remedy for breach of confidence by the media are relatively well explored. Because it is a legitimate aim to restrict freedom of expression in order to prevent disclosure of information received in confidence, and because UK law has a recognised cause of action for this purpose, attention is likely to focus on whether the particular restriction in the particular circumstances of the case is 'necessary in a democratic society'. In answering this question the Court will invoke the same principles as it does generally in relation to restrictions of expression (see Chapter 2). Thus, for instance, in *Fressoz and Roire* v *France* (1999) 5 BHRC 654, the French satirical magazine, *Le Canard Enchaine*, published the tax assessments of the head of Peugeot at the time of an industrial dispute at Peugeot over a pay claim. The assessments showed that the chairman's income had risen by about 45 per cent over two years, while the income of the workers had increased by only 6.7 per cent over the same period. The newspaper was found guilty of handling photocopies of the tax returns. The European Court noted that although the returns themselves were confidential, under French law local taxpayers could consult records for the taxable income and tax liability of others in their municipality. Thus the essential information contained in the assessments was accessible to a large number of people. The journalists acted in good faith. The article contributed to a debate on a matter of public interest. The publication of the extracts from the assessments was intended to corroborate the terms of the article and to show the credibility of its information. The Court found that the journalists' rights under Article 10 ECHR had been violated.

Although English law does not accord children any general right of privacy, there are occasions when it will grant injunctions to prevent media publicity or intrusion. A distinction is drawn (broadly speaking) between three situations (see the recent review in *Kelly* v *BBC* [2001] 1 All ER 323 (FamD)):

(a) Where the proposed publication does not deal directly with the care or upbringing of the child. Here the court will not intervene (e.g., *In Re X* [1975] Fam 47; *R* v *Central Independent Television plc* [1994] Fam 192).

(b) Where no positive approval of the media's activities is required, but the publication does impinge on the upbringing or care of the child. In these contexts, the court will sometimes grant injunctions, but the interests of the child do not have paramount importance. The value of the media's right of freedom of expression also has to be respected (e.g., *In Re M and N (Minors) (Wardship: Publication of Information)* [1990] Fam 211; *In Re W (A Minor) (Wardship: Restrictions on Publication)* [1992] 1 WLR 100).

(c) By contrast, if the approval of a parent (or the court) is required or sought, the interests of the child are taken to be of paramount importance (*Re Z (A Minor) (Identification and Restriction on Publication)* [1997] Fam 1). This principle was applied to prohibit a television programme concerning the rehabilitative treatment of the disabled child of a prominent politician and his former mistress. The broadcasters (and the mother) alleged that this violated Article 10 ECHR, but the Commission ruled the application inadmissible on the grounds that it was justifiable to give priority to the interests of the child (*A and Byrne and Twenty-Twenty Television* v *UK* (1997) 25 EHRR CD 159).

In UK law, breach of confidence is undergoing continuing expansion. In particular, the traditional requirement for a relationship of confidence between the claimant and, at least, the original person to whom the information was confided is becoming more and more attenuated. A sufficient relationship of confidence has been found to exist between people who are 'just good friends', so that the person who kisses and tells may be liable for breach of confidence (*Stephens* v *Avery* [1988] 1 Ch 449; *Barrymore* v *News Group Newspapers Ltd* [1997] FSR 600). Other courts have suggested that the thief who steals, or the innocent bystander who picks up, an obviously confidential document may be impressed with a duty of confidence (*X Ltd* v *Morgan Grampian (Publishers) Ltd* [1991] 1 AC 1 (theft); *English and American Insurance Co. Ltd* v *Herbert Smith* [1988] FSR 232, *Derby and Co. Ltd* v *Weldon (No. 8)* [1991] 1 WLR 73 and *A-G* v *Guardian Newspapers Ltd (No. 2)* [1990] 1 AC 109, at 281 (innocent acquisition of obviously confidential material)). Even more radically, another judge has suggested that a confidential relationship would exist between a photographer with a long-range telephoto lens and a subject who was engaged in some private act and not expecting to be observed (*Hellewell* v *Chief Constable of Derbyshire* [1995] 1 WLR 804, at 807 — see the quotation at 1.5 above). With these developments, English law is already covering more and more of the territory which in other jurisdictions would be protected by a generic law of privacy. These developments have been taken even further past–HRA (see 6.7 below). Together with this expansion of the scope of the cause of action has come some recognition that a defence of public interest is important.

Similarly, the courts ought not to allow a remedy for the further dissemination of information which (for good reasons or bad) has lost its confidential status. The ease with which information or copies of documents can be posted on the Internet has made this aspect of confidence claims particularly important. It was illustrated by an incident involving the arrest of William Straw, the son of the Home Secretary. Initially an injunction was granted to prevent publication of the boy's name. However, the injunction was lifted a very short time later when it became obvious that the name was widely available through the Net.

Now these features have been given a statutory basis. Under s. 12 of the HRA 1998, the court must have particular regard to the importance of the Convention right to freedom of expression; and, in relation to journalistic, literary or artistic material, it must have particular regard to the extent to which the material has (or is about to) become available to the public, or it is or would be in the public interest for the material to be published.

Remedies for breach of confidence are now supplemented by the Data Protection Act 1998 which was expressly concerned with the Convention right of privacy (see paras 2, 10, 11 and 17 of the preamble to EU Council Directive 95/46 on which the Act was based and Article 9 of the Directive) and which gives a statutory right to compensation against a data controller who contravenes the Act's requirements (s. 13). The rights of the media to freedom of expression are reflected in s. 32 of the Act.

6.3   PROTECTION OF CONFIDENTIAL SOURCES

Journalists who receive leaked documents or information from sources who wish to remain anonymous, will often find themselves facing demands for the return of the documents or for identification of their sources. The claim may be formulated as a simple demand for the return of the claimant's property or for the equitable relief which can be demanded of a person who through no fault of his own becomes mixed up in the tortious acts of others so as to facilitate their wrongdoing (*Norwich Pharmacal Co.* v *Commissioners of Customs and Excise* [1974] AC 133). The 'wrongdoing' will often be breaching a duty of confidence owed to the claimant.

In UK law, the media have the protection of Contempt of Court Act 1981, s. 10 of which provides:

No court may require a person to disclose, nor is a person guilty of contempt of court for refusing to disclose the source of information contained in the publication for which he is responsible; unless it be established to the satisfaction of the court that disclosure is necessary in the interests of justice or national security or for the prevention of crime or disorder.

The provision has been considered by the UK courts on numerous occasions and three appeals have reached the House of Lords. In *X Ltd* v *Morgan Grampian (Publishers) Ltd* [1991] 1 AC 1, Lord Bridge said of the 'interests of justice' exception that it called for a balancing exercise between the particular needs of the claimant and the journalist's presumptive right to preserve source anonymity: 'In this balancing exercise it is only if the judge is satisfied that disclosure in the interests of justice is of such preponderating importance as to override the statutory privilege against disclosure that the threshold of necessity will be reached.' Nonetheless, in that case, the House of Lords held that the journalist had been rightly ordered to disclose his source. The journalist, William Goodwin, persisted in his refusal and was fined £5,000. He complained that his rights under Article 10 ECHR were infringed, and in *Goodwin* v *UK* (1996) 22 EHRR 123 (followed in *De Haes and Gijsels* v *Belgium* (1997) 25 EHRR 1) the Court upheld the complaint. It said (at para. 39):

> Protection of journalistic sources is one of the basic conditions for press freedom, as is reflected in the laws and the professional codes of conduct in a number of contracting states and is affirmed in several international instruments on journalistic freedoms. Without such protection, sources may be deterred from assisting the press in informing the public on matters of public interest. As a result the vital public watchdog role of the press may be undermined and the ability of the press to provide accurate and reliable information may be adversely affected. Having regard to the importance of the protection of journalistic sources for press freedom in a democratic society and the potentially chilling effect an order of source disclosure has on the exercise of that freedom, such a measure cannot be compatible with Article 10 of the Convention unless it is justified by an overriding requirement of public interest.

On the facts of the case the Court was not persuaded that the interests of the claimant either in neutralising the threat from this particular leak, or of preventing similar leaks in the future were sufficient to outweigh the vital public interest in the protection of the journalist's source.

The language of the tests enunciated by the House of Lords and the European Court are very similar. However, the difference in their application can be striking. In the *Goodwin* case itself, of course, the House of Lords upheld the order that the journalist disclose his source, while the European Court found that this was not justified. In *Camelot Group plc* v *Centaur Communications Ltd* [1999] QB 124, the Court of Appeal commented on the similarity of the English and European tests and put down the difference in outcome to the different conclusions which different courts could come to on the facts. It must be doubtful as to whether this does justice to the European Court. The Court does not see itself as simply a court of further appeal. Its different reaction to the facts of the *Goodwin* case shows, it is submitted, a more acute appreciation of the importance of preserving the anonymity of sources (particularly in relation to the chilling effect of source disclosure orders on future informants) and the need to reserve encroachments on this principle to situations which are truly exceptional. The Court of Appeal has since agreed that the decisions of the European Court demonstrate that freedom of the press has in the past carried greater weight in Strasbourg that it has in this country (*Ashworth Security Hospital* v *MGN Ltd*, 18 December 2000 (CA), (2001) *The Times*, 10 January, para. 97. On the facts, the Court of Appeal did order the *Mirror* to identify its source).

A further pointer in that direction is a Recommendation of the Council of Europe Committee of Ministers which provides examples of where an order for source disclosure might be justifiable. They include the protection of human life, the prevention of major crime and the defence of a person accused or convicted of having committed a major crime.[1] Recommendations of the Council of Europe do not have the same status as judgments of the Court, but they are from time to time referred to by the Court as useful guides to the direction in which the Court should go (e.g., *Z* v *Finland* (1997) 25 EHRR 371: see 9.6.8).

In contrast to the importance which the Court has placed on preserving the anonymity of sources in the interests of freedom of expression, the Commission has been unresponsive to complaints by those insiders who have spoken out and who have suffered disciplinary action from their employers or other adverse consequences. The Commission has emphasised that civil servants owe a duty of discretion.[2] The reluctance of the Convention organs to intervene will be of less significance in the UK, because the Public Interest Disclosure Act 1998 already provides a degree of protection for 'whistleblowers'.

Goodwin's case concerned an attempt to compel the disclosure of confidential sources. The Commission took a different attitude to a complaint by the BBC that a witness order for it to produce untransmitted film to the defence in a criminal trial interfered with its rights under Article 10 ECHR. The BBC argued that its film crews would be exposed to greater risk if it was known that untransmitted film could be produced under compulsion in a criminal trial. The Commission was not persuaded: '[It] considers that any risk to film crews flows from their presence at such incidents as the Broadwater Farm riots and from the fact that they are filming such incidents, rather than from any possibility that untransmitted material may subsequently be made available to the courts' (*BBC* v *UK* (App. No. 25798/94), 84 DR 129).[3] The obligation to provide the film in response to the summons was part of the BBC's ordinary civic duty and was necessary for maintaining the authority and impartiality of the judiciary. The view, however, persists among cameramen and photographers that they are more at risk if such orders are made. Ultimately, the issue is one of evidence, and the position under Article 10 ECHR would no doubt be different if there were stronger evidence that such fears were well founded.

---

[1] Recommendation No. R (2000) 7 of the Committee of Ministers on the rights of journalists not to disclose their sources of information, 8 March 2000.

[2] See *Morissens* v *Belgium* (App. No. 11389/85) 56 DR 127; *X* v *Norway* (App. No. 9401/81) 27 DR 228; *Haseldine* v *UK* (App. No. 18957/91) 73 DR 225; *ES* v *Germany* (App. No. 23576/94) 84 DR 58. Where disciplinary action is taken against a *journalist* who has publicly criticised his or her employer the position may be different — see *Fuentes Bobo* v *Spain*, discussed above at 2.3.2.7 and 4.5.1.

[3] The case was decided after the Commission's decision in *Goodwin* but before the judgment of the Court in that case.

6.4   ARTICLE 8: STATE INTERFERENCE

Article 8 ECHR provides:

> 1.   Everyone has the right to respect for his private and family life, his home and his correspondence.
>
> 2.   There shall be no interference by a public authority with the exercise of this right except such as is in accordance with the law and is necessary in a democratic society in the interests of national security, public safety or the economic well-being of the country, for the prevention of disorder or crime, for the protection of health or morals, or for the protection of the rights and freedoms of others.

The opening words of Article 8(2) — 'there shall be no interference by a public authority . . .' — show that the guarantee is (at least primarily) concerned to restrict interferences with privacy by public or state authorities. This also fits with the nature of the ECHR, which is an international treaty between states. The obligations which are assumed are those of the contracting parties themselves. In this primary sense it will be unusual for the provision to have any direct effect on the journalistic activities of the media, since they are not (or not usually; but see 6.5 below) 'public authorities'.

The media may be beneficiaries of the protections which Article 8 ECHR provides against state interference. In at least some of its aspects, Article 8(1) is capable of protecting office or business matters. Thus, for instance, 'correspondence' can extend to business as well as personal correspondence (*Niemietz* v *Germany* (1992) 16 EHRR 97). It includes telephones as well as post (*Klass* v *Germany* (1978) 2 EHRR 214). There is no reason why it should not also include electronic mail. Accordingly, a police search of media premises or seizure of documents from the media would have to satisfy Article 8(2). As with Article 10(2), the intrusion must not only be for one of the aims set out in the second paragraph, but it must be in accordance with the law. Telephone tapping by the British police failed this requirement in *Malone* v *UK* (1984) 7 EHRR 14 (which led to the Interception of Communications Act 1985), and the Commission considered that the activities of the security services were vulnerable to an Article 8 challenge for the same reason (*Hewitt and Harman* v *UK* (1989) 67 DR 88, which led to the Security Service Act 1989). Intrusions must also be 'necessary in a democratic society'. This, in turn, brings in the requirement of proportionality, and over-broad search powers or warrants have been found to be incompatible with Article 8 (*Funke* v *France* (1993) 16 EHRR 297 and *Niemietz* v *Germany* (1992) 16 EHRR 97; *cf. Camenzind* v *Switzerland* (1999) 28 EHRR 458 and *Chappell* v *UK* (1989) 12 EHRR 1). In the UK the Interception of Communications Act and this aspect of the Security Service Act have now been repealed. The various forms of interception and covert surveillance by state authorities are now governed by the Regulation of Investigatory Powers Act 2000.

There will be times when the media can legitimately claim that a search by the police infringes their right to privacy under Article 8 ECHR and also constitutes a restriction on their right to freedom of expression. Up to now, the protection accorded to the media by the 'special procedure' in Schedule 1 of the Police and Criminal Evidence Act 1984 (see below) has been incomplete. The procedure does not, for instance, apply in Scotland, and a Scottish warrant can be executed in England even though it has not been shown to satisfy the 'access conditions' which are necessary under the special procedure (*R* v *Manchester Stipendiary Magistrate, ex parte Granada Television Ltd* [2000] 1 All ER 135 (HL)). These anomalies may need to be re-examined following the HRA 1998. Even though the statutes have been construed (in the case of the Scottish warrants, by the House of Lords), they have not been assessed in the light of the more demanding obligation to construe legislation as far as possible consistently with Convention rights.

The special procedure which is prescribed sets out two sets of access conditions. The first is commonly invoked by the police in seeking orders for unpublished photographs or unused film taken by the media at scenes of violent public disorder. This set of access of conditions does not allow the police to obtain information about confidential sources. A second set of access conditions does not carry this restriction. Where, prior to the 1984 Act, the police had a statutory power to obtain a search warrant, an order for production can be made even though the material might identify confidential sources (see Police and Criminal Evidence Act 1984, Schedule 1, para. 3). Following the HRA 1998, such an order would be compatible with the media's Convention rights only if the stringent tests in *Goodwin* could be satisfied by the police. This in turn would be material to the duty of the Crown Court judge who is asked to make a special procedure order, because even if one or other of the sets of access conditions is fulfilled the judge still has a discretion as to whether to accede to the application and make the order (Police and Criminal Evidence Act 1984, Schedule 1, para. 1). The value of this discretion and the importance of exercising it with due regard to the common law's principles of freedom of expression and the right to be left alone have already been discussed by the Divisional Court. This was in the context of an application against the media where the first set of access conditions was in issue (*R* v *Central Criminal Court, ex parte The Guardian, The Observer and Martin Bright* [2000] UKHRR 796). In addition to these common law principles, under the HRA 1998, s. 6(1), it would be unlawful for the Crown Court judge as a public authority to act in a way which is incompatible with a Convention right.

6.5 ARTICLE 8: PRIVACY INTRUSION BY PUBLIC SERVICE BROADCASTERS

In previous chapters, we commented on the meaning of the term 'public authorities'. We saw that it could be taken to include some media organisations which are owned ultimately by the public — in particular the BBC and Channel 4 (see 3.5.2). If they are public authorities then, like other public authorities, as a result of s. 6 of the HRA 1998, they are under a legal duty to act compatibly with Convention rights. If this were so, it would not be difficult to imagine a court finding that they were also public authorities for the purpose of Article 8 ECHR. Accordingly, their intrusions on private life, in order to be lawful, would have to conform to the requirements of Article 8(2).

In one sense, this would not (or ought not to) have a dramatic effect on the operation of the broadcasters. They are already subject to the code of Broadcasting Standards Commission (BSC). In the case of Channel 4, they are also required to observe the code of the Independent Television Commission (ITC). Both Codes contain substantial and detailed provisions on privacy matters.[4] Section 12 of the HRA 1998 would require the UK courts to have regard to these Codes to the extent that any issue concerning privacy violations by the broadcasters came before them. Yet while the norms which the BBC and Channel 4 would have to observe might not be that different, the consequences of breaching them and (perhaps as importantly) the process of investigating alleged breaches would be different. Instead of inquiries by the regulators leading perhaps (in the case of the BSC) to an obligation to publish the Commission's decision or (in the case of the ITC) to a fine, these public service broadcasters could face court action under s. 7 of the 1998 Act and claims for damages and injunctions.

6.6   ARTICLE 8: PRIVACY INTRUSION BY THE MEDIA

Although Article 8(2) ECHR envisages that the prohibited interference will be by a public authority, Article 8(1) speaks in general terms of everyone having the right to 'respect' for his private and family life, etc. As the Court said in *X and Y v Netherlands* (1985) 8 EHRR 235, at para. 23:

> The Court recalls that although the object of Article 8 is essentially that of protecting the individual against arbitrary interference by the public authorities, it does not merely compel the state to abstain from such interference: in addition to this primarily negative undertaking, there may be positive obligations inherent in an effective respect for private or family life (see the *Airey* judgment of 9 October 1979, Series A no. 32, p. 17, para. 32). These obligations may involve the adoption of measures designed to secure respect for private life even in the sphere of the relations of individuals between themselves.

The notion of 'positive obligations' has been employed particularly frequently in the context of Article 8. The Court has, for instance, found there to be positive obligations to provide for penal sanctions against those who engage in sexual

---

[4] See 6.6 below for the website references to these Codes.

abuse of a woman suffering from mental disorder (*X and Y* v *Netherlands*, above); to take positive measures to allow for the integration of illegitimate children into their families (*Marckx* v *Belgium* (1979) 2 EHRR 330); to provide legal aid so as to give effective protection to a woman against her alcoholic and violent husband by enabling her to divorce him (*Airey* v *Ireland* (1979) 2 EHRR 305); to provide information to those affected by environmental pollution (*Guerra and others* v *Italy* (1998) 26 EHRR 357); and, under Article 10 ECHR, to provide a remedy to a TV producer who was dismissed after criticising his management on a radio programme (*Fuentes Bobo* v *Spain*: see 2.3.2.7 and 4.5.1 above).

It is extremely difficult to draw any consistent theoretical basis for these decisions. Equally, it is difficult to predict how or whether they would be applied so as to require the UK to adopt a law of privacy. A novel feature of imposing a positive obligation in that particular context would be that it would potentially conflict with the rights of others — the rights of the media (or others) to freedom of expression. While this might make the Court more cautious, it would not necessarily prevent it from finding a positive obligation even in this area. Article 10(2) would be compatible with a right of privacy, at least one which was sensitive to the general conditions of legitimate aim, legality and necessity in a democratic society. Certainly, the laws of many other European countries include a provision for the protection of privacy, and they have not been challenged as fundamentally incompatible with Article 10.

Although the Court has not been confronted with this issue, the Commission has. In several cases from the UK, the applicants alleged that the absence of a law of privacy was a breach of the UK's positive obligations under Article 8 ECHR and accordingly a violation of their rights under the Convention. In *Winer* v *UK* (App. No. 10871/84) (1986) 48 DR 154, the applicant complained of the publication of a book which alleged that he was an agent of the South African Secret Service ('BOSS') and included intimate details concerning him and his wife. The Commission dismissed the complaint. The applicant had brought and settled defamation proceedings and the Commission considered that, in his case, English law had not shown a lack of respect for his private life. So too, the Commission rejected a complaint by Moors murderer, Ian Brady, that the UK's positive obligation to protect his privacy from media falsehoods had been broken. A national newspaper had published a story supposedly by his daughter, alleging that Brady had assaulted and tried to seduce her in prison. Brady alleged that the story was wholly untrue and infringed his privacy. The Commission accepted the government's argument that, despite the absence of a general law of privacy, specific remedies, notably actions for defamation and malicious falsehood provided some protection. Brady had been advised that a defamation action would fail because he had no reputation to protect. His malicious falsehood allegation had been struck out because he had suffered no financial loss. But the fact that Brady had met these insurmountable hurdles did not, in the Commission's view, mean that doubt was cast on the effectiveness of the remedies for protecting private life (*Stewart-Brady* v *UK* (App. Nos 27436/95 and 28406/95, 2 July 1997) (1997) 90 DR 45).

A later case, also involving Brady, had again challenged the UK's failure to protect his privacy. In this case a national newspaper had published a photograph of Brady in his Special Hospital. This had been taken with a long range telephoto lens. Brady had complained to the Press Complaints Commission which had found that the photograph illustrated a story which was in the public interest and that there had been no breach of its Code of Practice. A judicial review of the PCC's decision had failed. Again, the Commission said that this sequence of events did not show that the UK was in breach of any positive obligation under Article 8 (*Stewart-Brady* v *UK* (App. No. 36908/97, 21 October 1998).

More recently, Earl Spencer and his wife complained that the press had used a telephoto lens to take photographs of Countess Spencer while she was in a clinic for eating disorders. The pictures were published alongside stories about her treatment and the effect that the illness had on her marriage. A successful complaint was made to the Press Complaints Commission. Proceedings for breach of confidence against two friends of the Earl (who were suspected of being the newspapers' sources) were settled. The applications to the Commission argued that the UK was in breach of its positive obligations under Article 8 ECHR because its system of law failed to provide any effective remedy for the publication of material relating to their private affairs or the taking and publishing of photographs of Countess Spencer. The Press Complaints Commission had not been able to grant compensation or injunctions to restrain future breaches. The European Commission of Human Rights would not have rejected out of hand the claim that Article 8 did impose such positive obligations. However, it was unnecessary to express a final view because the applicants had failed to exhaust their domestic remedies. In particular, developments in the law of breach of confidence meant that the applicants might have obtained satisfaction in the UK courts. Their failure to pursue a case against the sources or to take any court proceedings against the newspapers, meant that their applications to Strasbourg were inadmissible (*Earl Spencer* v *UK* (App. Nos 28851/95 & 28852/95) (1998) 92 DR 56).

In another case, this time from Sweden (*N* v *Sweden* (App. No. 11366/85) (1986) 50 DR 173), the Commission again seemed prepared to contemplate that Article 8 ECHR might impose positive obligations to ensure respect for private life, though as it said: '... where a question arises of interference with private life through publication in mass media, the state must find a proper balance between the two Convention rights, namely the right to respect for private life guaranteed by Article 8 and the right to freedom of expression guaranteed by Article 10 of the Convention'. The applicant in that case had sued unsuccessfully for defamation, but the Commission was unpersuaded that Swedish law had failed to strike an inappropriate balance.

These cases provide some encouragement to the UK courts to develop the existing causes of action which provide some protection for privacy — notably breach of confidence. However, the experience of some other jurisdictions is that privacy rights have grown in ways which cannot be easily classified in terms of the present English torts. In California, for example, 'a right to privacy' is an omnibus way of describing a group of torts, some of which are recognisable in English terms (e.g., breach of confidence, trespass, harassment) but others of which are not. The latter include intrusion into private life, which is defined by the Restatement of the Law of Torts as being committed by 'one who intentionally intrudes, physically or otherwise, upon the solitude or seclusion of another or his private affairs or concerns, [and who] is subject to liability to the other for invasion of his privacy, if the intrusion would be highly offensive to a reasonable person'. This is notably a wrong which is directed at news gathering and is not dependent on subsequent publication. In Canada, the taking of photographs of a person — even in a public place — may be an actionable infringement of the subject's right to privacy (see *Les Editions Vice Versa Inc* v *Aubry* (1999) 5 BHRC 437 (SC)).

Even if the courts were to find that the ECHR did place the UK under a positive obligation to 'respect' the private life of individuals in these novel ways, it would not necessarily follow that the courts would be free to develop entirely new causes of action to protect privacy (see *Venables and Thompson* v *News Group Newspapers Ltd*, 8 January 2001, Butler-Sloss P, para. D4). There would be two objections in particular to this:

(a) The theory of positive obligations (if that is not too grand an expression for such a diffuse idea) is addressed to the obligations of the UK as the contracting party to the Convention. It is silent as to the means to achieve those obligations. That is left to the discretion of the state concerned (see *Abdulaziz, Cabales and Balkandali* v *UK* (1985) 7 EHRR 471, at para. 67). Within the UK's constitutional structure, the courts are not omnipotent and would not be able to invent a completely new cause of action beyond the incremental development of the law which common law doctrine permits.[5] The courts' duty as public authorities not to act in a way which is incompatible with Convention rights (see HRA 1998, s. 6(1)) would not alter that position. It would be for Parliament to respond to this positive obligation. Parliament's acts (or omissions to act) are excluded from the general obligation on public authorities (HRA 1998, s. 6(3)), as is the failure to introduce or lay before Parliament a proposal for legislation or a failure to make any primary legislation (HRA 1998, s. 6(6)).

---

[5] See, for instance, the comments of Hoffman LJ in *R* v *Central Independent Television plc* [1994] Fam 192.

(b)   The media defendant against whom such a new cause of action was first
       applied might well have a grievance under Article 10 ECHR. Even
       supposing the aim of the new cause of action was to 'protect the rights of
       others', it would be open to question whether it was a restriction
       'prescribed by law'. The Strasbourg Court has said that to comply with
       this requirement the 'law' must be reasonably foreseeable. A radical new
       cause of action might not satisfy this requirement.

In *Douglas* v *Hello!* (2001) *The Times*, 16 January (see further 6.7 below), the Court
of Appeal canvassed but did not finally reach a conclusion on any of these issues in
relation to the capacity of the courts to develop a new tort of privacy. Keene LJ
noted that the creation of a new cause of action would appear to circumvent the
restrictions on proceedings in s. 7(1) of the HRA 1998 and on remedies in s. 8(1)
(para. 166). Brooke LJ noted that a state's positive duty was founded on Article 1 of
the Convention, but this had not been included in the Convention Rights set out in
Schedule 1 to the HRA. Yet, he added (at para. 91), 'Where Parliament in this
country has been so obviously content to leave the development of the law to our
judges, it might seem strange if the absence of Article 1 from our national statute
relieved the judges from taking into account the positive duties identified by the
court at Strasbourg when they develop the common law.' Sedley LJ, however,
thought that if the step from confidentiality to privacy was a legal innovation, it was
justified by s. 6 of the HRA (fn para. 129). He relied also on s. 12(4) which required
particular regard to be paid to the Convention right of freedom of expression. He
said that this necessarily meant having regard to both Article 10 and Article 8.
   If a major innovatory cause of action faces these hurdles, it is to be expected
that the incremental development of the existing causes of action will continue.
In this respect (as well as in connection with the existing application of those
causes of action), the provisions in s. 12 of the HRA 1998 will be material. These
were discussed at 3.8 above. In brief:

(a)   On an application without notice to the defendant, relief cannot be given
       unless all practicable steps have been taken to notify the defendant or
       there are compelling reasons to dispense with notice.
(b)   Pre-trial relief is dependent on the court considering that the claimant is
       likely to establish a case for an injunction at trial. Thus the *American
       Cyanamid* approach — which led in the breach of confidence context to
       an emphasis on preserving the *status quo* pending trial — is replaced.
(c)   Courts must have particular regard to the importance of freedom of
       expression.
(d)   They must also have regard to the extent to which the material in question
       has become or is about to become available to the public, or is or would
       be in the public interest to be published.

(e)   Courts must also have regard to any relevant privacy code. Unlike the Data Protection Act 1998, the HRA 1998 does not give the Government the power to prescribe the codes which may be consulted. The Codes which have been prescribed for that purpose are an obvious source (the Data Protection (Designated Codes of Practice) Order 2000 (SI 2000 No. 418)) and so would include the codes of the ITC,[6] the BSC,[7] the Press Complaints Commission,[8] the Producers Guidelines of the BBC,[9] and the programme Code of the Radio Authority.[10] But in this context the courts could look more widely and take into account, for instance, the terms of any code which the paper or broadcaster had itself drafted and adopted.

6.7   MEDIA INTRUSION: COURT DECISIONS POST-HRA

6.7.1   *Douglas* v *Hello!*

The wedding of Michael Douglas and Catharine Zeta-Jones at the Plaza Hotel New York was a grand affair with 250 guests. However, the couple prohibited the taking of photographs because they had agreed to give *OK!* magazine exclusive rights to publish photographs of the occasion. Two days later they learnt that *Hello!* magazine was about to publish other, unauthorised, photographs of the event. They and *OK!* obtained an interim injunction over the telephone which was continued after a hearing on notice the following day. An appeal was heard very shortly after that by the Court of Appeal which set the injunction aside.

The essential reason for the Court of Appeal's decision was its view that the balance of convenience favoured *Hello!*. The magazine was on the verge of publication at the time of application, its losses would have been enormous and very difficult to calculate with precision. By contrast, if publication proceeded, the damage to *OK!*'s interests, while large, would not have been so hard to assess. Whatever rights the married couple might have had to confidentiality or privacy were not sufficient to support prior restraint given the agreement which they had made with *OK!*.

The interest of the case in the present context, however, is the opinions which were expressed as to any right of privacy distinct from a right to protect confidentiality. The judgments fizz with ideas, but none are very conclusive. In part this was because of the nature of the application (where the court had to consider likely success at trial rather than reaching a concluded and final view), in part because of the speed with which the litigation had been conducted

---

[6] See www.itc.org.uk
[7] See www.bsc.org.uk
[8] See www.pcc.org.uk
[9] See www.bbc.co.uk
[10] See www.radioauthority.org.uk

(although the judgment was reserved), and in part because the three judgments reflected differences in the views of the three members of the Court.

The claimants put their case in privacy as well as confidence because of the possibility that the photographs had been taken by an intruder rather than a guest. Brooke LJ noted the development of the tort of breach of confidence (including its use to restrain publication of unauthorised photographs (*cf Creation Records Ltd* v *News Group Newspapers Ltd* [1997] EMLR 444 (ChD) and *Shelley Films Ltd* v *Rex Features Ltd* [1994] EMLR 134). He considered the decision of the Supreme Court of Canada in *Les Editions Vice-Versa* (see above at 6.6), but noted important differences between the Convention and the Quebec Charter in relation to their 'horizontal effect' (i.e., as between two private parties). He referred to the capacity of the common law for organic growth (notably in developing the law of negligence) and the emphasis which the government in the *Spencer* case had placed on the scope for breach of confidence to grow. He saw that Strasbourg had invoked the doctrine of positive obligations often in the context of Article 8 but reflected on whether the absence of Article 1 from the list of 'Convention rights' in the HRA would be an obstacle to the UK courts doing the same (he thought it would be strange if it did). In the context of the dispute before him, he was able to rely on s. 12(4) of the HRA and its reference to relevant privacy Codes. He thought that, in the present case, the privacy claims of the couple were not particularly strong and they were likely to succeed in confidence or not at all. Ultimately he thought that the claimants were likely to succeed in confidence (para. 96).

Keene LJ also focused on confidence although he thought that because of the publicity which the couple had already sanctioned it was questionable whether they would succeed in obtaining a permanent injunction at trial (para. 171).

Sedley LJ was bolder. He concluded that the couple had at the lowest a powerfully arguable case to advance at trial that they had a right of privacy which English law would recognise and where appropriate protect (para. 125) and that this right had to protect, 'not only those people whose trust has been abused but those who simply find themselves subjected to an unwanted intrusion into their personal lives. The law no longer needs to construct an artificial relationship of confidentiality between intruder and victim: it can recognise privacy itself as a legal principle drawn from the fundamental value of personal autonomy.' (para. 126). The right was not, of course, absolute, but subject to the balancing and proportionality tests reflected in Article 8.

6.7.2 *Venables and Thompson* v *News Group Ltd*

Venables and Thompson at the ages of 11 were convicted of the murder of two-year-old Jamie Bulger and ordered to be detained during Her Majesty's pleasure. Although their anonymity was protected during the trial, on their conviction the trial judge lifted restrictions on reporting their identity. He did, however, use his inherent jurisdiction as a High Court judge and his powers under s. 39 of the Children and Young Persons Act 1933 to restrict publicity as to their detention or changes in appearance. The setting of their 'tariff' (i.e., the period they had to serve before the Parole Board considered their release) proved highly controversial. The trial judge had proposed eight years, the Lord Chief Justice had said ten years and the Home Secretary determined that it should be 15 years. The European Court held that the role of the executive in setting the tariff was contrary to the Convention. Subsequently, the matter was referred back to the Lord Chief Justice (for other aspects of the Court's decision see 9.6.7 below). In October 2000, Lord Woolf, who was by then the Lord Chief Justice, set a revised tariff which would permit the Parole Board to allow the release of Thompson and Venables in 2001. They applied to the court for a number of injunctions to protect their new identities and to continue the restrictions on reporting matters relating to their detention.

Lady Butler-Sloss, President of the Family Division, granted the injunctions regarding their new identities and appearances. Since they were now adults, this could not be done under the powers which the trial judge had used. However, she considered that the existing law of confidence was capable of extension to cover their cases. If information as to their new identities came to the media, they would be aware of its confidential character. It was crucial that the confidence be respected because of the risk (which she judged to be real and serious) of revenge attacks. By the nature of the case the matter could not be proved on a balance of probabilities, but it had been convincingly demonstrated. The absolute right to life guaranteed by Article 2 meant that the Court should give particular importance to trying to protect the new identities and distinguished this case from others where anonymity might merely be desirable. In giving pre-eminence to the right to life she followed the decision of the Court of Appeal in *R v Lord Saville of Newdigate, ex parte A* [2000] 1 WLR 1885 where the Court of Appeal had reversed a decision of the Bloody Sunday Tribunal of Inquiry that had required soldier witnesses to the Inquiry to give evidence without protection of anonymity. Furthermore, she granted the injunction against the world so that it would directly apply to newspapers who were not party to the proceedings, rather than in the indirect manner which the *Spycatcher* injunction was held to affect others. She directed that the injunctions should continue in force even if information as to their new identities was published abroad or on the Internet.

Chapter Seven

Racial Hatred

7.1 INTRODUCTION

UK statute law contains a number of provisions limiting freedom to express views and ideas which involve race hatred. These are summarised at 7.2 below. In the remainder of this chapter we consider how and why the ECHR allows governments to adopt such measures, notwithstanding the right to freedom of expression in Article 10(1), and indicate why the HRA 1998 is unlikely to lead to any significant changes in this area. We also consider how the European Court has approached the difficult issues which arise when the media report the views and activities of racists in the public interest.

7.2 DOMESTIC LAW

Abuse on grounds of race has long been recognised as a form of discrimination, usually described as 'racial harassment', for the purposes of the Race Relations Act 1976. The 1976 Act is mainly concerned with discrimination at work. It ensures that employers and principals are liable to pay compensation to victims of racial harassment within the workplace, unless they can show that they took reasonable steps to prevent it from occurring (s. 32). The bad publicity that results from media reporting of racial abuse cases in the employment tribunals is also important in ensuring that employers take these responsibilities seriously.

In addition, Part III of the Public Order Act 1986 contains a series of criminal offences involving acts intended or likely to stir up racial hatred. The best known of these is the use of words or behaviour or display of written material of a threatening, abusive or insulting nature (s. 18). However, publishing or distributing such written material is also an offence (s. 19), as are playing recordings of and broadcasting such material (ss. 21 and 22). It is also an offence under s. 23 of the 1986 Act to possess such racially inflammatory material with a view to its use in any of these ways. The Crime and Disorder Act 1998 further provides for the basic public order offences in the 1986 Act to be treated more severely where they are racially aggravated (s. 31). Again, media reporting of criminal proceedings for racist crimes is an important deterrent. Underlying all of these provisions is a recognition that there are fundamental rights of others which must be protected from the evils of racist sentiment. On the whole they have successfully limited the dissemination of racist propaganda in this country to material passing within closed racist groups or which is anonymous and furtively distributed.

7.3   DISCRIMINATION UNDER THE ECHR

The ECHR does not contain a free-standing right not to be discriminated against on grounds of race, or indeed any unlawful grounds. In this sense it lags well behind developments at a global level.[1] However, a new, Twelfth Protocol, requiring that the enjoyment of 'any right set forth by law shall be secured without discrimination', has recently been agreed by the Committee of Ministers of the Council of Europe.[2] At present the UK Government has no plans to ratify this general non-discrimination provision, or to include it as a 'Convention right' for the purposes of the HRA 1998.

There is some authority to suggest that discrimination based on race may of itself amount to degrading treatment for the purposes of Article 3 of the ECHR (*Abdulaziz, Cabales and Balkandali* v *UK* (1985) 7 EHRR 471, at para. 91), but the differences of treatment relied upon would have to be so extreme as to denote 'contempt', or be designed to 'humiliate or debase'. However, Article 14 does provide a 'subsidiary', or 'accessory', right to be free from discrimination by stating that:

> The enjoyment of the rights and freedoms set forth in this Convention shall be secured without discrimination on any ground such as sex, race, colour, language, religion, political or other opinion, national or social origin, association with a national minority, property, birth or other status.

This enables a complaint of unequal treatment to be made in conjunction with one or more of the substantive rights under the Convention or the Protocols. A

---

[1] See, in relation to race, in particular the 1965 UN Convention on the Elimination of All Forms of Racial Discrimination, Articles 4 and 5 of which require that the 'dissemination of ideas of racial superiority or hatred' be made an offence albeit with 'due regard to ... the right to freedom of opinion and expression'. See also Article 26 of the UN Covenant on Civil and Political Rights 1966.

[2] Agreed 26 June 2000, open for signature on 4 November 2000 and requiring ten ratifications for entry into force; the list of grounds constituting unlawful discrimination in Article 1 of the Twelfth Protocol are exactly the same as in Article 14 of the Convention.

violation of Article 14 coupled with the provision creating the substantive right will be established if the complainant can show that the facts in issue in the complaint 'fall within the ambit of' the substantive provision (*Abdulaziz*, at para. 71) or, put differently, that there has been discrimination in the context of one of the rights or freedoms guaranteed. The connection between the substantive Convention right and the discrimination may be a loose one and it is not necessary to establish a violation of the substantive right in order for a claim under Article 14 to succeed. For example, if a contracting party were to grant a series of new broadcasting licences, this would enhance freedom of expression. But if it resolved to give them only to its own nationals, although the measure would not involve any interference with the Article 10(1) rights of those excluded, the rights given by Articles 10 and 14 together would be violated.

Article 14 does not prohibit all differential treatment between those in a comparable situation. The Court has accepted that discrimination may be justified on a 'reasonable and objective' basis (*Belgian Linguistics Case (No. 2)* (1968) 1 EHRR 252, at para. 9). This requires the Government to demonstrate a legitimate aim and that the discriminatory measure is proportionate. In any case where the discrimination is because of differing race or nationality, the contracting state will almost certainly fail in any attempt to justify the differential treatment. (See, for example, *East African Asians* v *UK* (1981) 3 EHRR 76.)

7.4   LIMITING RACIST EXPRESSION

Although the ECHR does not yet contain a substantive right to be free of discrimination, it does contain provisions which enable contracting parties to control race hate expression. In addition to the limitations on the right of freedom of expression in Article 10(2), which include the protection of the rights of others, Article 17 ECHR provides that:

> Nothing in this Convention may be interpreted as implying for any state, group or person any right to engage in any activity or perform any act aimed at the destruction of any of the rights and freedoms set forth herein or at their limitation to a greater extent than is provided for in the Convention.

In *Lawless* v *Ireland (No. 3)* (1961) 1 EHRR 15, a complaint was made by a member of the IRA who had been detained without trial for some five months in the Republic. The Irish Government contended that the IRA's terrorist activities in Ireland at that time, both north and south of the border, were such that the applicant's membership of the organisation deprived him of the fundamental rights of liberty and a fair trial in Articles 5 and 6 ECHR. It relied upon Article 17. In rejecting this argument the Court stated that:

> ... the purpose of Article 17, in so far as it refers to groups or to individuals, is to make it impossible for them to derive from the Convention a right to engage or perform any act aimed at destroying in any activity any of the rights and freedoms set forth in the Convention ... This provision which is negative in scope, cannot be construed ... as depriving a physical person of the rights guaranteed by Articles 5 and 6 of the Convention ... (at para. 7)

7.4.1 Race hate propaganda

The Commission has consistently drawn on Articles 10(2), 14 and 17 to resist attempts by propagandists to allege violations of Article 10(1). In 1979, in the applications of *Glimmerveen and Hagenbeek* v *Netherlands* (App. Nos 8348/78 & 8406/78) (1979) 18 DR 187, the Commission considered Article 17 in the context of a conviction for possessing, with a view to distribution, leaflets inciting racial discrimination. The two applicants held senior positions in a political party, the '*Nederlandse Volks Unie*' (NVU), which sought an ethnically homogeneous population without any racial mixing. The previous year the NVU had been declared a prohibited organisation under the Dutch Civil Code. The leaflets advocated the 'removal' of all 'Surinamers, Turks and other so-called guest workers from the Netherlands'. In one of two applications, Glimmerveen contended that his conviction violated his rights under Article 10(1) ECHR. While the Dutch Government accepted that it interfered with his right of freedom of expression, it argued that Article 17 of the Convention prevented him from exploiting Article 10(1) to enable him to disseminate racist material. The Commission agreed, restating the *Lawless* principle thus: 'The general purpose of Article 17 is to prevent totalitarian groups from exploiting in their own interests the principles enunciated by the Convention.' It went on:

> ... To achieve that purpose it is not necessary to take away every one of the rights and freedoms guaranteed from persons found to be engaged in activities aimed at the destruction of any of those rights and freedoms. Article 17 covers those rights which, if invoked, will facilitate the attempt to derive therefrom a right to engage personally in activities aimed at the destruction of any of the rights and freedoms set forth in the Convention ... (at 195)

Even without a free-standing right not to be discriminated against on racial grounds, the Commission had no difficulty finding that the views expressed in Glimmerveen's leaflets were aimed at the destruction of precisely such rights. These were identified as the subsidiary right under Article 14, the possibility that race discrimination might amount to degrading treatment under Article 3 (see 7.3

above) and the provisions of the Fourth Protocol prohibiting collective or individual expulsion of nationals and collective expulsion of aliens.[3] The Commission concluded that:

> ... The Netherlands' authorities in allowing the applicants to proclaim freely and without penalty their ideas would certainly encourage the discrimination prohibited by [these] provisions of the Convention ... [such activities being] contrary to the text and spirit of the Convention ... (at 196)

The application under Article 10 was therefore ruled inadmissible by reason of Article 17.

In *Kuhnen* v *Federal Republic of Germany* (App. No. 12194/86) (1988) 56 DR 205), the applicant was a neo-Nazi journalist who had been convicted of an offence prohibiting the dissemination of anti-democratic propaganda which challenged 'the notion of understanding amongst peoples' by unconstitutional organisations. His leaflets proclaimed that his organisation, the 'ANS', was '*against*: capitalism, communism, Zionism, estrangement by means of masses of foreign workers ...'. The conviction was based on a finding that the ANS was unconstitutional as an organisation which sought the revival of the Nazi party (NSDAP) and national socialism in Germany, and with it 'the state of violence and illegality which existed in Germany between 1933 and 1945'. The criminal court also found that the material could revive anti-Semitic and racist sentiments. Like Glimmerveen, Kuhnen argued that the conviction violated his rights under Article 10(1) ECHR. He contended that Article 17 did not apply in his case because the ANS only advocated the reinstatement of NSDAP as a constitutional party by legal means. The Commission declared the application to be manifestly ill-founded. It stated that the interference with Kuhnen's Article 10(1) rights represented by the conviction, which was prescribed by law, had legitimate aims under Article 10(2), namely the interests of national security and public safety and the protection of the rights of others. It also considered that the applicant was indeed trying to use Article 10 in the way prohibited by Article 17 because, as the criminal court had found, by the very act of advocating Naziism his publications 'aimed at impairing the basic order of freedom and democracy' (at 209–10). Because of this, the interference was 'necessary in a democratic society'.

The Commission's approach in these two cases has been applied consistently in other race hate propaganda cases, and the new Court, having taken over the role of assessing admissibility, is now taking a similar line. (See, for example, *Schimanek* v *Austria* (App. No. 32307/96, 1 February 2000).)

Similarly, in a human rights case from Scotland, Lord Steyn said, 'It is also noteworthy that Article 17 of the Convention prohibits among others, individuals

---

[3] See Articles 3 and 4 of the Fourth Protocol; although note that the UK is not a party to the Fourth Protocol so that its guarantees are not 'Convention rights' for the purposes of the HRA 1998.

from abusing their rights to the detriment of others. Thus notwithstanding the danger of intolerance towards ideas, the Convention system draws a line which does not accord the protection of free speech to those who propagate racial hatred against minorities.' (*Stott (Procurator Fiscal, Dunfermline) v Brown*, 5 December 2000 (PC))

The Court will, however, look closely at the material to ensure that it contains provocative or hate speech. In *Ceylan v Turkey* (1999) 30 EHRR 73, the applicant, a prominent Marxist trade unionist, had been convicted for inciting hatred and hostility through a polemical newspaper article. The piece virulently criticised the government for using supposed 'anti-terrorist' measures to attack Kurds fleeing into Turkey from Iraq. But it had not advocated violence in retaliation and had called for the plight of the Kurds to be seen as part of a working class struggle against oppression. The Court acknowledged the racial and other tensions caused by the influx of Kurdish refugees but characterised the article as strong political invective rather than hate speech. On this basis it found a violation of the applicant's Article 10 rights.

7.4.2 Holocaust denial

The Commission and Court have also consistently rejected as manifestly ill-founded, complaints asserting the right to engage in holocaust denial. In *X v Federal Republic of Germany* (1982) 29 DR 194, the applicant had been successfully sued in defamation by a Jewish neighbour after he displayed a pamphlet on his garden fence describing the holocaust as a 'Zionist swindle'. The Commission agreed with the domestic court that this was an attack on the reputation of his neighbour, whose grandfather had died in Auschwitz, and that the ruling therefore pursued the legitimate aim of protecting the others specified in Article 10(2) ECHR. The restriction was considered proportionate because the pamphlet failed to observe the principles of tolerance and broadmindedness upon which democratic society rests (at 197). In *T v Belgium* (App. No. 9777/82) (1983) 34 DR 158, the applicant had edited a pamphlet which sought to minimise and justify Nazi atrocities, particularly at Auschwitz. The author, Degelle, had forfeited his right to publish political work through committing wartime national security offences. The applicant had been convicted of availing herself of his forfeited right. She was imprisoned for a year, heavily fined and all the pamphlets were destroyed. The Commission accepted that these severe measures were aimed at preventing disorder and maintaining the authority of the judiciary within the meaning of Article 10(2) ECHR, and that the interference was necessary in a democratic society 'two hallmarks of which are tolerance and broadmindedness' (at 170–71).

A series of Court and Commission decisions since *T v Belgium* have adopted essentially the same approach, but have also made clear that Article 17 removes any denial of the objectively established facts of the holocaust from the protection of Article 10. (See, for example, *Honsik* v *Austria* (App. No. 25062/94) (1995) 83 DR 77 at 84, and recently *Witzsch* v *Germany* (App. No. 41448/98, 20 April 1999), in which the Court applied the reasoning in *Lehideux and Isorni* v *France* (see 7.4.3 below).) Although the Court has never been asked to rule directly on specific holocaust denial legislation in one of the countries where it exists, it seems clear from these cases that in principle such laws can be regarded as pursuing legitimate aims under Article 10(2) and that it would be possible to defend their application as 'necessary in a democratic society'. Indeed, in *Faurisson* v *France* (1997) 2 BHRC 1, the UN Human Rights Committee cited *Glimmerveen* and *X* v *Federal Republic of Germany* (above) in finding that such legislation is compatible with Article 19 of the International Covenant on Civil and Political Rights 1966 (which closely corresponds to Article 10 ECHR). The applicant had been convicted under the French Gayssot Act, passed in 1990, for denying the holocaust in a magazine interview. The conviction was found to be a necessary restriction on his freedom of expression, the Committee noting in particular evidence that in France 'denial of the Holocaust [is] the principal vehicle for anti-semitism' (at para. 9.7).

7.4.3   *Lehideux and Isorni* v *France*

In this important case (*Lehideux and Isorni* v *France* (1998) 5 BHRC 540), the Court considered a conviction for 'making a public defence of crimes of collaboration with the enemy'. The applicants were representatives of two lawful associations which sought to overturn the conviction of the leader of the wartime Vichy government, Marshal Pétain, for acts of collaboration with the Nazis. They had placed an advertisement in a newspaper which presented him in a positive light and suggested that Pétain had been playing a 'double game' in the interests of the French people. While expressly disapproving of the Nazi atrocities, it made no mention of the collusion and involvement in Nazi persecution of French Jews which had caused Pétain's conviction. The applicants' convictions were based on findings that by omitting to mention the latter and 'putting forward an unqualified ... eulogy of the policy of collaboration [they] were justifying the crimes committed in furtherance of that policy'.

   The Court re-emphasised that any justification of a pro-Nazi policy or denial of 'clearly established historical facts — such as the Holocaust' would be removed from the protection of Article 10 ECHR by Article 17 (at paras 47 and 53), and described the omissions in the text 'about events directly linked with the Holocaust' as 'morally reprehensible'. However, these omissions had to be considered in the context of (in particular) the passage of time since the war, the need for 'every country to debate its own history openly and dispassionately' (at para. 55) and the fact that the applicants' aims in inserting the advertisement were the same as their organisations' which were lawfully constituted and had never been prosecuted (at para. 56). In the light of these considerations, the Court did not consider that conviction for a criminal offence in connection with the advertisement met a 'pressing social need'. In reaching this conclusion the Court invoked the *Handyside* principles of 'pluralism, tolerance and broadmindedness' against the state rather than (as in the cases referred to above) the polemicist applicants.

Lehideux v *France* indicates the Court's concern to limit the use of Articles 10(2) and 17 to interfere with freedom of political expression in areas other than race hate speech and denial of the established facts of the holocaust, in particular where controversial areas of a state's history are being debated. The decision may prove to be of considerable significance in the context of freedom of expression not only about the Second World War, but also the subsequent history of many eastern European states.

7.5 EXPOSING RACISM IN THE PUBLIC INTEREST

Different issues arise where racist statements are reproduced by the media in the process of reporting on the activities of racists. A balancing exercise is required between two important principles: (i) freedom of dissemination of information; and (ii) the protection of the rights of racial minorities.

This exercise was undertaken by the full Court in its decision in the important case of *Jersild* v *Denmark* (1994) 19 EHRR 1. The applicant had compiled a television documentary about a group of openly racist youths in Copenhagen known as the 'Greenjackets'. The broadcast included a few minutes of an interview with them which had lasted several hours, most of which had been filmed. In these extracts the youths made a series of derogatory and racist comments about 'niggers'. Together with all 'foreign workers', black people were said to be 'animals'. The youths were subsequently convicted of an offence of disseminating racist statements. The applicant was convicted for having 'assisted' the offence. He argued that the conviction and sentence violated his Article 10(1) rights. Denmark disputed this. It had ratified the 1965 UN Convention (see 7.3 above) and relied upon this fact to argue that although the conviction interfered with the applicant's Article 10(1) rights, the interference was 'necessary in a democratic society' to protect the rights of others within the meaning of Article 10(2).

The Court noted that the case had split the UN Committee on the Elimination of Racial Discrimination, when it was presented to it by the Danish Government, over the issue of whether 'due regard' had been paid to the applicant's right of freedom of expression as a journalist (at para. 21). It had also split the Commission, which had found a violation by 12 votes to four. It is perhaps therefore not surprising that the Court itself was divided on the difficult issue of proportionality. It held, by 12 votes to seven, that the applicant's rights had been violated, the conviction and sentence being disproportionate to the aim of protecting the rights of others.

The majority gave considerable weight to the case law of the Court establishing the unique role of the press as a responsible 'public watchdog' (see, for example, *Observer and Guardian* v *UK* (1991) 14 EHRR 153, at para. 59), and emphasised once again that '... it is ... incumbent on it to impart information and ideas of public interest. Not only does the press have the task of imparting such information and ideas: the public also has a right to receive them ...'. It acknowledged that the potential impact of the particular medium was an important factor in assessing whether the press had complied with its 'duties and responsibilities' and that the audio-visual media often had 'a much more immediate and powerful effect than the print ... conveying through images meanings which the print media are not able to impart'. But it reiterated that the rights provided for under Article 10 ECHR extend to the form as well as to the substance of the expression, so that the courts could not '... substitute their own views for those of the press as to what technique of reporting should be adopted by journalists ...' (at para. 31)[4] and the journalist had a discretion as to the way in which the racist sentiments might be counter-balanced (at para. 37). It also observed, in a passage that may assist in protecting journalists who republish defamatory statements by interviewees, that:

> ... News reporting based on interviews, whether edited or not, constitutes one of the most important means whereby the press is able to play its vital role of 'public watchdog'. The punishment of a journalist for assisting in the dissemination of statements made by another person in an interview would seriously hamper the contribution of the press to discussion of matters of public interest and should not be envisaged unless there are particularly strong reasons for doing so ... (at para. 35)

The majority found that, on any objective view, the programme could not have appeared:

> ... to have as its purpose the propagation of racist views and ideas. On the contrary, it clearly sought — by means of an interview — to expose, analyse and explain this particular group of youths, limited and frustrated by their social situation, with criminal records and violent attitudes, thus dealing with a matter that already then was of great public concern ... (at para. 33)

It also noted that the broadcast was a serious Danish news programme intended for a well-informed audience (at para. 34) and that it was undisputed that the applicant's aims in compiling the broadcast were journalistic and not racist (at para. 36). In the light of these findings of fact, it felt that the conviction of the applicant was disproportionate.

---

[4] See also *Oberschlick* v *Austria* (1991) 19 EHRR 389, at para. 67.

Even the dissenting opinion in the case was split. Four judges began their opinions by observing poignantly that this was 'the first time that the Court has been concerned with a case of dissemination of racist remarks which deny to a large group of persons the quality of "human beings"', and concluded that the Danish authorities had acted inside the margin of appreciation. They considered it particularly significant that the short section of interview used in the programme represented the 'most crude remarks' made by the youths, '. . . so it was absolutely necessary to add at least a clear statement of disapproval' (at 31, para. 3), which the applicant had failed to do. The other three dissenting judges came down even more strongly against the applicant, observing that the absence of any 'significant reaction on the part of the commentator' to the remarks rendered the statements 'an incitement to contempt not only of foreigners in general but more particularly of black people'. This being so, the defence that the programme would provoke a 'healthy reaction of rejection amongst viewers [displayed] an optimism, which to say the least is belied by experience' (at 32).

The decision in *Jersild* v *Denmark* establishes that the media can report the activities of racists. However, there are certain ground rules. They must take care to maintain their distance and ensure that the presentation does not suggest endorsement of racists' views.

7.6   THE FUTURE

It is unlikely that the implementation of the HRA 1998 will have any significant effect on the provisions of UK law referred to at 7.2 above. Our courts, like the Strasbourg Court, will remain 'particularly conscious of the vital importance of combating racism in all its forms and manifestations' (*Jersild* v *Denmark*, at para. 30) and will accept that government may indeed control the expression of views and ideas where they involve race hate to protect the rights of others.

This broad UK and European consensus is reflected in Canadian constitutional law (see *R* v *Keegstra* [1990] SCR 697, where the Supreme Court, albeit by a margin of only four to three, upheld the conviction of a teacher found guilty of making anti-Semitic statements to his pupils). In the United states, by contrast, the Supreme Court has used the First Amendment to the Bill of Rights to protect expression from interference by government because of its racist content alone. In *Colin* v *Smith* 439 US 916 (1978), a local ordinance which banned assemblies that would incite hatred of an ethnic, religious or racial group (intended to prevent the Neo-Nazi party of America marching in Chicago) was struck down. Fourteen years later, in the landmark case of *R.A.V.* v *City of St Paul* 505 US 377 (1992), the Supreme Court considered a conviction of a minor, Viktoria, for the act of burning a cross on the lawn of a black family. The conviction was under a municipal ordinance which penalised placing:

... on public or private property a symbol, object, appellation, characterization or graffiti, including but not limited to, a burning cross or Nazi swastika, which one knows or has reasonable grounds to know arouses anger, alarm or resentment in others on the basis of race, colour, creed, religion or gender ...

All nine judges found that the ordinance was unconstitutional because of its width. Five of them, while registering their belief that Viktoria's action had been 'reprehensible', nonetheless found that the ordinance was unconstitutional because it proscribed expression purely on the basis of its content.

Chapter Eight

Obscenity and Blasphemy

8.1 INTRODUCTION

Obscene and blasphemous speech (together with racist speech, discussed in depth in Chapter 7) are regulated, at least in part, because of their ability to offend and shock some or all of the population. Indeed, the protection of individuals from offence as a result of attacks on their religion is really the only justification for prohibiting blasphemous speech.

A number of additional rationales have been advanced for proscribing obscene speech, including the harm caused to the individual who is exposed to the obscene material (moral corruption), harm caused by the exploitation of individuals in the making of the obscene material and more general harms to the population (particularly the female population), by the widespread availability of such material. In relation to restricting expression because it offends, the European Court in *Handyside* v *United Kingdom* stated:

> Freedom of expression constitutes one of the essential foundations of a society, one of the basic conditions for its progress and for the development of every man. Subject to paragraph 2 of Article 10, it is applicable not only to 'information and ideas' that are favourably received or regarded as inoffensive but also to those that offend, shock or disturb the state or any sector of the population. Such are the demands of pluralism, tolerance and broad mindedness without which there is no 'democratic society'. ((1976) 1 EHRR 737, at para. 49)

Unfortunately, this worthy sentiment has too often been forgotten by the European Court when deciding cases concerning obscene or blasphemous speech. Obscene and blasphemous speech usually occur in the artistic rather, than the political or commercial, fields. The Court has consistently granted states a substantial margin of appreciation in this regard, first, because the expression in question (unlike political speech) is not considered to be of central importance (see 2.3.3.6) and secondly, because the Court is particularly deferential to state regulation of expression where protection of morals is in issue. This is perhaps not surprising given the scope of the European Court's jurisdiction, extending as it does from liberal Northern European states such as The Netherlands to the socially conservative Turkey. The Court in *Müller* v *Switzerland* (1988) 13 EHRR 212 stated:

> It is not possible to find in the legal and social orders of the Contracting states a uniform conception of morals. The view taken of the requirements of morals varies from time to time and from place to place, especially in our era, characterised as it is by a far reaching evolution of opinions on the subject. (at para. 35)

As in the field of commercial speech (see Chapter 2), the regular recourse to the doctrine of margin of appreciation means that the existing jurisprudence provides little coherent guidance to assist English courts when, as they undoubtably will be, they are faced with challenges to prosecutions in the obscenity and perhaps the blasphemy fields. Before discussing the ECHR case law in detail, we briefly outline the domestic law of obscenity and blasphemy.

8.1.1   Domestic law: obscenity

The law relating to obscenity and indecency derives from some 20 different statutes and from the common law.[1] It was described by the Williams Committee on Obscenity and Film Censorship as 'a mess'.[2] The simplification that the Williams Committee advocated has, unfortunately, not been adopted by subsequent legislation. Such legislation has, if anything, further complicated the law.

The common law test for obscenity was laid down in *R* v *Hicklin* (1868) LR QB 360:

> ... whether the tendency of the matter charged as obscenity is to deprave and corrupt those whose minds are open to such immoral influences and into whose hands such a publication might fall.

This definition was closely followed by that provided in s. 1, Obscene Publications Act 1959:

---

[1] See Shorts, E. and de Than, C., *Civil Liberties, Legal Principles of Individual Freedom* (London, Sweet & Maxwell, 1998), chap. 5 for a detailed discussion of the statute and common law in this field.
[2] (1979) Cm. 7772.

... an article shall be deemed to be obscene if its effect or (where the article comprises two or more distinct items) the effect of any one of its items is, if taken as a whole, such as to tend to deprave and corrupt persons who are likely, having regard to all relevant circumstances, to read, see or hear the matter contained or embodied in it.

Obscene speech is traditionally viewed as relating to sexually explicit material, but the definition is wider than this and extends to, for example, encouraging the use of dangerous drugs (see, e.g., *Calder v Powell* [1965] 1 QB 509 and *R v Skirving* [1985] QB 819) or the use of violence (*Director of Public Prosecutions v A & BC Chewing Gum Ltd* [1968] 1 QB 159).

8.1.2 Domestic law: blasphemy

The common law offence of blasphemous libel relates to comments about God, holy personages or articles of the Anglican faith, and is constituted by vilification, ridicule or indecency. Lord Scarman in *Whitehouse v Gay News Ltd and Lemon* [1979] AC 617, held that the modern law of blasphemy was correctly formulated in Article 214 of *Stephen's Digest of the Criminal Law* (9th edn), which stated:

Every publication is said to be blasphemous which contains any contemptuous, reviling, scurrilous or ludicrous matter relating to God, Jesus Christ or the Bible, or the formularies of the Church of England as by law established. It is not blasphemous to speak or publish opinions hostile to the Christian religion, or to deny the existence of God, if the publication is couched in decent and temperate language. The test to be applied is as to the manner in which the doctrines are advocated and not to the substance of the doctrines themselves.

Thus, the offence relates to 'immoderate or offensive treatment of Christianity or sacred subjects' rather than to moderate and reasoned criticism. The offence is one of strict liability, there being no requirement that the defendant intended to blaspheme.

The rationale for making blasphemers criminally punishable is:

Their manner, their violence, or ribaldry, or, more fully stated, for their tendency to endanger the peace then and there, to deprave public morality generally, to shake the fabric of society and to be a cause of civil strife. (*Bowman v Secular Society* [1917] AC 406)

The Law Commission recommended that the offence of blasphemy and blasphemous libel be abolished, but no Government has seen fit to follow up this recommendation.[3]

---

[3] Law Commission, Working Paper No. 79, *Offences Against Religion and Public Worship* (1981).

8.2 OBSCENITY: ECHR

8.2.1 'Interference by a public authority'

In all the cases concerning obscene speech, the existence of an interference with the applicant's right to freedom of expression has not been seriously disputed. The manner of the interference has included seizure or forfeiture of the offending material (*Müller* v *Switzerland* (1988) 13 EHRR 212), and a criminal conviction followed by a fine (see *Müller*) or imprisonment (*Hoare* v *United Kingdom* (App. No. 31211/96) [1997] EHRLR 678). The only argument that could have been invoked by governments to deny an interference with the right to freedom of expression is that obscene publications are not 'expression' within the meaning of Article 10 ECHR. Such an approach has gained some academic[4] and judicial support in the USA, partly as a result of the absolutist nature of the text of the First Amendment (protecting freedom of speech) (see, e.g., *Roth* v *United States* 354 US 476 (1957)). However, the European Court has, sensibly, rejected this artificial approach, stating in *Müller* v *Switzerland* that Article 10 did not distinguish between the various forms of expression and that artistic expression, including indecent or obscene art, affords the opportunity to take part in the public exchange of cultural, political and social information and ideas (at para. 27).

8.2.2 'Prescribed by law'

Defining what matters are obscene is notoriously difficult. What to one individual is innocuous, to another is a threat to society. Justice Potter Stuart, in a concurring opinion in *Jacobellis* v *Ohio* 378 US 184 (1964), at 197, acknowledged that obscenity was difficult (if not impossible) to define, but considered that 'I know it when I see it.' However, this impossibility has not prevented the European Court and Commission from concluding in all cases that the restriction, whatever it may be, is sufficiently certain and predictable to be 'prescribed by law'.

8.2.3 'Legitimate aim'

In all the cases concerning obscene speech the legitimate aim is the 'protection of morals'. In *Müller* (see 8.2.1), the Court intimated that the 'protection of the rights of others' might also be engaged when, as in *Müller*, the obscene material was available by way of exhibition to the general public without adequate warnings. This conclusion was reached in part because individuals had complained about the exhibition of the obscene paintings (see para. 30).

8.2.4 'Necessary in a democratic society'

One of the first Article 10 ECHR cases to be heard by the European Court concerned English obscenity legislation. In *Handyside* v *United Kingdom* (1976)

---

[4] See, e.g., Schauer, F., *Free Speech: A philosophical Enquiry* (Cambridge, CUP, 1982) chap. 12.

1 EHRR 737, the European Court enunciated a number of general principles in relation to the right to freedom of expression. *Handyside* concerned a book entitled *The Little Red School Book*, which was designed to be a reference book for 12–18-year-old children. It contained chapters on, *inter alia*, sex (both heterosexual and homosexual), use of drugs and pornography. The book adopted an anti-authoritarian approach to these topics; for example, when discussing relationships no mention was made of marriage. The police seized both copies of the book and the book matrix. The applicant was convicted under the Obscene Publications Acts 1959 and 1964 and was fined. The magistrates had concluded that the book, bearing in mind its target audience, was likely to 'deprave and corrupt' a substantial proportion of that audience. The magistrates placed reliance, in reaching their conclusion, on the anti-authoritarian nature of the work and the likelihood that it would undermine teaching by parents, the Church and others in authority. Both the Commission and the Court concluded that the prosecution, conviction and seizure of the book was 'necessary in a democratic society' and within the state's margin of appreciation. The Court noted that when interferences with freedom of expression are for the 'protection of morals', the state has a significant margin of appreciation. *A fortiori*, where the protection of children is in issue. The applicant contended that the seizure, prosecution and conviction were not 'necessary in a democratic society' as the book was on sale in a large number of other European states. It had also not been the subject of prosecution in the Isle of Man or Northern Ireland. A prosecution under the Scots law of obscenity had been brought, but it had been unsuccessful. The Court brushed this argument aside by relying on the state's margin of appreciation. The Court noted that a revised edition of the book with the offending passages taken out had been allowed to circulate freely which, notwithstanding the applicant's arguments to the contrary, indicated that the national authorities wished to limit themselves to what was strictly necessary.

A similar approach was taken by the Court in *Müller* v *Switzerland* (1988) 13 EHRR 212, which concerned three paintings in a public exhibition. The national courts considered the paintings obscene as they depicted (amongst other things) sexual relations between men and animals. The national courts convicted the applicants of publication of obscene items, fined them and ordered the confiscation of the paintings. These paintings were returned eight years later. The Court concluded that both the fine and the confiscation were within Switzerland's margin of appreciation. particularly as the public had free access to the paintings since they were displayed in an exhibition which sought to attract the public at large.

The Commission, in *Scherer* v *Switzerland* (App. No. 17116/90, 14 January 1993), concluded that a conviction of a sex-shop owner who exhibited pornographic films for a homosexual audience in his unmarked shop was *not* 'necessary in a democratic society'. *Müller* was distinguished on the grounds that the pornography was exhibited only to adults who wished to see it and were aware of the content. *Scherer* was struck out of the list by the Court as the applicant died shortly after the Commission decision ((1994) 18 EHRR 276).

The European Commission refused to follow its earlier decision in *Scherer* in *Hoare* v *United Kingdom* (App. No. 31211/96) [1997] EHRLR 678, which concerned the sale of hard-core pornographic videos. The applicant advertised his videos in *The Sport* newspaper. Individuals who responded to the advert were sent a catalogue from which they could order films. The applicant was convicted for publishing obscene articles under s. 2, Obscene Publications Act 1959 and was sentenced to 30 months' imprisonment. He argued that this procedure ensured that the videos would be seen only by consenting adults who were aware of their content. The Commission rejected this argument on the ground that videos, unlike the films shown in *Scherer*, could easily be viewed by people (including children) other than those who ordered them.[5] The prosecution was therefore proportionate to the legitimate aim of 'protecting the rights of others' (see 8.2.3 above).

8.2.5 Selective enforcement

In *W and K* v *Switzerland* (App. No. 16564/90, 8 April 1991) the applicant challenged a prosecution for selling and renting obscene material on the basis that the enforcement measures taken by the state were arbitrary and unfair since a number of other film shops rented similar films but were not prosecuted. The Court concluded that the enforcement was proportionate to the legitimate aim pursued and that as the applicants had failed to demonstrate that their prosecution and conviction stemmed from a particular ground of discrimination stated in Article 14 ECHR, the complaint was inadmissible.

8.3 BLASPHEMY: ECHR

8.3.1 'Interference by a public authority'

An interference with the right to freedom of expression was not disputed in all four of the decisions relating to blasphemous speech under Article 10 ECHR. The nature of the interference included subsequent prosecution of published blasphemous speech (*Gay News Ltd and Lemon* v *United Kingdom* (1982) 28 DR 77; (1982) 5 EHRR 123), the seizure and forfeiture of a film prior to its exhibition (*Otto-Preminger-Institut* v *Austria* (1994) 19 EHRR 34) and the prevention of distribution of a video by the refusal to classify it (*Wingrove* v *United Kingdom* (1996) 24 EHRR 1). Both the seizure and the refusal to certify the film in question prevented the expression reaching an audience and thus amounted to a prior

---

[5] This approach mirrors that of the Court in *Wingrove* v *United Kingdom* (1996) 24 EHRR 1, in relation to blasphemous videos.

restraint. Prior restraints are, theoretically, more difficult to justify, although in both cases the Court concluded that such interferences were justifiable.

8.3.2 'Prescribed by law'

The first opportunity for the European judicial bodies to consider the English law of blasphemous libel arose in the case of *Gay News Ltd and Lemon* v *United Kingdom* (1982) 28 DR 77; (1982) 5 EHRR 123. Mrs Mary Whitehouse, in the first prosecution for blasphemy since 1922, brought a private prosecution against the magazine, *Gay News*, which had published a poem about a homosexual's conversion to Christianity which metaphorically attributed homosexual acts to Jesus Christ. Leave was obtained[6] for a private prosecution, the jury deciding that both the editor and the publishing company 'unlawfully and wickedly published or caused to be published a blasphemous libel concerning the Christian religion, namely an obscene poem and illustration vilifying Christ in his life and in his crucifixion' (*R* v *Lemon and Gay News Ltd* [1979] AC 617). The European Commission concluded that the application brought by the convicted defendants was inadmissible. It considered that the law of blasphemous libel was sufficiently certain to be 'prescribed by law', even though four out of five Law Lords had stated that the issue of whether intention to blaspheme was a necessary requirement of the offence was unclear. Their Lordships decided by 3:2 that intention to blaspheme was not a necessary element of the offence. Two of the judges in the majority (namely, Lords Russell and Scarman) and the two dissenting judges (Lords Diplock and Edmund-Davies) were of the view that the state of the law was unclear. The only judge to regard the law as clear on this issue was Viscount Dilhorne. Furthermore, the Law Commission had criticised the state of the law with regard to its lack of clarity (para. 10). The European Commission noted that the offence of blasphemy cannot by its very nature lend itself to precise legal definition. The Commission viewed the conclusion of the majority of the House of Lords on the issue of the requisite *mens rea* as not overstepping the limits of an acceptable clarification of the law. It further concluded that the law was sufficiently accessible to the applicants and that the interpretation was foreseeable with appropriate legal advice. The existence of this certainty is doubtful when one recalls that the definition of the offence requires the publication to be 'contemptuous' or 'ludicrous' — inherently subjective terms, particularly when these matters are questions for the jury.

The European Commission's view as to accessibility and foreseeability was reiterated by the European Court in the case of *Wingrove* v *United Kingdom* (1996) 24 EHRR 1, which arose out of the refusal of the British Board of Film Classification (BBFC) to classify a short film called 'Visions of Ecstasy' on the

---

[6] Leave from a High Court judge is necessary for prosecutions of newspapers: see Law of Libel Amendment Act 1888.

grounds that it violated the criminal law of blasphemy. The BBFC acted within its statutory powers under s. 4(1) of the Video Recordings Act 1984. The Commission found no distinguishing features which would enable it to depart from its earlier conclusion, the common law of blasphemy not having materially changed. The refusal to grant a certificate for distribution of the film on the grounds that it was blasphemous was predictable because the BBFC was enjoined by the Home Secretary to avoid classifying works that 'infringed provisions of the criminal law' and the work in question was, on the advice of counsel, blasphemous.

8.3.3 'Legitimate aim'

The United Kingdom Government in *Gay News* advanced three potential 'legitimate aims': 'prevention of disorder', 'protection of morals' and 'protection of the rights of others'. The Commission rightly rejected the first two justifications, noting that the public authorities had not viewed it as necessary to prosecute the applicants. This left protection of the rights of others as the only justification. The Commission, ignoring the Court's *dicta* in *Handyside* v *United Kingdom* that Article 10 ECHR extended to offensive and shocking expression (see 8.1), concluded that the protection of the rights of citizens not to be offended in their religious feelings by publications was a legitimate aim.

The European Court adopted the same approach in *Otto-Preminger-Institut* v *Austria* (1994) 19 EHRR 34, which concerned the public exhibition of a satirical film with religious subject matter entitled 'Council of Heaven'. Before its first showing the Public Prosecutor instituted criminal proceedings against the manager of the applicant association and a judicial order for seizure of the film was made. Subsequently an order of forfeiture was made. The European Commission — taking a far more robust approach than in *Gay News* v *United Kingdom* — concluded by a majority of 9:5 that the seizure was a violation of Article 10, and by 13:1 that the forfeiture was also a violation of Article 10. The Commission concluded that provisions of the Austrian Penal Code were aimed at protecting the 'rights of others' and 'the prevention of disorder', namely preserving religious peace. The Commission did not, therefore, need to decide whether the forfeiture and seizure were also aimed at the 'protection of morals'. The Court adopted a similar analysis, emphasising the importance of freedom of religion in a democratic society. The Court stated that certain methods of opposing or denying religious beliefs could 'inhibit those who hold such beliefs from exercising their freedom to hold and express them'. It concluded that the respect for religious feelings of believers as guaranteed in Article 9 ECHR, can be violated by provocative portrayals of objects of religious veneration.

This approach was attacked by the applicant in *Wingrove* v *United Kingdom* (see 8.3.2 above). The applicant contended that the rights of others only extended to an actual, positive right not to be offended and did not include a hypothetical right held by some Christians to avoid disturbance at the prospect of other people viewing the video work without being shocked. Both the Commission and the Court rejected this narrow definition of 'rights of others', although their analysis is somewhat lacking.

8.3.4 'Necessary in a democratic society'

The Commission in *Gay News* concluded that the law and the prosecution were 'necessary in a democratic society' and not disproportionate. The Commission explicitly stated that the strict liability nature of the blasphemous libel did not mean that it was disproportionate. The lack of any defence similar to the 'public good' defence under s. 4, Obscene Publications Act 1959 also did not trouble the Commission.

The Commission, in *Otto-Preminger*, quoted the *Handyside dicta* relating to the need to protect offensive speech, and concluded that the seizure was not 'necessary in a democratic society'. The film was being shown in an art cinema addressed to a specially interested public, an admission fee was charged, the film was shown late at night and, most important of all in the Commission's view, there was an adequate but inoffensive warning about the contents of the film. The majority of the Commission were of the view that these restrictions were adequate to protect the rights of others by preventing the attendance of children and individuals who might be offended by the content of the film. The Commission went on to conclude that the state's reaction of a complete ban was therefore disproportionate because the measures adopted to limit the viewing were sufficient. The forfeiture, which produced permanent effects in Austria for everyone who wished to receive and impart ideas, was, *a fortiori*, disproportionate. The Court, by a majority of 6:3, however, found that both the seizure and forfeiture of the film were 'necessary in a democratic society' to protect the rights of the majority of the population from gratuitous insults to their religious feelings. The seizure of the film to 'ensure religious peace' was proportionate and within Austria's margin of appreciation.

The majority judgment in *Otto-Preminger* has been cogently criticised[7] as unconvincing because, first, it is for viewers or readers rather than the judiciary to assess whether or not a film makes a contribution to any form of public debate capable of furthering human affairs;[8] secondly, the judgment fails to understand that social development in art often proceeds from assertion of offensive ideas to established views — freedom of expression that is limited to inoffensive speech is of little value; thirdly, penalisation of dissent against strong, established religion is particularly dangerous in religious societies such as Austria where the

---

[7] David Pannick QC, 'Religious feelings and the European Court' [1995] PL 7.
[8] This criticism reflects the views of Hoffman LJ in *R* v *Central Independent Television plc* [1994] Fam 192, where he stated: 'But a freedom which is restricted to what judges think to be responsible or in the public interest is no freedom.'

power of religion is great. The Court should have protected dissenting voices from an intolerant majority.

However, ignoring such criticism, the Court in *Wingrove* adopted a similar approach to that in *Otto-Preminger*, concluding that both the law of blasphemy and the BBFC's refusal to certify the film were 'necessary in a democratic society'. The applicant attacked the BBFC's actions on a number of grounds. First, he argued that there was not a 'pressing social need' to ban a video work on the uncertain assumption that it would violate the law of blasphemy, particularly when the video could potentially be prosecuted after distribution under a panoply of laws including the offence of blasphemy. Secondly, he contended that a complete ban of the video work, which contained no obscenity and no element of vilification of Christ, was disproportionate to the aim pursued ((1996) 24 EHRR 1, at para. 54). The Court rejected the applicant's submissions and concluded that the ban was both 'necessary in a democratic society' and within the state's 'margin of appreciation'. The Court acknowledged that there were strong arguments for the abolition of the crime of blasphemy and that a number of states had abolished it, but it found that there was insufficient common ground in the legal and social orders of the member states of the Council of Europe to conclude that the imposition of restrictions on such material was unnecessary in a democratic society (at para. 57).

8.3.5 'Discrimination'

The English law of blasphemy was subject to further scrutiny, albeit pursuant to Article 9 ECHR (the right to freedom of religion) and Article 14 (concerning a prohibition of discrimination) by the Commission in *Choudhury* v *United Kingdom* (App. No. 17439/90, 5 March 1991). The case arose out of the failed private prosecution for blasphemy brought against Salman Rushdie, the author of *Satanic Verses*, and his publisher. The prosecution failed on the ground that the criminal offence of blasphemy did not extend to the Moslem religion. The applicant argued that this was a violation of his right to freedom of religion and the right not to be discriminated against. The application was unanimously declared inadmissible on the grounds that Article 9 ECHR did not extend to a right to bring any specific form of proceedings against those who, by authorship or publication, offend the sensitivities of an individual or a group of individuals. Given this conclusion that Article 9 was not engaged, Article 14 ECHR was also of no assistance because it applies only when a Convention right is in issue.

This discriminatory nature of the English law of blasphemy was invoked by the applicant in *Wingrove* v *United Kingdom* (see 8.3.4 above) in support of his argument that the law did not pursue a legitimate aim. The Court brushed this argument away, stating that the case related to the Christian faith and the extent to which English law protects other beliefs was not in issue. The Court would not rule in the abstract as to the compatibility of domestic law with the Convention.

8.4 THE LIKELY IMPACT OF THE HRA ON DOMESTIC LAW

8.4.1 Obscenity

The jurisprudence of the European Court of Human Rights in this field is of limited assistance in assessing the likely impact of the HRA 1998, because of the Court's consistent resort to the margin of appreciation, which is of no relevance to domestic law (see 3.2.2). The common law offences of outraging public decency, conspiracy to outrage public decency and conspiracy to corrupt public morals are all likely to violate Article 10 ECHR.[9] The lack of any clear indication as to what types of expression will be covered by these offences[10] suggests that they may not be 'prescribed by law'. The fact that they admit of no defence that the dissemination of the material was for the public good, nor require that the material will tend to 'deprave and corrupt', suggests a real question as to whether they are necessary in a democratic society.

The statutory offences under the Obscene Publications Acts 1959 and 1964, although not without fault, are likely to survive challenge pursuant to Article 10 ECHR. The statutory defence of 'public good' allows a publication to be justified even though the material is obscene, and the further but limited safeguard provided by the bureaucratic input of the Director of Public Prosecutions into prosecutorial decisions is likely to weigh in favour of the statutory offences. There is a possible argument that the requirement to show a 'tendency to deprave and corrupt' (1959 Act, s. 1(1)) is insufficiently precise, though the Court's case law suggests that this argument is unlikely to be successful (see para. 2.3.3.2). There may, however, be some scope for contending that the use of 'forfeiture' provisions under s. 3 of the Obscene Publications Act 1959 is disproportionate and therefore not 'necessary in a democratic society'.

The Protection of Children Act 1978 makes it an offence to take or make any indecent photograph or pseudo-photograph of a child (s. 1(a)), to distribute such photographs (s. 1(b)), or to possess such photographs with a view to their being distributed or shown by the individual himself or others (s. 1(c)). There is a defence in relation to the distribution or possession of such photographs if the individual 'has a legitimate reason for distributing or showing the photographs or having them in his possession'. However, this defence does not apply to the taking of or making of any indecent photograph under s. 1(a). The lack of a defence in relation to the taking and making of indecent photographs of children may give rise to difficulties under Article 10 ECHR, as the courts have interpreted s. 1(a)

---

[9] *Cf. S and G v UK* (App. No. 17634/91, 2 September 1991), which ruled inadmissible a challenge to a conviction of outraging public decency.

[10] In 1976 the Law Commission recommended that the common law offence of outraging public decency should be abolished because of the vagueness of the definition of the offence. See generally Feldman, D., *Civil Liberties and Human Rights in England and Wales* (Oxford, Clarendon Press, 1993), at 712–3.

very broadly to include downloading such pictures from the Internet (*R* v *Graham-Kerr* (1989) 88 Cr App R 302 (CA)). There may be legitimate reasons for such downloading; for example, a journalist investigating the extent of child pornography on the Internet might download such pictures. The journalist would have no defence open to him. Prosecutions in such circumstances may well be regarded as disproportionate and unnecessary in a democratic society.

8.4.2 Blasphemy

The Law Commission concluded that the offence of blasphemy was arguably a violation of the Convention in two respects. First, it was impossible to predict in advance whether a particular publication would constitute the offence[11] and, secondly, the offence extended only to the Christian faith and thus discriminated against other faiths.[12] The lack of a 'public good' defence also indicates that the offence is overbroad and therefore arguably disproportionate. Such arguments were rejected by the European Court in *Wingrove* (see 8.3.4 above). However, it is to be hoped that the English courts will take a more robust approach to prosecutions for blasphemy and apply the principle, already established in the case law of the European Court of Human Rights, that speech cannot be criminalised merely because it is offensive to a sector of the population. (See *Handyside* v *UK* at 8.1 above, and Sedley LJ in *Redmond-Bate* v *DPP* (1999) 7 BHRC 375.)

8.4.3 Cinema regulation

The regulation of cinemas under the Cinema Act 1985 is a function of local authorities. Most will allow any film to be shown which is certified by the British Board of Film Classification. However, that does not prevent the local authority intervening to prevent the showing of a particular film. One recent example is Westminster City Council's ban on the film 'Crash', which could be viewed lawfully at cinemas in the neighbouring borough of Camden. If such a localised ban is challenged by a distributor or even a potential viewer of the film, councils may well have difficulty persuading a court that such a ban is 'necessary in a democratic society'.[13]

---

[11] Law Commission, Working Paper No. 79, *Offences Against Religion and Public Worship* (1981).

[12] Article 10, read together with Article 14, prevents states from discriminating between religions in respect of the extent to which their Convention rights are protected.

[13] *Cf. Handyside* v *UK*, where the Court found that the conviction and fine were 'necessary in a democratic society' even though the book was available throughout Europe and in Scotland and Northern Ireland. However, *Handyside* is an early decision of the European Court and may not (in this respect) be followed today. Furthermore, the Court granted the UK a considerable margin of appreciation which would not be available to the council if it were sued in domestic courts.

Chapter Nine

Court Reporting and Contempt of Court

9.1 INTRODUCTION

Court reporting is part of the staple diet of newspapers and broadcasters in the UK and in the other states who are party to the ECHR. From the perspective of Article 10, the starting point is the right of freedom of expression which the media, like all members of the public, have as a result of Article 10(1). From the perspective of defendants, the right to a fair trial which is guaranteed by Article 6 includes the right to a 'public hearing' and to a publicly pronounced judgment. However, as the UK domestic experience repeatedly demonstrates, there is ample scope for free reporting to conflict with the interests of defendants or others involved in the judicial process. Article 10(2) recognises that those exercising freedom of expression have 'duties and responsibilities' and that restrictions or penalties may be imposed for a variety of reasons, including 'for the protection of the ... rights of others' and 'for maintaining the authority and impartiality of the judiciary'. Article 6(1) accepts that:

> ... the press and public may be excluded from all or part of the trial in the interests of morals, public order or national security in a democratic society, where the interests of juveniles or the protection of the private life of the parties so require, or to the extent strictly necessary in the opinion of the court in special circumstances where publicity would prejudice the interests of justice.

The recognition of these competing interests is, however, only the beginning. This chapter will examine how they have been worked out in particular situations which are most likely to affect the court reporting activities of the media.

9.2 WHOSE RIGHT?: STANDING TO COMPLAIN

9.2.1 Article 10

There is no doubt that media organisations or individual journalists can rely on the freedom to receive and impart information in Article 10(1) ECHR. Court orders prohibiting or restricting reporting will constitute 'interferences' even though the media or journalists are not formally party to the proceedings. For professional organisations, such as the National Union of Journalists, the position is more difficult. As has previously been explained, Strasbourg will accept that a complainant is a 'victim' for the purposes of Article 34 ECHR only if he or she (or it) has been directly affected by the alleged violation of the Convention. The union would be able to demonstrate that this was so if its own freedom of expression was affected (e.g., by what it could publish in its own magazine or on its own website), but otherwise it would be insufficient that it was indirectly affected because of the impact of the restriction on its members (see *Hodgson, D. Woolf Productions Ltd and National Union of Journalists* v *UK* (App. Nos 11553/85 and 11685/85) (1987) 51 DR 136).

9.2.2 Article 6

The requirements that trials be in public are a protection for the parties, but there is also a public interest in being able to observe how justice is being administered. Thus, while in principle the right to a public hearing can be waived, this is subject to the proviso that waiver does not run counter to any important public interest (*Hakansson* v *Sweden* (1990) 13 EHRR 1, at para. 66). Although the right to a public trial includes the right for the public to attend trials, for the vast majority of people what is more important is the ability to learn about trials through the media. Does this mean that the media can claim to be victims of violations of Article 6 if they are improperly excluded from trials which ought to have been held in public? The Court has not ruled on this issue, but we would expect it to decide that the context of Article 6 makes clear that it is establishing a bundle of rights for litigants, not for others. The public interest in open justice may provide part of the underpinning justification for those rights, but they remain rights which can be claimed only by those who are party to the proceedings. But if the media are not able to rely on Article 6 directly, they may be able to do so indirectly. In particular, the public interest justification for open trials, may buttress their claims to argue for a right under Article 10 to have access to trials unless one of the qualifications on the right to a public trial in Article 6(1) can be established (see further at 9.6.6 below).

Of course, if reporters or media organisations are themselves party to legal proceedings, they will be able to claim the protections of Article 6. If they are subject to contempt proceedings, these would almost certainly amount to 'criminal charges' for the purpose of the Article. This is an autonomous concept which is not dependent on how the proceedings are classified in domestic law and, therefore, the anomalous character of contempt in UK law is not determinative.

Article 6 also applies to proceedings which will determine a person's 'civil rights and obligations'. This is also an autonomous concept, but one which remains ill-defined. The Commission decided in 1987 that a court ruling as to reporting restrictions did not determine a reporter's 'civil rights and obligations' (see *Hodgson, D. Woolf Productions Ltd and NUJ* v *UK* (above); *Atkinson, Crook and The Independent* v *UK* (App. No. 13366/87) (1990) 67 DR 244) and that therefore a complaint that the ruling was made without allowing the reporter to be heard was manifestly unfounded and inadmissible. The meaning of 'civil rights and obligations' is an area of the Strasbourg case law which is still developing so that this may not be the final word on the issue. In addition, the practice of the UK courts has changed since the trial judge in that case refused to hear from the media, and it is now common for courts to hear media representations as to why reporting restrictions should not be made or should be lifted. It is important to remember that the HRA 1998 expressly provides that the rights which it creates are in addition to any other rights which the person concerned may have (s. 11).

9.3 'INTERFERENCE'

An issue related to standing is whether there has been an 'interference' with the applicant's 'freedom of expression'. Again, in many cases this will be undisputed. The Court has accepted that the manner and means of publication are essentially a matter of choice for the publishers: Article 10 ECHR protects not only the content of the information or ideas but also the form in which they are presented (*Jersild* v *Denmark* (1994) 19 EHRR 1, at para. 31, discussed further at 7.5). Thus, in *News Verlags* v *Austria* (unreported) 11 January 2000, the Court rejected an argument of the Government that an Austrian court order prohibiting a newspaper from publishing a suspect's picture in conjunction with a report of his arrest on criminal charges did not interfere with the publisher's freedom of expression because the picture had no information value.

However, the Commission's conclusion in *Loersch* v *Switzerland* (App. No. 23868/94) (1995) 80 DR 162, that there had been no interference with the journalist applicant's freedom of expression, was the reason why it ruled the application inadmissible. In that case the journalist had been refused accreditation with a court because he had refused to provide a *curriculum vitae* or police record, or proof of legal training. Even without accreditation the journalist was as free as any other member of the public to attend court and obtain a copy of the judgment. He could not get the readier access to judgments, or the advance notification of hearings or copies of unpublished judgments that accredited journalists could, but the Commission said that none of these rights was guaranteed by Article 10 ECHR and therefore their denial did not constitute a violation of the Convention.

9.4   'LEGITIMATE AIM'

Any interference with freedom of expression has to be for the purpose of one of the permitted exceptions listed in Article 10(2) ECHR, i.e. the 'interests of national security, territorial integrity or public safety, ... the prevention of disorder or crime, ... the protection of health or morals, ... the protection of the reputation or rights of others, ... preventing the disclosure of information received in confidence ... maintaining the authority and impartiality of the judiciary'. Although from time to time the other interests may be served by reporting restrictions, 'maintaining the authority and impartiality of the judiciary' has particular importance in the present context. The European Court has said that:

> The term 'judiciary' ('*pouvoir judiciaire*') comprises the machinery of justice or the judicial branch of government as well as the judges in their official capacity. The phrase 'authority of the judiciary' includes, in particular, the notion that the courts are, and are accepted by the public at large as being, the proper forum for the ascertainment of legal rights and obligations and the settlement of disputes relative thereto; further, that the public at large have respect for and confidence in the courts' capacity to fulfil that function ... in so far as the law of contempt may serve to protect the rights of litigants, this purpose is already included in the phrase 'maintaining the authority and impartiality of the judiciary': the rights so protected are the rights of individuals in their capacity as litigants, that is as persons involved in the machinery of justice, and the authority of that machinery will not be maintained unless protection is afforded to all those involved or having recourse to it. (*Sunday Times* v *UK* (1979) 2 EHRR 245, at paras 55 and 56)

There is no reported case in this area in which the Court or Commission has held that an interference was not pursuing one or more of the aims permitted by Article 10(2).

9.5   'PRESCRIBED BY LAW'

The Court has said that the requirement that any restriction must be 'prescribed by law' means that it must be possible to ascertain with reasonable certainty whether freedom of expression in a particular context is amenable to restriction (*Sunday Times* v *UK* (1979) 2 EHRR 245, at para. 49). However, in the present context it has never found a violation because this requirement has been unsatisfied. One might find this surprising given the remarkably protean character of the common law concept of contempt of court. In one of the cluster of cases concerning *Spycatcher* the Attorney-General took proceedings for contempt against the *Independent* for publishing information which other newspapers were injuncted from publishing. A preliminary hearing was held to determine whether such behaviour could constitute contempt. The Vice-Chancellor ruled that it could not (*Attorney-General* v *Newspaper Publishing plc* [1988] Ch 33). His decision was subsequently overturned by the Court of Appeal, but it might be thought that Sir Nicolas Browne-Wilkinson's decision called into question whether this extension (or 'application' as the Court of Appeal described it) was reasonably foreseeable. Nonetheless, the Commission ruled inadmissible the complaint by Times Newspapers that its Article 10 right had been violated by its conviction for contempt of court in publishing extracts from *Spycatcher* when other papers (but not *The Times* or any of the other titles of its publishers) had been enjoined from publishing extracts (*Times* v *UK* (App. No. 18897/91, 12 October 1992)). It noted that the paper had been repeatedly warned by the Government's lawyers that publication in these circumstances would be contempt. Although the paper had received contrary advice, it had been well aware of the risks that it ran.

9.6 'NECESSARY IN A DEMOCRATIC SOCIETY'

9.6.1 *Sunday Times* v *UK:* the thalidomide articles injunctions

As is so often the case in connection with Article 10 ECHR, the critical issue is whether the restriction conforms to the requirement that it is 'necessary in a democratic society'. One of the earliest cases in which the Court had to consider this phrase was *Sunday Times* v *UK* (1979) 2 EHRR 245. This followed the decision of the House of Lords to uphold an injunction against the newspaper, so preventing it from continuing with its series of articles about thalidomide. Essentially, their Lordships considered that the articles prejudged the litigation which was ongoing between alleged victims of the drug and the manufacturers. In a seminal judgment, the European Court held that this ruling violated the rights of the publishers under Article 10. Many of its propositions are of general application in cases concerning Article 10 and are referred to elsewhere in this book, but of particular importance in the present context are the Court's following comments:

(a) Although the Court allows the contracting states a margin of appreciation in deciding whether restrictions on freedom of expression are necessary, the scope for discretion varies according to the subject matter: more latitude is allowed in relation to restrictions thought necessary to protect morals, less in relation to the 'far more objective notion of authority of the judiciary' (at para. 59). Because the margin of appreciation plays a lesser role in this context, there is correspondingly less need for UK courts to make allowance for this international concept in applying the judgments of the Court and the decisions of the Commission.

(b) Whatever the historical origin of the phrase concerning the judiciary (and some suggested that it was specifically designed to cover the unique common law institution of contempt of court), 'necessity' was a Convention concept with an autonomous meaning, and thus even contempt measures had to satisfy that yardstick (at para. 60).

(c) Freedom of expression is one of the essential foundations of a democratic society. Subject to Article 10(2), it applies to information or ideas which offend, shock or disturb the state or any sector of the population:

> These principles are of particular importance as far as the press is concerned. They are equally applicable to the field of the administration of justice, which serves the interests of the community at large and requires the co-operation of an enlightened public. There is general recognition of the fact that courts cannot operate in a vacuum. Whilst they are the forum for the settlement of disputes, this does not mean that there can be no prior discussion of disputes elsewhere, be it in specialised journals, in the general press or amongst the public at large. Furthermore, whilst the mass media must not overstep the bounds imposed in the interests of the proper administration of justice, it is incumbent on them to impart information and ideas concerning matters that come before the courts just as in other areas of public interest. Not only do the media have the task of imparting such information and ideas: the public also has a right to receive them. (at para 65)

(d) The task is not to choose between conflicting principles but to apply 'a principle of freedom of expression that is subject to a number of exceptions which must be narrowly interpreted' (at para. 65).

It was because of this ruling that the UK Government introduced the Bill which became the Contempt of Court Act 1981 and which, for the purpose of strict liability contempt, replaced the 'prejudgment' test with that of 'serious risk of substantial prejudice'.

9.6.2 Prejudicial publicity: other cases

In *Worm* v *Austria* (1997) 25 EHRR 454, the applicant was a journalist who had published an article on Hannes Androsch, a former Vice-Chancellor of Austria and Minister of Finance, who was facing criminal charges alleging tax evasion. Worm was convicted of exercising prohibited influence on the criminal proceedings. It was noted that his article had assumed the guilt of Androsch, and indeed implied that no result other than a conviction was possible. The case against Androsch was due to be tried by a panel, which included lay judges who were more likely to have been influenced by the publication. Although the European Court found that there had been no violation of Article 10 ECHR, its judgment built on the principles of *Sunday Times* v *UK*:

(a) *Sunday Times* v *UK* spoke of litigation not precluding 'prior' discussion of the same issues in the media. *Worm* added that court proceedings did not mean that there could be no contemporary discussion, and that reporting 'including comment' on court proceedings contributes to their publicity and is thus perfectly consonant with the requirement under Article 6(1) that hearings be in public (at para. 50).

(b) The media's task of imparting information to the public and the public's right to receive this 'is all the more so where a public figure is involved ... Such persons inevitably and knowingly lay themselves open to close scrutiny by both journalists and the public at large. Accordingly the limits of acceptable comment are wider as regards a politician as such than as regards a private individual (at para. 50). The last comment is interesting because it carries over into the context of contempt a principle which the Court had previously articulated in the context of defamation. However, the Court qualified its remarks by recalling that public figures are still entitled to a fair trial, including the right to an impartial tribunal, on the same basis as every other person and 'the limits of permissible comment may not extend to statements which are likely to prejudice, whether intentionally or not, the chances of a person receiving a fair trial or to undermine the confidence of the public in the role of the courts in the administration of justice' (at para. 50).

In *News Verlags* v *Austria* (unreported) 11 January 2000, a newspaper had publicised the arrest of a bomb suspect in lurid prose which clearly assumed guilt, and accompanied the article with his pictures. Austrian legislation prohibited the publication of a person's picture if this was contrary to his legitimate interests. An injunction was granted against any use of the suspect's picture in conjunction with a publication about the criminal proceedings. The European Court found this to be disproportionate since the prohibition was not confined to publications which impinged on a suspect's right to a presumption of innocence.

At the time of the Birmingham Six appeal in 1987, Channel 4 proposed to broadcast nightly news reports with actors taking the part of judges, counsel and witnesses. The plan was stopped by the Court of Appeal which granted an injunction on the grounds that, although the broadcast would not affect the judgment of the court, the public might perceive that it had been influenced which would undermine confidence in the court's decision. Channel 4 complained that this violated its rights under Article 10 ECHR. The Commission found that the restriction did answer a pressing social need and dismissed the application as manifestly ill-founded (*C* v *UK* (App. No. 14132/88, 13 April 1989)). Subsequently, the High Court of Justiciary has said that while the Court of Appeal's decision might not have infringed Article 10, it was not compatible with the strict liability test in the Contempt of Court Act 1981, s. 2 (*Al Meghrahi* v *Times Newspapers Ltd*, 10 August 1999; see the Scots Courts website at http://www.scotcourts.gov.uk).

9.6.3 Pre-trial injunctions

The *Sunday Times* thalidomide case concerned an injunction to prevent the newspaper publishing what the domestic courts considered would be a contempt of court. It was implicit in the European Court's judgment that a prior restraint on publication was not by itself enough to constitute a violation of Article 10 ECHR. The Court said this expressly in *Observer and Guardian* v *UK* (1991) 14 EHRR 153, at para. 60. However, 'the dangers inherent in prior restraints are such that they call for the most careful scrutiny on the part of the Court. This is especially so as far as the press is concerned for news is a perishable commodity and to delay its publication, even for a short period, may well deprive it of all its value and interest.' The Court's examination of the injunction in this case (which concerned Peter Wright's book *Spycatcher*) is considered in Chapter 13. In brief, it held that there was no violation prior to the publication of the book in the USA, but the continuation of the injunction after that date was no longer necessary in a democratic society.

9.6.4 Criticism of the judiciary

Several judgments of the Court have concerned alleged violations of Article 10 arising out of criminal or civil proceedings against the media for critical attacks on judges. In principle, the Court has accepted that the public watchdog role of the press includes raising questions concerning the functioning of the system of justice. The press is one of the means by which politicians and public opinion can verify that judges are discharging their heavy responsibilities in a manner which is in conformity with the aim which is the basis of the task entrusted to them (*Prager and Oberschlick* v *Austria* (1995) 21 EHRR 1, at para. 34). However, at the same time, the Court has had regard to the special role of judiciary and the need for it to enjoy public confidence: 'It may therefore prove necessary to protect such confidence against destructive attacks that are essentially unfounded, especially in view of the fact that judges who have been criticised are subject to a duty of discretion that precludes them from replying.' In *Prager and Oberschlick* itself, the Court found no violation because the complainants had been unable to prove the factual assertions which they had made, or demonstrate that their value judgments were fair comment.

In *Barfod* v *Denmark* (1989) 13 EHRR 493, the Court found no violation of Article 10 ECHR in the conviction of a Greenlander for criminal defamation. He had published an article criticising two lay members of a court which had ruled in favour of the local government entity of which they were employees. They had done their duty, the article said, by which, the Greenland courts had inferred, the complainant meant that they had acted partially and in contravention of their professional duty. Although the Greenland court had also accepted that the lay members should not have sat in such a case, there was nothing to show that they had in fact been influenced by bias in their result. The Court has been criticised for this decision and for failing to give more weight to the fact that the article raised a matter of genuine public concern. It relied on the margin of appreciation, and the Court may have felt obliged to show deference to a domestic court which was protective of the position of lay members of the judiciary. This again illustrates the care with which UK courts must treat the Strasbourg jurisprudence when it depends on the margin of appreciation.

A much more robust approach was taken by the Court in *De Haes and Gijsels* v *Belgium* (1997) 25 EHRR 1. The applicants there were the authors of articles which had severely criticised the Antwerp Court of Appeal for giving custody of children to their father, a public notary, despite allegations that the notary had been guilty of incest and other assaults on the children. The notary had been acquitted of the criminal charges, but his defamation action against his wife and her parents was dismissed because there was no bad faith in their complaints. The Court of Appeal judges and Advocate-General who had been involved in the custody case took proceedings against the journalists complaining that the articles accused them of bias. The Belgian courts upheld the complaints. The European Court found that the journalists' rights under Article 10 ECHR had been violated. Their articles contained a wealth of detail drawn (apparently) from the original medical reports on the children. They were unable to produce the reports themselves for fear of prejudicing the anonymity of their sources. The European Court accepted that the domestic courts ought to have looked at the copies of the reports contained in the court files. The articles were in essence comments and (unlike *Prager and Oberschlick*) it could not be said that the journalists lacked a factual foundation for their opinions. The Court did not approve of the polemical (even aggressive) tone of the articles, but it recognised that the form of expression was a matter for the journalists not the judges (whether domestic or European). The one area where the Court found that criticism was justified was a reference to the conviction of the father of one of the judges for collaboration with the Nazis. The Court said that this was an impermissible intrusion into private life. The case also needed to be seen against the backdrop of concern over child abuse in the country and the public interest in the integrity of the country's legal system. However, whereas the latter point in other cases had been a factor weighing in favour of restrictions on expression, in this case (where, as has been said, the journalists were able to persuade the Court that there was a substantial foundation for their opinions) it told in favour of free reporting.

9.6.5 Criticism by lawyers

Lawyers, like everyone else, enjoy the presumptive right of freedom of expression, but the Court has said that the special status of lawyers gives them a central position in the administration of justice as intermediaries between the public and the courts; and because of this role it is legitimate to expect lawyers to contribute to the proper administration of justice, and thus to maintain public confidence therein. When, Schopfer, a Swiss lawyer, held a press conference to publicise what he regarded as the improper behaviour of the local prosecutor's office, he was disciplined by his professional body. The Court found that the relatively modest fine which had been imposed did not breach Article 10 ECHR. At the time of the press conference, there were still legal avenues of redress open to the lawyer's clients, and these subsequently proved at least partially successful. This rather undermined the lawyer's case that he had had no alternative but to take his complaints (expressed in strong language) to the media (*Schöpfer* v *Switzerlnd* [1998] EHRLR 646).

Similar comments were made by the Commission in ruling the complaint inadmissible in *Zihlman* v *Switzerland* (App. No. 21861/93) (1995) 82 DR 12. By contrast with cases such as *De Haes and Gijsels* (9.6.4 above), the Strasbourg institutions have been influenced by the tone of the language which the lawyer/complainant chose to use. The lawyer's position, said the Commission, obliged him to be 'discreet in his statements and, more specifically, to show objectivity and to keep the tone of his comments neutral' (at 19). However, *Zihlman*, like *Schopfer*, emphasised two other features. In the first place, this was an area where the margin of appreciation was particularly important:

> As they have direct and continuous contact with lawyers and the administration of justice, these councils [i.e. professional associations] and the national courts are in a better position than an international court to determine how, at a given time, the right balance can be struck between the various interests involved, namely the requirements of the proper administration of justice and the dignity of the profession. (ibid., referring to *Casado Coca* v *Spain* (1994) 18 EHRR 1)

In the second place, both bodies emphasised the small penalty which had been imposed in deciding that the interference with freedom of expression had not been disproportionate. The Commission adopted a similar approach in finding a complaint from an Austrian judge to be inadmissible. Remarks about his colleagues to a journalist, including the view that the 'judiciary is a whore', lacked a factual basis, and anyway had attracted only the relatively mild punishment of a reprimand (*Leiningen-Westerburg* v *Austria* (App. No. 26601/95) (1997) 88 DR 85).

9.6.6 Access to courts and tribunals

Can journalists rely on Article 10 ECHR to claim a right of access to trials? We noted at 9.2.2 that Article 6 does require a public as well as a fair hearing of a criminal charge or the determination of a civil right or obligation. However, Article 6 appears to confer rights on the parties to the legal proceedings rather than on outsiders such as the press. If (as may often be the case) the immediate parties positively want to avoid media attention, or are indifferent to whether the trial is heard in public, it may only be the media themselves who are able to make the case for open justice. Can they invoke Article 10 in their cause?

While the Court has developed the concept of 'positive obligations' in other contexts (see Chapter 2), it has resisted the idea that Article 10 gives a right of access to information. Ordinarily, Article 10 assumes a willing supplier of information and a willing recipient. It does not create a positive right to demand access to information from an unwilling supplier (see *Leander* v *Sweden* (1987) 9 EHRR 433 and *Guerra and others* v *Italy* (1998) 26 EHRR 357). In the present context the position may be different. The Court itself has recognised that the normal obligation to hold trials in public often serves a public interest as well as being intended to protect the parties. Similarly, while the parties may waive their right to a public trial, this is dependent on there being no countervailing public interest. The media are the obvious candidates to put forward the views as to why there might be such a countervailing public interest, or why the exceptions to a public trial which Article 6 expressly permits are not made out. In Convention terms, the media can only do this if Article 10 is, in these limited circumstances at least, construed as conferring a positive right of access to courts which would ordinarily sit in public.

This argument was presented to the Commission in *Atkinson, Crook and The Independent* v *UK* (App. No. 13366/87) (1990) 67 DR 244. The Commission was at least prepared to assume (without deciding) that the argument had merit. In the UK the Administrative Court has alluded to the difficulty of ordinary members of the public establishing standing to complain under Article 6 of a decision by a court to sit in private (*The Queen (on the Application of Pelling)* v *Bow County Court* [2000] UKHRR 165 at para. 30) The Court did not decide the point and the position of the media to raise the matter may, in any case, be somewhat stronger. Of course, as with other Article 10 cases, the right is not absolute and must give way if there is a pressing social need in pursuit of one of the aims listed in Article 10(2) ECHR. The occasions listed in Article 6(1) when a trial can be determined other than in public are not directly relevant to Article 10, but they provided the Commission with a useful benchmark, and on the facts of the *Atkinson and Crook* case it was persuaded that any interference with the journalists' right of access was justified in a democratic society.

Access of a more general kind was sought in *Grupo Interpres SA* v *Spain* (App. No. 32849/96) (1997) 89 DR 150. A commercial organisation had wished to obtain access to archives of court decisions in order to compile a database which it would then sell to financial institutions who needed to conduct credit checks. The local courts had refused this request and the organisation argued that Article 10 had thereby been violated. The Commission rejected the application as inadmissible. It recalled that Article 10 generally did not give a right of access to information against an unwilling supplier. The court records were not generally accessible to the public since a legitimate reason had to be furnished, and this was intended to protect the private lives of litigants. All these are factors which are consistent with other parts of the Strasbourg jurisprudence. However, the emphasis on the commercial nature of the applicant's operation is more troubling. It has not elsewhere been considered a material factor that newspapers, for instance, compile their stories in order to be able to market their products. As we discuss at 2.3.3.6 and in Chapter 12, even purely commercial speech is protected by Article 10.

Where the government sets up an inquiry to investigate a particular issue, Article 6 ECHR may not be immediately applicable, since the function of the inquiry is not to determine civil rights and obligations. However, Convention rights may still be material. In July 2000, the Divisional Court considered a judicial review challenge to the Health Secretary's decision to hold the inquiry into Dr Harold Shipman's activities in private (*R v Secretary of State for Health, ex parte Associated Newspapers Ltd*; *R v Secretary of State for Health, ex parte Wagstaff* [2000] UKHRR 875 (QBD)). One of the objections was that this conflicted with Article 10. The Government argued, following *Leander*, that there was no 'interference' with freedom of expression. However, the court preferred the view that the decision to hold the inquiry in private 'restrict[ed] a family witness waiting to give evidence from receiving information that others who are currently giving evidence wish or may be willing to impart to him, namely an accurate account of what they are saying not based simply on their own imperfect recollection after they have finished'. The media had the right to rely on Article 10 since they had their own right to receive information. What was important in this respect was that at least some of the potential witnesses before the inquiry were anxious that it should take place in public. The Government later announced that the investigation would be conducted as a tribunal of inquiry, which must be heard in public unless it is expedient in the public interest to take evidence in private (Tribunals of Inquiry (Evidence) Act 1921, s. 2).

9.6.7 Article 6 and the extent of the obligation to hold 'public hearings'

Article 6 ECHR may be important for the media even though it does not confer rights directly on them. For this reason, they may need to explore its limits. It clearly applies to first instance trials of criminal and civil cases. The UK's practice of holding small claims arbitrations in private was in the process of being successfully challenged in Strasbourg when the Government agreed to change the procedural rules to provide for a presumption in favour of a public hearing (see *Scarth* v *UK* [1999] EHRLR 322). There is more doubt as to whether hearings of pre-trial applications must be in public. An old Commission decision said they did not because they did not 'determine' civil rights or obligations (*X* v *UK* (1970) 30 CD 70, but subsequent judgments of the Court indicate that this may not represent the Court's view (see, e.g., *Robins* v *UK* (1997) 26 EHRR 527, at para. 28). In any case, the UK Court of Appeal has already indicated that as a matter of domestic law, greater accommodation must be made for the interests of the media in interlocutory matters (*Hodgson* v *Imperial Tobacco* [1998] 2 All ER 673) and this is now reflected in the Civil Procedure Rules (CPR Part 39, r. 39.2).

Other tribunals which determine civil rights and obligations will need to look to their procedural rules to see whether adequate provision is made for public hearings. In *Diennet* v *France* (1995) 21 EHRR 554, the Court found a violation of Article 6 ECHR in the general rule of a French medical disciplinary tribunal that it should always sit in private. Such proceedings might well involve private matters, but the procedure should allow for a public hearing unless and until a private matter emerged. Where a hearing is required to be in public, the opportunity for public access must be real and not illusory (see, e.g., *Riepan* v *Austria*, 14 November 2000 (European Court)).

We have seen that Article 6(1) itself envisages that there are circumstances where the usual principle of publicity may be abrogated. The ECHR does not in terms say how these should be approached, but in *Campbell and Fell* v *UK* (1984) 7 EHRR 165, which considered the practice of holding prison disciplinary hearings in prison and in private, the Court found the practice to be proportionate and its language in this sense thus echoed its approach to Article 10(2). There will be an opportunity for the Court to examine this issue further when it considers the case of *Pelling* v *UK* (App. No. 35974/97, 14 September 1999). The Commission has held admissible a complaint that the virtually automatic practice of hearing custody disputes in chambers is contrary to the right of litigants (in this case the father) to a public hearing and publicly pronounced judgment. Because reporting restrictions apply to family proceedings held in private, the Commission also declared admissible the father's consequential complaint under Article 10. (See also the companion case *Bayram* v *UK* (App. No. 36337/97, 14 September 1999).) The Practice Direction under the Civil Procedure Rules has, in any case, now expressly recognised that a judge considering an application to sit in private must consider the requirements of Article 6(1) (CPR, PD 39, para. 1.4A). In view of this, it is unsurprising that a challenge to the *vires* of the Rules on the grounds of their incompatibility with the requirements of Article 6(1) was dismissed (*The Queen (on the Application of Pelling)* v *Bow County Court* [2000] UKHRR 165 (QBD)).

T v *UK* (2000) 7 BHRC 659 had to consider the converse position. The two children accused of murdering the baby James Bulger were tried in an adult court.

Although some adjustments were made for their age (eleven years old at the time), they still went through a three-week public trial which attracted widespread media attention. The European Court referred to the UN Convention on the Rights of the Child and Beijing Principles, both of which emphasised the general principle that the privacy of a child (even one accused of a criminal offence) should be respected. The Government had argued that public trials (particularly of notorious crimes) served a general interest in open justice. The Court considered that a modified procedure could have coped with this by providing for selective attendance and judicious reporting. The public character of the trial was one of the reasons for the Court to conclude that the defendants had been denied the opportunity to participate effectively in the criminal proceedings, and that they had therefore been denied a fair trial. In consequence of this decision the Lord Chief Justice issued a *Practice Direction* as to the trial of children and young persons in the Crown Court ([2000] 1 WLR 659).

The position is less clear in relation to appeals. Strasbourg has been willing to find private appeal hearings compatible with Article 6 ECHR, but only if there has been a public hearing at first instance, and then only if there are 'special features' of the appeal procedure (*Ekbatani* v *Sweden* (1988) 13 EHRR 504). In *Axen* v *Germany* (1983) 6 EHRR 195, a private hearing was justified on the ground that it helped reduce the court's case load, but, importantly, the first instance hearing had been in public, the appeal only concerned issues of law and, furthermore, the position would have been different if the appellate body was minded to overturn rather than approve the lower court's decision.

Separately from requiring a public hearing, Article 6 also obliges a court to pronounce its judgment publicly. This is not taken literally. If the judgment is deposited in the court registry to which the public has access, this will suffice (*Pretto* v *Italy* (1983) 6 EHRR 182; *Sutter* v *Switzerland* (1984) 6 EHRR 272). On the other hand, if inspection is reserved to those who can demonstrate a legitimate interest, this will not be an adequate substitute for public pronouncement of the judgment (*Werner* v *Austria* (1997) 26 EHRR 310, at paras 56–59; *Szucs* v *Austria*, 24 November 1997).

9.6.8   Publicity of court proceedings and witnesses' privacy interests

Judicial proceedings can often intrude into the most intimate matters of a person's private and family life. Article 8 ECHR guarantees the right to respect for a person's private and family life, his home and correspondence. How are these interests to be reconciled? In *Z* v *Finland* (1997) 25 EHRR 371, the Court had to consider the case of a woman whose husband was accused of attempted manslaughter by deliberately subjecting women to the risk of infection with the HIV virus which he carried. An issue arose as to when the husband knew that he was infectious. In this connection the police investigated the medical records of both the husband and his wife. These were added to the court's file. The Court considered that these measures were justified in terms of Article 8(2) as being necessary in the interests of the protection of the rights of others and the prevention of crime. The husband was convicted of certain counts, but the matter went to the Court of Appeal. Although the Court had power to omit the woman's name and to publish only an edited version of its reasoning, and although the Court was aware that she would have preferred this, it chose not to do so. Its judgment (which was made available to the press) named her and disclosed her infection. The European Court found that this publication was not necessary and infringed her rights under Article 8.

The Court was clearly influenced by the extreme sensitivity of these particular data. Not only did they concern the complainant's health, but they related to a highly dangerous disease. As the Court said:

> The disclosure of such data may dramatically affect his or her private and family life, as well as social and employment situation, by exposing him or her to opprobrium and the risk of ostracism. For this reason it may discourage persons from seeking diagnosis or treatment and thus undermine any preventative efforts by the community to contain the pandemic. The interests in protecting the confidentiality of such information will therefore weigh heavily in the balance in determining whether the interference was proportionate to the legitimate aim pursued. Such interference cannot be compatible with Article 8 unless it is justified by an overriding requirement in the public interest. (at para. 96)[1]

9.6.9   Infringement of court secrecy requirements

Where court proceedings or documents are confidential, disclosure may lead to penalties. In principle this is likely to be seen as pursuing the legitimate aim of maintaining the authority of the judiciary. However, the position is different if the material is no longer confidential. In *Harman* v *UK* (App. No. 10038/82) (1984) 38 DR 53, Harriet Harman (then legal officer for the National Council of Civil Liberties) had shown to a journalist a bundle of documents which had been produced by the Home Office in an action which her client had taken for false imprisonment. The significant feature of the case was that all the documents had been read out in open court in the course of the opening speech of her client's counsel. Nonetheless, the House of Lords found her to be in contempt of court for infringing the implied undertaking to use discovered documents only for the purpose of the proceedings. Showing them to a journalist was external to that purpose. The Commission declared her complaint admissible. The matter went no further because, as part of a friendly settlement, the Government agreed to change

---

[1] It is worth noting that this is an example of where the Court drew on other instruments of the Council of Europe — a recommendation adopted by the Council of Ministers (R89) and the Convention for the Protection of Individuals with Regard to Automatic Processing of Personal Data.

UK law by introducing an amendment to the Rules of the Supreme Court. A companion complaint by David Leigh, the journalist concerned, was found to be inadmissible since he was not a victim of any violation. No proceedings for contempt had been taken against him (although he had published an article on the basis of the documents). His claim that the House of Lords ruling would make it more difficult for him to operate as a journalist in the future was regarded as being too distant an impact to constitute an interference (*Leigh* v *UK* (App. No. 10039/82) (1984) 38 DR 74).

Somewhat similarly, in *Weber* v *Switzerland* (1990) 12 EHRR 508 (see also *Vereinging Weekblad Bluf!* v *Netherlands* (1995) 20 EHRR 189, discussed at 13.2.2) the complainant had been prosecuted for holding a press conference at which he had disclosed details of a criminal investigation being conducted against him by a judge. Swiss law required these investigations to remain confidential. The Court found this to be a violation of Article 10 ECHR because nine months earlier the same man had held another press conference at which he had referred to virtually the same details. This had led to no prosecution. Thus, by the time of the incident which did found the charge against him, the details were in the public domain. The Court seemed unconcerned by the fact that they had been put there by the complainant.

UK law prohibits the disclosure of jury deliberations (Contempt of Court Act 1981, s. 8). In *Attorney-General* v *Associated Newspapers Ltd* [1994] 2 AC 238, the House of Lords held that 'disclosure' should be given a broad meaning and included a newspaper putting into the public domain previously unpublished details of a jury's deliberations. It upheld a fine for contempt of court against the newspaper publisher, editor and journalist for infringing this prohibition. The European Commission of Human Rights dismissed their allegation of a violation of Article 10 ECHR as manifestly unfounded. The newspaper argued that because the restriction applied in an absolute form, the national courts had not had to assess the proportionality of the restriction. It submitted that this could not be compatible with the principles of what is 'necessary in a democratic society'. The Commission rejected this argument. It said that the purposes of the prohibition on jury disclosures was to encourage frankness of exchanges in the jury room, and any possibility of intrusion on this privacy could undermine that confidence. The absolute character of the restriction was thus intimately connected with its purpose (*Associated Newspapers Ltd* v *UK* (App. No. 24770/94, 30 November 1994)).

In *Du Roy and Malaurie* v *France*, 3 October 2000, the Court was also concerned with an absolute prohibition on reporting aspects of court proceedings. In this case it was a French law that did not allow publication of information concerning the joinder of civil parties to a criminal prosecution. The applicants were the editor and a journalist on a French magazine which had publicised the fact that the new management of a public company for the management of residential centres for emigrants had lodged a criminal complaint and had applied to be a *partie civile* in criminal proceedings against the former head of the company. The applicants had been fined despite arguing before the French courts that the general and absolute prohibition conflicted with Article 10 ECHR. The applicants had lost in the French courts all the way up to and including the *Cour de Cassation*, on the basis that the French law was intended to guarantee the presumption of innocence and to prevent external influence on the course of justice. However the European Court upheld the complaint under Article 10. It said that the law was anomalous: it prevented publication of proceedings instituted by a *partie civile* but not where the prosecution was brought by the state prosecutor or an ordinary complainant. There was no objective basis for this differential treatment. Furthermore, this particular case concerned a matter of public interest and the absolute ban was disproportionate.

9.7 EFFECT ON ENGLISH LAW

9.7.1 The Human Rights Act 1998

As with the other specific areas covered in this book, the effect of the HRA 1998 on the law of contempt and reporting restrictions is difficult to predict. However, it is unlikely to be dramatic for several reasons.

In the first place, the law of contempt has already been significantly affected by the Convention. *Sunday Times* v *UK* (1979) 2 EHRR 245 led to the introduction and enactment of the Contempt of Court Act 1981. Notably, this defined more precisely the period during which the '*sub judice*' period lasted when the media were vulnerable to prosecution for strict liability contempt. It established a test for strict liability contempt (see s. 2 of the 1981 Act) which eliminated the prior 'prejudgment test' and relied exclusively on a test based on risk of prejudice. Even in relation to this test, the feared prejudice has to have been serious and the risk that such prejudice would occur has to have been substantial. If the risk of prejudice is incidental to a good faith discussion of public affairs or other matters of general public interest, there is no contempt under the strict liability rule (s. 5). There is a defence that the publication was a good faith, contemporaneous, fair and accurate report of court proceedings held in public (s. 4(1)). Given the genesis of the 1981 Act, it is unsurprising that the English courts have interpreted it with Article 10 ECHR in mind. However, the trend has been to find that a Convention analysis produces a result that is no different to that which would result from a domestic approach to the legislation (see, for instance, *Attorney-General* v *Guardian Newspapers Ltd* [1999] EMLR 904). The same is true of those parts of the Act which deal with protection of sources (see *Camelot Group plc* v *Centaur Communications Ltd* [1999] QB 124) and the prohibition on jury disclosures (*Attorney-General* v *Associated Newspapers Ltd* [1994] 2 AC 238).

Secondly, as this chapter has already shown, with some notable exceptions, the Commission has frequently rebuffed complaints that the UK law of contempt and reporting restrictions is contrary to Article 10 ECHR. It is the case, of course, that decisions of the Commission do not have the same weight as judgments of the European Court, and in the Article 10 field particularly, outcomes have turned on the particular sets of facts which individual cases have thrown up. Nonetheless, these inadmissibility decisions discourage the idea that the HRA 1998 will lead to a wholesale rewriting of the law of contempt or discarding of reporting restrictions.

Thirdly, in the run-up to commencement of the HRA 1998 there have been some significant shifts in law and practice, in part to accommodate the Convention's requirements. We have already referred to the changed attitude of the Court of Appeal to the privacy of interim hearings in the Queen's Bench Division and the continuation of this trend by the Civil Procedure Rules.

Fourthly, while all courts will be required to see that their actions comply with Convention rights (including Article 10), the extra obligations in s. 12, HRA 1998 (and which are designed to further protect freedom of expression) do not apply to orders in criminal proceedings (see further Chapter 3). The law of contempt, of course, does not apply exclusively to criminal proceedings, but it is in this context that problems most frequently occur.

Nonetheless, the HRA 1998 is likely to be influential. It would be rash to attempt a comprehensive analysis, but some examples of possible situations where this could occur follow.

9.7.2 The power of a superior court to deal with alleged contempt itself of its own motion

Present authority strongly encourages judges not to deal themselves with allegations that proceedings which they are trying have been put at risk by prejudicial publications. Instead, the preferred alternative is for the judge to refer the matter to the Attorney-General, who will (if he thinks it appropriate) institute proceedings for contempt in the Divisional Court. The guarantee in Article 6(1) ECHR that in the determination of a criminal charge everyone is entitled to an *impartial* tribunal means that this practice should now become the invariable rule, since a judge who has instituted the criminal proceedings can hardly be regarded as impartial.

However, in a case which did not concern the press (but a verbal attack on a prosecution witness by a defendant), the Court of Appeal said that Article 6 did not add to or alter the normal requirements under English law that the proceedings be conducted fairly. It upheld the finding of contempt even though it was 'regrettable' that the judge had taken the witness through her evidence in chief. The situation in this case was marked by a witness who had been put in fear by the defendant's behaviour and so will be distinguishable from most alleged contempts by the press where there will rarely be such a strong need for immediate action by the judge dealing with the matter himself or herself (*R* v *MacLeod* (2000) *The Times*, 20 December (CA)).

9.7.3 Scandalising the court

This is a form of contempt which is intended to protect the judiciary from attacks on its integrity. It has not been successfully invoked in the UK for decades, despite occasional press and media campaigns against the judges. Given that the legal system has survived without the aid of prosecutions for scandalising the court, any future resurrection of this ancient relic would no doubt meet the challenge that the restriction did not answer a 'pressing social need' and was therefore incompatible with Article 10 ECHR. The challenge would, though, have to address the survival of scandalising the court in many parts of the Commonwealth. As recently as 1999, the Privy Council had to consider whether a prosecution for scandalising the court was compatible with the Mauritian Constitution (*Ahnee* v *DPP* [1999] 2 AC 294). This was largely based on the European Convention and guaranteed freedom of expression in almost identical terms to Article 10. Lord Steyn noted the limitations on 'scandalising the court'. The words had to concern a judge or judges in their official capacity and pose a real risk to public confidence in the judiciary. Good faith criticism would not be an offence, neither would the exposure and criticism of judicial misconduct. He thought that hedged in this way the offence was 'reasonably justifiable' in the terms of the Constitution. The decision does not necessarily mean that the same result would follow if this form of contempt were used in England. Lord Steyn specifically commented that this form of contempt was particularly useful in small jurisdictions where confidence in the administration of justice could more readily be put in jeopardy.

9.7.4 Reporting restrictions which are absolute and which cannot be lifted even if the public interest would favour reporting

Absolute restrictions on reporting which cannot be altered if the circumstances demand are relatively unusual. Where they do exist they are not necessarily incompatible with the ECHR, as Associated Newspapers' unsuccessful challenge to the ban on jury disclosures showed. However, as *Du Roy and Malaurie* showed, they will call for examination against the standards of Article 10 which we have discussed in this chapter. If they have continued as a historical anachronism with no continuing objective justification, they will be vulnerable to challenge as incompatible with Article 10. This will be particularly so where they apply so as to hinder the publication of reports of cases with a real public interest.

One particular example is the complete ban on the taking of photographs in court imposed by the Criminal Justice Act 1925, s. 41. In a suitable case, this effective prohibition on televising courts may be vulnerable to challenge on Article 10 grounds. Because the section is expressed in such stark terms it may prove impervious to even the new methods of interpretation which the HRA 1998 requires, and thus lead to an application for a declaration of incompatibility. Interestingly, s. 41 does not apply to Scotland. However, the settled practice of the Scottish courts has been not to allow proceedings to be televised. Practice Directions in 1992 suggested that in certain cases this might change, but not for criminal trials. The issue came to the fore in connection with the trial of two Libyan suspects for the Lockerbie bombing. They were being tried in The Netherlands, but by three judges from Scotland in accordance with Scots law. Broadcasters were refused permission to film the proceedings with their own cameras. Their challenge (*inter alia*) on Article 10 grounds failed (*BBC's Petition*, judgment of Lord MacFadyn, 7 March 2000 (HCJ)). The court held that televising the proceedings would risk prejudicing the trial of the accused. In a second attempt, the broadcasters referred to the fact that the proceedings were in fact being televised for reception in a limited number of sites around the world with access being allowed only to a limited category of persons — principally relatives of the victims. In these proceedings the broadcasters sought access to this encrypted feed. Again the challenge failed. The court referred to the *Leander* line of authorities that Article 10 presumed a willing supplier of information. In this case the people responsible for the limited broadcasting facilities did not wish the signal to be made more widely available. Their refusal of access did not amount to an 'interference' in terms of Article 10 (*BBC Petition (No. 2)*, 20 April 2000 (HCJ)). Neither case is likely to be the last word on the compatibility of the prohibition on televising the courts and Article 10.

9.7.5 The Strasbourg requirements

More generally, before action is taken against the media for infringing reporting restrictions or for contempt, it will be necessary to consider the common themes which run through the Strasbourg case law. In particular, did the story pursue a matter of genuine public interest? Was it published in good faith? Is the interference proportionate to the legitimate end to be served?

Attorney-General v *Punch Ltd*, 6 October 2000, gives an early example of how these principles will be applied. Silber J found the publishers and editor of *Punch* to be in contempt of court for publishing a column by the ex-MI5 employee, David Shayler, which was contrary to the terms of an injunction obtained by the Attorney-General against Associated Newspapers. The judge found that the contempt application pursued a legitimate aim (protection of the rights of others and preventing the disclosure of information received in confidence), that the principle of liability was 'prescribed by law' and that it was necessary in a democratic society. The judge noted that there was a high threshold for the

Attorney-General to cross — there had to be an interference with the
tion of justice in a substantial way, the case had to be establish
reasonable doubt, and there had to be a deliberate intention to co
injunction (recklessness would not do). The judge considered separately whether
a finding of contempt would be disproportionate but concluded that it would not
since the court order had allowed an exception for publications to which the
Attorney-General did not object and, if anyone had been dissatisfied with the
Attorney-General's view, they could have applied to the court for the order to be
varied. The publisher and editor were fined for contempt.

Chapter Ten

Reporting on Elections and Parliament

10.1 INTRODUCTION

Until the Political Parties, Elections and Referendums Act (PPERA) 2000, many of the most familiar features of modern elections were unregulated. Election law did not even recognise the existence of parties or their national campaigns and election broadcasts. All this is now changing. As PPERA 2000 comes into force, financial and other controls are being imposed on national campaigning by political parties and third parties. The Electoral Commission established under Part I of PPERA 2000 is required to oversee most aspects of our electoral process. Parties fielding candidates must register their name and emblem with the Commission, which may refuse registration on grounds of similarity with an existing party, obscenity or offensiveness.[1] The Representation of the People Act (RPA) 1983, with some important amendments resulting from PPERA 2000, continues to regulate elections at constituency and local level in a way that has remained largely unchanged for many years.

The rules of Parliamentary procedure are similarly old-fashioned. Indeed, the House of Commons can still banish journalists from the precincts of the Palace of Westminster for contempt of Parliament. The only significant concession to modernisation has been the decision to admit television cameras in 1989.

In this chapter we consider both the domestic and Convention law in these areas, and how the HRA 1998 might have an effect.

---

[1] See PPERA 2000, ss. 28 and 29, replacing provisions in the Registration of Political Parties Act 1998. These were introduced to prevent unscrupulous candidates using descriptions which were designed to trick careless party voters into marking their box on the ballot paper. This was becoming an increasing problem with many 'Conversative' candidates, in particular, appearing. A genuine candidate or organisation refused registration of the style of their choice might seek to challenge the decision under Article 10 ECHR and/or Article 3 of the First Protocol.

10.2 ELECTIONS

Article 3 of the First Protocol to the ECHR guarantees the right to free elections and provides:

> The High Contracting Parties undertake to hold free elections at reasonable intervals by secret ballot, under conditions which will ensure the free expression of the opinion of the people in the choice of the legislature.

The 'conditions' under which our Parliamentary, European and local elections are held are mainly set out in the PPERA 2000, the RPA 1983 and the rules made under the two Acts. There are a number of provisions which bear upon the reporting of elections by press and broadcasters.

10.2.1 Campaigning

Advertisements and one-off publications which support one candidate or undermine another, are strictly controlled by the RPA 1983 if the cost exceeds a specified sum. They may be published only with the authorisation of a candidate at the election, and the costs must then be included in that candidate's statutory election expenses (RPA 1983, s. 75(1) and (5)). The specified sum has been fixed at £5 for many years. It will rise when an amendment to s. 75(1) of the RPA 1983, resulting from s. 131 of PPERA 2000, takes effect. The new figure will be £500 for Parliamentary elections and will be a variable amount (depending on the size of the electorate) of at least £50 for local elections. However, even if the cost does not exceed this amount, the expenditure will still be unlawful if it is part of a 'concerted' arrangement to promote or disparage a particular candidate. The only type of publication caught by the new financial limits on national third party campaigning is political advertising through the print or broadcast media (PPERA 2000, s. 87(2)(a)). A breach of s. 75 is a criminal offence known as a 'corrupt practice', punishable by fine, imprisonment for up to a year and mandatory disqualification from public office for five years (ss. 168(a)(ii), 173(a) and 160(4)). Newspapers must therefore take care to ensure that the advertiser is the candidate or an election agent. The RPA 1983 allows the media to promote or 'disparage' candidates (s. 75(1)(c)(i)). However, in the case of the print media this protection is limited to a 'newspaper or other periodical'. In one recent Parliamentary by-election, a national tabloid exposed itself to the risk of prosecution (as well as incurring the wrath of the other parties) when its normal edition was distributed in the constituency on election day with a special 'wrap around' front and back page urging voters to support the candidate of a particular party. These extra pages were not published anywhere else in the country and were arguably not part of 'the newspaper'. The practice has not been repeated in subsequent by-elections.

It is currently unlawful during an election period to broadcast an item about a particular constituency or electoral area in which a candidate takes part without his or her consent (s. 93(1)). However, this provision applies only where there is active participation in the item by one or more of the candidates. It does not apply, for example, to a film showing a public appearance or canvassing exercise even if the candidate co-operates (*James Marshall* v *BBC* [1979] 1 WLR 1071, at 1073). Even if the featured candidate consents, the item cannot be broadcast until after the close of nominations and all of the other candidates have also consented (s. 93(2)). Effectively, therefore, one candidate can block a programme, and if not already featured can threaten to do so unless allowed air time. Section 93 also presents difficulties, and risks, for candidates. Under s. 93(1)(a), it is an election offence to take part in such an item in order to promote your candidacy and then agree that it can be broadcast, unless all the other candidates have similarly consented. A candidate who commits the offence will be incapable of holding public office for five years and will, in consequence, be unseated if victorious in the election (ss. 160(5) and 173). This places a heavy onus on a candidate who gives an interview in this way, to be absolutely sure that all rivals are happy to have it broadcast before finally consenting himself or herself. Section 144 of the PPERA 2000, when in force, will change all of this. An entirely new s. 93 will be introduced into the RPA 1983 in place of these complicated provisions. The broadcasting authorities will simply adopt Codes of Practice for local coverage. The Codes, to be approved by the Electoral Commission, will be designed to ensure fair and balanced coverage.

Section 106(1) of the RPA 1983 renders it a summary offence to make or publish a false statement of fact about the personal character or conduct of a candidate 'for the purpose of affecting the return' of that candidate, unless it can be shown that there were reasonable grounds for believing the statement to be true. In addition an injunction can be obtained, on prima facie proof of falsity, preventing publication of such a statement during the campaign (s. 106(3)). Urgent injunction applications are often made by candidates aggrieved about an opposition leaflet which has suddenly appeared in the constituency,[2] though they sometimes use this provision to prevent the media running groundless stories about them in an attempt to influence the result. However, there are important limitations. The statement must be about the candidate's 'personal' character or conduct, rather than public conduct or political views. Although there is no reported case law, injunction applications can be defeated by adequate written evidence showing reasonable grounds for believing that the story is true within the meaning of s. 106(1).

---

[2] Statements by candidates in an election are not made on an occasion of qualified privilege; see Defamation Act 1952, s. 10.

10.2.2 Broadcasting balance during election campaigns

The BBC and the licensed commercial channels are under a duty to do all they can to ensure 'due impartiality' in their coverage of politics. The BBC assumes the obligation through its Licence and Agreement with the Heritage Secretary.[3] Commercial channels are bound by the terms of their licences under the Broadcasting Act 1990 and are subject to regulation by the Independent Television Commission (ITC) and Radio Authority (RA) (see the Broadcasting Act 1990, s. 6(1)). In practice, therefore, broadcasters cannot take sides as between candidates or parties at elections. The BBC and the two regulatory bodies each maintain a code giving guidance on the 'due impartiality' requirement, in particular to broadcasters and editors. Political parties sometimes complain to these bodies, or to the Broadcasting Standards Commission (formerly the Broadcasting Complaints Commission), about unfair treatment in the form of lack of balance in coverage of the parties. However, they are very reluctant to trespass upon the editorial policy of the programme-maker concerned, where political matters are involved. The courts have, in turn, been unwilling to require intervention (see *R* v *Broadcasting Complaints Commission, ex parte Owen* [1985] QB 1153), although they have recognised the particular importance of the impartiality principle at election time (*James Marshall* v *BBC* [1979] 1 WLR 1071, at 1073).

10.2.3 Party election broadcasts

Political advertising on television and radio has always been prohibited in this country, even at election times (see now Broadcasting Act 1990, ss. 8 and 92). In 1971, the Commission rejected a complaint under Article 10 ECHR seeking to challenge this principle, holding that the provision for Government licensing of radio and television broadcasting in Article 10(1) allowed contracting parties to impose such a blanket ban (*X and the Association of Z* v *United Kingdom* (App. No. 4515/70, 11 July 1971)).

The party political, or election, broadcast is the alternative. The importance of election broadcasts has grown progressively through the mass-media age, to the point where the parties now regard them as central to their election strategy. Political parties have no specific statutory entitlement to election broadcasts, although in practice they are an established part of the electoral process and the ITC and RA can require licence-holders to carry them (see the Broadcasting Act 1990, s. 36; though under the PPERA 2000, s. 37, a party must be registered in order to have a broadcast). The BBC, ITC and RA determine how much air time should be given to election broadcasts and, even more importantly, how the due impartiality requirement should be met in allocating the air time. In the past the

---

[3] See clause 5.1(c) of the Agreement of 25 January 1996.

allocation rules have been heavily influenced by informal agreements reached by the political parties represented in the current Parliament through their 'Committee on Party Political Broadcasting'. Under the rules, a broadcast is offered only to a party fielding a minimum number of candidates, with extra slots allocated strictly according to past electoral performance.

This approach was adopted at the 1997 general election, albeit with the authorities maintaining that they had taken their own decisions as to allocation, uninfluenced by the parties in Parliament. Although it discriminates against new parties, it was upheld by the Divisional Court in *R* v *BBC, ex parte Referendum Party* [1997] EMLR 605. The court accepted that the BBC and ITC had indeed reached their own decisions and held that impartiality in this context could not be 'equated with parity or balance as between political parties of different strengths, popular support and appeal'. It simply meant 'fairness of allocation' of air time, taking into account such factors and with proper allowance being made for changes in the political landscape and the potential for television to influence such changes (at 618). Broadcasters must now take into account the views of the Electoral Commission in setting their allocation rules (PPERA 2000, s. 11).

10.2.4   *Bowman* v *United Kingdom*

In the important decision of *Bowman* v *United Kingdom* (1998) 26 EHRR 1, the Court considered the restrictions placed on freedom of expression at election time by s. 75 of the RPA 1983.

The applicant complained that a prosecution brought against her under s. 75 of the 1983 Act violated her Article 10(1) ECHR rights. Immediately before the 1992 general election, she had arranged the distribution of 1.5 million leaflets in selected constituencies on behalf of the Society for the Protection of the Unborn Child. These put the case against abortion and summarised the views of the main local candidates on the issue. She was prosecuted for the leaflet put out in the constituency of Halifax, where the candidates had strong pro- and anti-abortion views. Although the applicant was acquitted on a procedural technicality, the Court accepted that she was a victim because the decision to prosecute operated as a warning that she would be prosecuted for doing the same thing again at any future election (at para. 29). The Court acknowledged that s. 75 helped to secure equality between candidates, and therefore pursued the legitimate aim of protecting the rights of the candidates and the electorate (at para. 38). The case therefore turned on the proportionality issue.

The Court emphasised once again the crucial importance of freedom of political speech in the democratic process (see, for example, *Castells* v *Spain* (1992) 14 EHRR 445, at paras 65 and 67) and that the free elections guaranteed by Article 3 of the First Protocol are 'secured in part' by freedom of expression so that 'it is particularly important in the period preceding an election that opinions and information of all kinds are permitted to circulate freely' (at para. 42). But it also recognised, as is implicit in s. 75, that on occasion the two rights may come into conflict during a campaign:

> ... so that it may be considered necessary, in the period preceding or during an election, to place certain restrictions, of a type which would not usually be acceptable, on freedom of expression. (at para. 43)

The Court could not accept that this was necessary in Mrs Bowman's case, observing that s. 75, and the five-pound expenditure cap in particular, operated 'for all practical purposes, as a total barrier to Mrs Bowman's publishing information with a view to influencing voters of Halifax in favour of an anti-abortion candidate'. In particular, it was not satisfied of the necessity for this strict interference with her freedom of expression in a democracy where the media were free to support or oppose particular candidates, and national or regional advertising on political issues at election time was unregulated (at para. 47).

Section 75 of the 1983 Act is a relic of the distant days when a local leaflet or advertisement could really influence the outcome of an election. As the Court in *Bowman* found, the blanket prohibition on all local publication which may influence voters for or against a particular candidate, is difficult to justify in an era when millions of pounds are spent by parties and other organisations on national and regional election campaigns. A law preventing the media from using their influence in this way, outside of normal election coverage, may be justifiable in principle as an attempt to maintain the sort of level playing field between candidates that the Court referred to in *Bowman*. However, a fair balance must be struck between the rights of non-candidates to campaign impartially on public issues at a local level and the need to maintain this level playing field. The increase in the prescribed limit (see 10.2.1 above) will undoubtedly allow more scope for local campaigning. Problems may still arise, however, particularly where it is viewed as a 'concerted' attempt to promote a particular candidate. Section 75 applies only where the campaigning is 'with a view to promoting or procuring the election of a candidate at an election' (s. 75(1)). The solution, short of further amendment to the RPA 1983, may be for the domestic courts to interpret these words in a way which excludes genuine campaigning on issues of public interest, as distinct from supporting a candidate who is preferred *because of* his or her identity or party allegiance.

10.2.5   Election law: other areas of possible challenge

The scope for politicians and electors to complain about lack of balance or biased reporting at election time may be limited. It is well established in the Convention case law that Article 10 ECHR does not give a citizen or private organisation a 'general and unfettered right' to put forward an opinion through the media or to be interviewed in a particular way, although the same cases acknowledge that a complaint about denial of access to broadcasting time could in principle be made out in 'exceptional circumstances' if one political party was excluded while others were given broadcasting time (see *Haider* v *Austria* (App. No. 25060/94) (1995) 83 DR 66, at 74, and the cases referred to there). However, there would have to be clear evidence of bias, arbitrariness or unjustifiable discrimination. In *Huggett* v *United Kingdom* (App. No. 24744/94) (1995) 82 DR 98, the Commission rejected a complaint about the BBC's threshold requirement that a party should be standing candidates in at least 12.5 per cent of the seats in an election before it could qualify for an election broadcast. The threshold was justified by the need to ensure that air time was given only to political opinions which were 'likely to be of general interest and command some public support' (at 101). In the earlier case of *X and the Association of Z* v *United Kingdom* (App. No. 4515/70, 11 July 1971), a similar complaint by an organisation which was not fielding any candidates at all was rejected by the Commission. Although in principle, therefore, a political party could seek to challenge the allocation of election broadcast time as discriminatory, asking the Divisional Court to take account of its Article 10(1) rights in conjunction with Article 14,[4] the result would probably be the same as in the *Referendum Party* case (see 10.2.3). In *Haider* v *Austria* (at 74), the Commission also rejected a complaint of bias by the politician against a statutory Broadcasting Supervisory Body which had declined to question legitimate editorial and journalistic decisions taken at election time. In *Bader* v *Austria* (App. No. 26633/95) (1996) 22 EHRR CD 213, a complaint alleging failure by the Austrian authorities to provide sufficient information to help electors to vote in the referendum on accession to the EU was rejected. The Commission reiterated that while the right to receive information under Article 10(1) ECHR prohibits restrictions on the passage of information, it cannot be used to force public authorities to disclose information against their wishes. (See further *Gaskin* v *UK* (1989) 12 EHRR 36 and *Leander* v *Sweden* (1987) 9 EHRR 433.)

Section 93 of the RPA 1983 reflects the general obligation of impartiality under which broadcasters work. As indicated at 10.2.4 above, both the European Court and our own courts have emphasised the importance of maintaining this sort of level playing field at election time. The scope for a broadcaster to argue that its operation has resulted in a violation of Article 10(1) is therefore, probably, limited to a case where one candidate has unreasonably withheld the necessary consent, perhaps having participated in the recording but not liking the outcome. A successful *candidate* unseated by s. 93(1)(b) for having given an interview could,

---

[4] The challenge would be to the regulatory authorities and the BBC which, is undoubtedly carrying out a public function in reaching its allocation decision; see 3.4.3 above.

however, allege a violation of Article 10(1) rights, particularly if there was a clear victory in an otherwise fair election.[5] The new Codes of Practice, when they replace the existing s. 93 (see 10.2.1 above), should remove most of these problems. While s. 106 of the 1983 Act limits freedom of expression speech at election time, it may not be incompatible with Convention rights, seeking as it does to protect candidates from wholly unfounded allegations of fact about their private lives and, thereby, to preserve the integrity of the electoral process. However, the provision that 'prima facie proof' of falsity is sufficient for the purpose of granting an interim injunction (RPA 1983, s. 106(3)) may conflict with the higher test for prior restraint in s. 12(3), HRA 1998 and the close scrutiny which the European Court requires (see 2.3.3.6 above).

10.3 PARLIAMENT

10.3.1 Parliamentary privilege

Article 9 of the Bill of Rights of 1688 provides that 'the freedom of speech, and debates or proceedings in Parliament ought not to be impeached or questioned in any court or place outside of Parliament'. The effect is that there is a 'blanket prohibition' on the examination of Parliamentary proceedings in court. The court cannot hear evidence, cross-examination or argument challenging the truth or propriety of anything done in the course of Parliamentary proceedings (see *Hamilton* v *Al Fayed* [2000] 2 All ER 224 (HL), *per* Lord Browne-Wilkinson at 231B). There is therefore an absolute privilege against suit in defamation which extends to speech and publication incidental to the proceedings themselves, for example giving evidence to a committee or the Parliamentary Commissioner for Standards (see Defamation Act 1996, s. 13(5)). In so far as it protects political speech in matters of public interest, this aspect of our constitutional law is in harmony with Convention law which, as indicated in Chapter 5, gives a high level of protection to such speech and the rights of elected representatives. As the Court explained in *Castells* v *Spain* (1992) 14 EHRR 445, at 476: '... While freedom of speech is important for everybody, it is especially so for an elected representative of the people. He represents his electorate, draws attention to their preoccupations and defends their interests ...' (reiterated by the Court in *Piermont* v *France* (1995) 20 EHRR 301, at para. 76.)

In *Young and O'Faolain* v *Ireland* (App. Nos 25646/94 and 29099/95) [1996] EHRLR 326, the applicants complained under Articles 6(1) and (8) ECHR that Irish Parliamentary immunity denied them an effective domestic remedy in respect of statements made by TDs in the Dail. The Commission rejected the

---

[5] A complaint to this effect is currently before the Court, albeit in a case where the result was close; see *Loveridge* v *United Kingdom* (App. No. 39641/98).

complaints on the grounds that the protection of free debate in the public interest was a legitimate aim, and that a reasonable relationship of proportionality existed between this aim and the absolute immunity. Under Article 6(1), the Commission found that Parliamentary immunity involved denial of access to the maker of the statement as a defendant in legal proceedings, rather than to the court itself (see also *Golder* v *United Kingdom* (App. No. 4451/70, 1 June 1973)). There may, however, be scope to challenge the absolute nature of the privilege in cases where the statement in Parliament does not genuinely relate to a matter of public interest.

However, the rule also prevents any direct criticism by the courts about the propriety of a member's actions in connection with such proceedings (*Hamilton* v *Al Fayed*, at 231J). This will hamper the defence in a libel action brought *by* a Parliamentarian, if it involves any direct criticism of anything said or done in Parliament. Where it does, the claim will be stayed unless the privilege is waived by the claimant under s. 13(1) of the Defamation Act 1996 (see *Prebble* v *Television New Zealand* [1995] 1 AC 321).[6] This provision probably succeeds in ensuring that the rights of both parties to a fair trial under Article 6(1) ECHR are protected. A fair and accurate report of proceedings in either House or a committee of Parliament has qualified privilege in defamation and proceedings for contempt of court (*Wason* v *Walter* (1868) LR 4 QB 73; see also *Attorney-General* v *Times Newspapers Ltd* [1973] 1 All ER 815, at 823). The media can also comment honestly upon statements made in Parliament under cover of privilege, whether they are true or not, provided the report gives an accurate account of the making of the statement.[7] Again this rule is broadly consistent with Convention law (see 5.6.1 above).

10.3.2 Contempt of Parliament

Each House of Parliament still has the power to impose a range of possible punishments for contempt — from mild censure, through banishment from the precincts of the Palace, to imprisonment. The definition of Parliamentary contempt is predictably loose, and would include any act which has a 'tendency' to 'obstruct or impede' the House, or its members and officers, in the exercise of their functions. This could extend to acts, in the form of articles or broadcasts, tending to diminish the respect due to them and lower their authority.[8] There is no clearly established defence of truth of fair comment and there are no procedural safeguards for the person accused.

---

[6] The right to waive in s. 13(1) of the Defamation Act 1996 was introduced into the Defamation Bill in the House of Lords after the proceedings against the *Guardian* in *Hamilton and Greer* v *Hencke and others* were stayed by the High Court in 1995.

[7] See *Gatley on Libel and Slander*, Milmo, P. and Rodgers, W. V. H. (eds), 9th edn (London, Sweet & Maxwell, 1998), at para. 12.20 and the cases referred to.

[8] See *Erskine May's Parliamentary Practice*, 22nd edn (London, Butterworths, 1997), chap. 8.

It is almost inconceivable that this power would be used today to stifle criticism or disrespectful comment by the media. Indeed, by its own resolution, the House of Commons will now lay a charge of contempt only where there is some 'substantial interference with its functions'.[9] If it did, the proceedings would be open to successful challenge in Strasbourg under Articles 5, 6 and 10 ECHR. Ironically, the HRA 1998 would not assist a journalist facing such proceedings, since the courts will not pass judgment on the fairness or otherwise of Parliament's procedures for protecting its 'established privileges'.[10]

---

[9] 234 Commons Journals 170.

[10] See *per* Lord Browne-Wilkinson in *Prebble* v *Television NZ*, at 332D, and the cases referred to; and HRA 1998, s. 6(3) makes clear that Parliament is not a 'public authority' for the purposes of the Act.

Chapter Eleven

Licensing and Regulation of the Media

11.1 INTRODUCTION

Other chapters have considered the application of the guarantee of freedom of expression to specific subject matters. In this chapter we consider the impact of the ECHR in connection with prior licensing and subsequent regulation of the media. In particular we consider the possible impact of the requirements of procedural fairness under Article 6 ECHR upon the activities of media regulators.

11.2 BROADCAST LICENSING AND REGULATION

11.2.1 The proviso for licensing in Article 10(1)

Article 10(1) ECHR provides:

> Everyone has the right to freedom of expression. This right shall include freedom to hold opinions and to receive and impart information and ideas without interference by public authority and regardless of frontiers. This Article shall not prevent states from requiring the licensing of broadcasting, television or cinema enterprises.

The third sentence does not exclude licensing of broadcasting and cinemas entirely from the guarantees in the opening two sentences. The Court has explained that the origins of the third sentence were the technical limitations on broadcasting frequencies which made some form of regulation inevitable. Although there are still technical aspects, broadcasting licensing has other functions. It was recognised that the electronic media had the potential for much greater impact than the print media, and licensing controls sought to regulate content. A literal reading of the third sentence of Article 10(1) might suggest that any licensing restrictions were excluded from the Article's guarantees. However, the jurisprudence of the Court has developed so that restrictions imposed by way of broadcasting licensing are compatible with the Convention only if they satisfy two of the requirements for restrictions on freedom of expression in Article 10(2) — they must be prescribed by law and they must be necessary in a democratic society. In effect, the licensing of broadcasting, television and cinema has become a further 'legitimate aim' which restrictions on freedom of expression may pursue. Licensing regimes may still be directed at technical aspects of broadcasting, but they may have wider public interest objectives as well. As with restrictions imposed for the other aims (specified in Article 10(2)), they are neither automatically a violation nor automatically valid. In particular, the Government must demonstrate their necessity in a democratic society (*Groppera Radio AG and others* v *Switzerland* (1990) 13 EHRR 321; *Autronic AG* v *Switzerland* (1990) 12 EHRR 485 and *Informationsverein Lentia and others* v *Austria* (1993) 17 EHRR 93).

The Court recently had to consider a complaint by a religious organisation that it had not been allowed to compete for a national radio licence. The complaint was made under Articles 10 and 14. The Court found that both complaints were manifestly unfounded. Technical limitations did still mean that national licences had to be rationed and the UK had a margin of appreciation as to how to allocate these so as to satisfy as many listeners as possible (*United Christian Broadcasting Ltd* v *UK* (App. No. 44802/98, 7 November 2000).

In the UK, the provisions of the Broadcasting Acts 1990 and 1996 (in relation to digital programme services) provide for the regulation of independent broadcasting services by the Independent Television Commission and the Radio Authority through the licensing system. General requirements as to standards are prescribed by ss. 6 (television) and 90 (radio) of the 1996 Act. These are incorporated into licences and include the familiar requirements as to good taste and decency, due accuracy and impartiality in news and politics, as well as respect for religious beliefs.[1] The regulators promulgate codes of guidance and have wide powers of enforcement through notices, fines and ultimately revocation of licences. In addition, the 1996 Act created the Broadcasting Standards Commission with powers to adjudicate upon complaints as to standards (covering violence, sex, taste and decency) and fair treatment (including unwarranted infringements of privacy).

The general requirements represent long-established standards widely accepted as being in the public interest. They have not been challenged in Strasbourg. They are unlikely to be affected by the arrival of the HRA 1998 in so far as they apply to mass broadcasting accessible by switching on a television or radio. The advent of 'personalised' broadcasting access through use of a password or pin number

---

[1] The BBC undertakes to comply with comparable standards by its Licence and Agreement with the Heritage Secretary; see in particular the latter, Cm 3152 (1996), para. 5.1.

known only to a consenting adult may, however, make it harder to justify some of them.

The phrase 'regardless of frontiers' in the second sentence of Article 10(1) makes it clear that the restrictions on broadcasts which originate abroad will also infringe the guarantee of freedom of expression unless they are prescribed by law and necessary in a democratic society (see *Groppera Radio* and *Autronic*, above).

11.2.2 Public service broadcasting

The existence of publicly owned broadcasters does not infringe Article 10 ECHR, but in one of its most important cases the Court held that the right to freedom of expression was violated if the publicly owned stations had a monopoly on broadcasting from within the state. In *Informationsverein Lentia and others* v *Austria* (1993) 17 EHRR 93, the Court repeated the fundamental part that freedom of expression played in a democracy and the media's role of imparting information and ideas of general public interest which the public was also entitled to receive. It said: 'Such an undertaking cannot be successfully accomplished unless it is grounded in the principle of pluralism, of which the state is the ultimate guarantor' (at para. 38). Austria argued that the state monopoly was necessary to guarantee the objectivity and impartiality of the audio-visual media and to achieve a diversity of programmes, balanced programming and impartiality and independence. The Court was not persuaded. It saw state ownership as the most restrictive means of achieving these aims and observed that other European states sought to pursue similar aims by measures which allowed a mix of publicly and privately owned stations to coexist. The working out of a new regime in Austria was protracted. At one stage only two private radio stations were permitted for the Vienna region. In a subsequent case the Court said this was 'surprising', but did not need to rule on whether it was compatible with the Convention since the law allowing this had been declared null and void by the Austrian courts (*Radio ABC* v *Austria* (1997) 25 EHRR 185).

11.2.3 Broadcasting bans

Under the BBC's Licence and Agreement and under the Broadcasting Act 1990, s. 10(3), the Home Secretary can direct broadcasters not to include any prescribed material in their programmes. Between 1988 and 1994 this power was exercised to prohibit the broadcasting of the voices of anyone who was a member of or a supporter of a number of organisations, including Sinn Fein. Consequently, if Gerry Adams, the President of Sinn Fein, was interviewed on the television or radio, his words had to be blanked out and replaced with the voice of an actor and/or subtitles. The domestic legal challenge to these directions by various journalists and TV producers led to the House of Lords decision in *Brind* v *Secretary of State for the Home Department* [1991] AC 696. Having lost in the domestic courts, they pursued their challenge in Strasbourg. However, the European Commission on Human Rights held that their application was inadmissible as manifestly unfounded. It agreed that the broadcasting bans did interfere with the applicants' freedom of expression, but the restrictions were prescribed by law and were pursuing the legitimate aim of combating terrorism. They had a limited effect on the broadcasters' freedoms and the court had recognised the particular difficulties of taking measures against terrorism. For these reasons, and taking account of the margin of appreciation, it was not reasonably arguable that the Government had failed to show that the measures were necessary in a democratic society (*Brind* v *UK* (App. No. 18714/91) (1994) 77 DR 42). This decision followed a rejection of complaints from Ireland which had sought to argue that similar broadcasting bans in that country were contrary to Article 10 (*Purcell* v *Ireland* (App. No. 15404/89) (1991) 70 DR 262).

Although the particular broadcasting bans thus survived a Convention challenge, the introduction of the HRA 1998 will require a reversal of the principle which the House of Lords set out in *Brind*. That case has come to stand for the proposition that administrative decisions could not be challenged as unlawful on the grounds that they were contrary to the Convention. From 2 October 2000, public bodies are under a duty to act compatibly with Convention rights. Any future broadcasting ban would therefore have to be measured against the demands of Article 10 ECHR in order to assess its lawfulness.

11.2.4   Access to broadcasting

Article 10 ECHR guarantees a right to impart ideas and opinions, but access to the airwaves is in practice controlled by the broadcasters and anyone who wishes to 'impart ideas or opinions' on television or radio must pass these gatekeepers. Does Article 10 control the way in which they exercise these powers?

In general the answer is 'No'. In a case brought by Jorg Haider against Austria (*Haider* v *Austria* (App. No. 25060/94) (1995) 83 DR 66) the Commission held that Article 10 ECHR does not give a general and unfettered right for any private citizen or organisation to have access to the broadcasting media.[2] There may be exceptional circumstances where one political party is excluded from broadcasting facilities to which others are given access. Even here, the Commission has declared inadmissible an application under Article 10 from an independent candidate for the European Parliament who was not allowed to make a party political broadcast (see *Huggett* v *UK*, at 10.2.5 above; see also *Tete* v *France* (App. No. 11123/84) (1987) 54 DR 52). The Commission recognised that air time

---

[2] The Commission's previous decisions were to the same effect. See, e.g., App. No. 4515/70, 12 July 1971; *X* v *Sweden* (App. No. 9297/81) 28 DR 204; and *Sundberg* v *Sweden* (App. No. 12439/86, 15 October 1987).

was inevitably limited and found that the threshold test used to decide which parties would be allowed a broadcast was compatible with Article 10(2). In the *Haider* case, the applicant also complained about the hostile manner in which he had been interviewed. The Commission commented, 'with regard to interviews of politicians, it is in the interests of freedom of political debate that the interviewing journalist may also express critical and provocative points of view and not merely give neutral cues for the statements of interviewed persons, since the latter can reply immediately'.

11.2.5   Advertising restrictions

We consider controls on commercial speech and advertising in particular in Chapter 12. Many countries with public broadcasting bodies restrict advertising to commercial channels. In a 1993 case from the Netherlands, the applicant had been fined by the Dutch broadcasting regulator for violating the restrictions on advertising by including incidental references to two products in the course of a children's information programme (*Nederlandse Omroepprogramma Stichtung* v *Netherlands* (App. No. 16844/90, 13 October 1993)). The Commission accepted that this was an 'interference' (and not, as the Government argued, merely an enforcement of the condition on which the licensed programme had been permitted to be aired). The Commission thought that the restriction had the legitimate aim of protecting the rights of others, namely the rights of children to be protected from indirect advertisements in TV programmes directed at a young audience. This, incidentally, illustrates the broad and non-technical way in which the Strasbourg organs have interpreted the concept of 'rights of others' (see also *Ahmed* v *UK* (1998) 29 EHRR 1). In all the circumstances it considered that the restriction had been proportionate and necessary in a democratic society. It ruled the application to be inadmissible. The applicant also complained that the Dutch attitude to incidental inclusion of product names was much stricter than in other European countries. Dutch audiences would be exposed to programmes made outside the Netherlands but picked up or retransmitted into the Netherlands. Consequently, the applicant argued, it was subjected to restrictions which were discriminatory and contrary to Article 14 ECHR. The Commission rejected this argument as well. It held that the position of a programme made or broadcast from inside the Netherlands was not comparable to one from outside.

The Court is due to hear a case from Switzerland concerning the rejection of a television advertisement on the grounds that it had a clear 'political character' (*VgT Vereingegen Tierfabriken* v *Switzerland* (App. No. 24699/94, 6 February 2000)). The advertisement had been submitted by a pro-animal organisation which wished to encourage people to eat less meat. The advertisement compared the position of wild pigs in the forest with the industrially reared variety. The application has been declared admissible in connection with Article 10. The organisation also complained under Article 14 on the grounds that advertisements from the meat industry encouraging people to eat more meat had been accepted. This, too, has been declared admissible.

11.3 NEWSPAPER LICENSING

The press in the UK has not been licensed for centuries. There is still a requirement for the printers and publishers of every newspaper which is not owned by a company registered under the Companies Acts to submit an annual return to Companies House with the title and name of the proprietor (Newspaper Libel and Registration Act 1881).

The European Commission has held that a system of registration for the press is not incompatible with the Convention as long as there is no discretion to refuse registration (if the requirements are complied with) and as long as the requirements are purely formal. Even in these circumstances, a penalty for non-compliance would have to satisfy Article 10(2) ECHR (*H.N.* v *Italy* (App. No. 18902/91) (1998) 94 DR 21). A complaint from Poland concerning a refusal to register two periodicals is now pending before the Court (*Gaweda* v *Poland* (App. No. 261229/95, 4 December 1998)).

11.4 MEDIA REGULATORS

There are various contexts in which the media are regulated either in advance of publication (e.g., the system for classification of videos by the British Board of Classification), or after the event (such as by the Broadcasting Standards Commission, the Press Complaints Commission and the Advertising Standards Authority, as well as through the broadcast licensing system referred to at 11.2 above). We consider in other chapters the approach which the ECHR requires to be taken to substantive matters. Thus, for instance, Chapter 8 considers the issues which are raised by the control of material which might be considered obscene or blasphemous. Here we deal briefly with the procedural issues which might arise under Article 6 ECHR in connection with such regulatory activities.

11.4.1 Article 6: applicability

Article 6 ECHR applies: 'In the determination of [a person's] civil rights and obligations or of any criminal charge against him.' These two alternatives — 'civil rights and obligations' and 'criminal charge' — need to be considered separately.

11.4.1.1 Civil cases
For the Article 6 protections to apply, the case must concern a 'civil right', there must be an arguable basis for that right in domestic law (a dispute or

'*contestation*' in French) and the procedure must lead to the 'determination' of the right.

The phrase 'civil rights or obligations' is an example of an 'autonomous concept', that is a term which is defined and developed by the Court in the context of the Convention and its case law. Whether a dispute concerns a civil right is influenced, but not conclusively resolved, by its categorisation in the domestic legal system (*König* v *Germany* (1978) 2 EHRR 170). Ultimately this question must be answered 'by reference to the substantive contents and effect of the right' in issue (at para. 89). Comments about this particular autonomous concept have to be tentative, in part because the Court appears to have shied away from providing a comprehensive definition and in part because its attitude has evolved over time and is still developing. Early cases from the Court referred to the distinction between rights in private law (which were treated as 'civil') and those in public law (which were not) (*Ringeisen* v *Austria* (1971) 1 EHRR 455). Paradigmatic cases can be identified in this way. Thus litigation between two private parties (e.g., over libel, breach of confidence or copyright) clearly concerns 'civil rights or obligations'. Conversely, disputes of a purely public law character which do not directly affect a private law right are not within Article 6(1) ECHR. On this basis, complaints have been dismissed in relation to the admission or expulsion of aliens, the recruitment or dismissal of civil servants and the validity of election expenses, even though, in the last case, the applicant might have lost his seat and the payments which went with elected office (*Pierr-Bloch* v *France* (1997) 26 EHRR 202). However, disputed public law decisions which decisively affect the relationships of private legal personalities in civil law, may involve the determination of civil rights (see *Ringeisen* v *Austria*, which concerned an administrative approval of a transfer of land between the applicant and a vendor).

The form or the venue of the dispute is clearly not decisive. In particular, disputes which directly affect pecuniary rights or obligations, or which concern the use of property, are likely to be classified as 'civil'. Of particular significance in the context of the regulation of media activities are cases which have held that the withdrawal of a licence to engage in a commercial activity is a 'civil' matter (*Pudas* v *Sweden* (1987) 10 EHRR 380; *Tre Traktörer Aktiebolag* v *Sweden* (1989) 13 EHRR 309; and see *Benthem* v *Netherlands* (1985) 8 EHRR 1) and others which have held that refusal of planning permission to develop privately owned land also concerned civil rights (*Fredin* v *Sweden* (1991) 13 EHRR 784). It is likely that the refusal of a BBFC video certificate would concern a civil right in this sense. The Court has held that disciplinary proceedings by a professional body which can lead to the loss of the right to continue in the profession would engage Article 6(1) (*Le Compte, Van Leuven and De Meyere* v *Belgium* (1981) 4 EHRR 1; *Diennet* v *France* (1995) 21 EHRR 554; *Kingsley* v *United Kingdom* (App. No. 35605/97, 7 November 2000)). Decisions by the Radio Authority or the

ITC which might lead to the revocation of a broadcasting licence would similarly be likely to involve a 'civil right or obligation'.

In order for Article 6 to apply through the gateway of 'civil rights and obligations', there must also be an arguable basis in domestic law for the right. This in part reflects the principle that Article 6 is concerned with procedural rather than substantive rights, although the borderline between procedural bars and substantive ineligibility can sometimes be elusive (see, e.g., *Osman* v *UK* [1999] 1 FLR 198).

Furthermore, the dispute must concern a 'right' rather than a discretionary grant, so that the ability to apply for an *ex gratia* payment would not attract Article 6 procedural protections. Yet here, too, firm guidance is difficult. There have been cases where a dispute concerning the initial grant of a government licence has been held to be within Article 6 (see *Benthem* v *Netherlands* (1985) 8 EHRR 1 — licence to run a petrol station granted then removed on basis of unknown opposition at the time of determination, the applicant continued to trade while an appeal went through the administrative system and then to court; *Jorbedo Foundation of Christian Schools* v *Sweden* (App. No. 11533/85) (1987) 61 DR 92 — extension of licence to an existing private middle school to allow it to teach older children). Although these have involved some element of ongoing commercial activity, this is not necessary in principle. On the face of it, therefore, even 'first time' or speculative applications for broadcasting licences would involve the determination of a civil right, however odd this may look.[3]

Lastly, the proceedings must lead to a 'determination' of the right or obligation. On this basis the Al-Fayed brothers' complaint about the alleged unfairness of inspectors appointed under the Companies Acts was unsuccessful: the inspectors reported to the Department of Trade and Industry but determined nothing (*Fayed* v *UK* (1994) 18 EHRR 393). On the same basis, the Court of Appeal has concluded that the procedure by which a person's name was included on the Department of Health's list of people about whom there are doubts as to their suitability to work with children, did not have to conform with Article 6 ECHR. Although inclusion on the register would be highly detrimental to the prospects of a person gaining employment in a post that involved contact with children, it did not in itself determine anything (*R* v *Secretary of State for Health, ex parte C* [2000] UKHRR 639 (CA)).

11.4.1.2   Criminal charge
Once again the concept of 'criminal' proceedings is autonomous. Here, though, if the domestic system does classify the proceedings as criminal that is determinative. Thus, unsurprisingly, Article 6(1) ECHR will apply if a broadcaster is

---

[3] A Channel 3 licence, for example, is awarded to the highest bidder unless there are exceptional reasons relating to quality; see Broadcasting Act 1990, s. 17.

prosecuted for an offence under the Broadcasting Act 1990 (e.g., broadcasting without a licence contrary to s. 13), or if a person is charged with an offence under the Video Recordings Act 1984.

However, this is not the limit of the applicability of Article 6. Even if domestic law would regard the proceedings as non-criminal, they may involve the determination of a 'criminal' charge for the purposes of Article 6 (*Engel and others* v *Netherlands* (1976) 1 EHRR 706). Contempt proceedings may not be strictly criminal as a matter of domestic law, but since they potentially involve imprisonment and/or substantial fines, they are criminal for the purposes of Article 6 (see *Harman* v *UK* (App. No. 10038/82) (1984) 38 DR 53).

The Court will look at the nature of the conduct in question and the severity of the possible penalty. The fines which the Radio Authority and the ITC can impose can be (and have been) very large. However, there must be doubt as to whether the proceedings which lead to these penalties come within the Strasbourg concept of 'criminal'. It is only licensees who can face these proceedings. Previous cases before the Court have distinguished between regimes which have a general application (e.g., for collection of the community charge or poll tax and penalties for non-payment) which have been held to be 'criminal' (*Benham* v *UK* (1996) 22 EHRR 293), and those applying a disciplinary scheme to a particular group, such as prisoners or the armed forces, or civil servants or professionals who face proceedings before their association. None of the latter has been held to involve the 'criminal' procedural protections.

11.4.2　Article 6(1): rights granted

Assuming that Article 6(1) ECHR applies either because the proceedings concern the determination of a person's civil rights or obligations, or because they involve the determination of a criminal charge, it provides the following guarantees:

(a)　a fair and public hearing;
(b)　within a reasonable time;
(c)　by an independent and impartial tribunal established by law, with;
(d)　judgment to be pronounced publicly.

The judgment must be reasoned, but the duty to give a public hearing is not absolute. Article 6(1) provides that the:

> public may be excluded from all or part of the trial in the interest of morals, public order or national security in a democratic society, where the interests of juveniles or the protection of the private life of the parties so require, or to the extent strictly necessary in the opinion of the court in special circumstances where publicity would prejudice the interests of justice.

Article 6(1) underpins the fundamental principle of the rule of law and is to be construed broadly (*Delcourt* v *Belgium* (1969) 1 EHRR 355). Yet the decisions of the European Court indicate that the touchstone, as with the common law duty, is overall fairness, rather than particular technical failings. The case law of the Court under Article 6(1) is extensive, but the following features may be of importance in the context of media regulation.

11.4.2.1   The 'tribunal'

If not a court, this must exercise essentially judicial functions. The fact that it has other non-judicial, perhaps administrative, functions does not necessarily prevent it being a tribunal (see *Campbell and Fell* v *United Kingdom* (1984) 7 EHRR 165, concerning the disciplinary functions of a prison Board of Visitors), neither does the fact that the members are not professional judges (*Ettl* v *Austria* (1987) 10 EHRR 255). Where a decision affecting civil rights or obligations is taken by a body which does not meet Article 6(1) requirements, the procedure can be saved by a right of appeal or review before a court or tribunal which does so (*Albert and Le Compte* v *Belgium* (1983) 5 EHRR 533, at para. 29). A full reconsideration of the merits may be required (as in *Albert and Le Compte* v *Belgium*, where an appeal to the Court of Cassation against a decision of a medical disciplinary tribunal, on a point of law only, was regarded as insufficient), though not necessarily. The Court has accepted that in certain specialised areas of law, where issues of policy arise, Article 6(1) may be satisfied by a two-stage procedure under which an administrative body reaches a decision, making findings of fact and exercising judgment, which is then subject to an appeal or review on a point of law. In *Bryan* v *UK* (1995) 21 EHRR 342, the Court found that a planning inquiry was procedurally fair, but that the inspector lacked the necessary independence from the Secretary of State. The subsequent judicial review proceedings cured this defect, however, since the inspector's findings of fact were not disputed and the procedure enabled the applicant to challenge fully the policy decisions in issue.

11.4.2.2   Independence and impartiality

In considering independence, 'regard must be had, *inter alia*, to the manner of appointment of [the tribunal's] members and to their term of office, to the existence of guarantees against outside pressures and to the question whether the body presents an appearance of independence' (*Bryan* v *UK* (1995) 21 EHRR 342, at para. 37; three-year terms of office were upheld in *Campbell and Fell*, see para. 80). Appointment by the executive does not, *per se*, deny independence, though a right to dismiss during the appointee's terms of office would do so (*Campbell and Fell* v *United Kingdom* (1984) 7 EHRR 165, at paras 79 and 80). In *Zand* v *Austria* (App. No. 7360/76) (1978) 15 DR 70, at 80) the Commission observed that 'the irremovability of judges during their term of office, whether it be for a limited period of time or for a lifetime, is a necessary corollary of their independence from the Administration and thus included in the guarantees of Article 6(1) of the Convention'. In one of the early Scottish cases under the HRA 1998, an objection to criminal trial by a temporary sheriff, who could be removed from office at any time for any reason by a member of the executive (the Lord Advocate), was upheld (*Starrs and Chalmers* v *Procurator Fiscal, Linlithgow* 2000 JC 208).

Impartiality is simply the absence of bias. This may be actual bias, for which the Court applies a subjective test to establish the 'personal conviction of the given adjudicator', or perceived bias ('the lack of the necessary appearance of impartiality'). In the latter case the Court looks for 'sufficient guarantees to exclude any legitimate doubt' (*Piersack* v *Belgium* (1982) 5 EHRR 169, at para. 30; *Langborger* v *Sweden* (1989) 12 EHRR 416 and *Kingsley* v *UK* (App. No. 35605/97, 7 November 2000)). In *Kingsley* v *UK*, the applicant's licence to manage in the gaming industry had been removed following a Gaming Board hearing tainted by an appearance of bias. The Board had already resolved that he was not a 'fit and proper person' to hold a licence, which was the issue at the revocation hearing. However, the applicant failed to quash the decision in judicial review proceedings and was denied leave to appeal by the Court of Appeal. Both Courts held that the Board had no power to delegate the revocation hearing to an independent tribunal. The applicant was therefore denied his remedy on grounds of necessity. The European Court held that in this case judicial review was plainly inadequate to cure the defect since 'the concept of full jurisdiction involves that the reviewing court not only considers the complaint but has the ability to quash the impugned decision' (at para. 48).

11.4.2.3   Protections specific to 'criminal charges'

If the proceedings constitute the determination of a criminal charge, Article 6 guarantees certain specific procedural protections in addition to the general requirements of Article 6(1). Thus Article 6(2) provides:

> Everyone charged with a criminal offence shall be presumed innocent until proved guilty according to law.

Article 6(3) says:

> Everyone charged with a criminal offence has the following minimum rights:
> (a)   to be informed promptly, in a language which he understands and in detail, of the nature and cause of the accusation against him;
> (b)   to have adequate time and facilities for the preparation of his defence;
> (c)   to defend himself in person or through legal assistance of his own choosing or, if he has not sufficient means to pay for legal assistance, to be given it free when the interests of justice so require;

(d)   to examine or have examined witnesses against him and to obtain the attendance and examination of witnesses on his behalf under the same conditions as witnesses against him;

(e)   to have the free assistance of an interpreter if he cannot understand or speak the language used in court.

In addition, Article 7 prohibits the imposition of retrospective criminal liability or a more severe penalty than prevailed at the time the criminal offence was committed.

A considerable body of case law has elaborated these rights and the specialist books on criminal procedure should be consulted if the proceedings in question are likely to be classified as the determination of a criminal charge.

11.4.3   Article 6: issues for media regulation

As indicated above, there are number of statutory and industry-imposed regimes for the regulation of television, radio, cinema/video, the press and advertising. The status of these bodies under the HRA 1998 is dealt with at 3.4.3. The impact that their decisions can have on the interests of media organisations (as well as complainant consumers) is varied. They will have to be alive to decisions which engage Article 6(1) rights. Some, such as denial/revocation of a licence or a requirement to cease an advertising campaign, will obviously do so. Others may be less obvious.

Where these rights are engaged, regulators should not assume that the possibility of a judicial review challenge to the proceedings after the event will cure all defects, as it did following the planning inquiry in *Bryan* v *UK* (1995) 21 EHRR 342 (see 11.4.2.1). They will have to ensure that their procedural arrangements meet the Article 6 requirements, particularly in respect of the fairness of the fact-finding exercise. This may not be too traumatic. They have been subject to the public law duty of fairness for many years. In broad terms this corresponds with the Article 6 protection, in particular the requirement to accord a fair hearing. Indeed, in some respects the common law duty is broader. It applies, for instance, to all parties (including the person presenting a complaint or opposing an application for a licence or renewal). The duty to give a public hearing would have been novel in many regulatory contexts some years ago, but there has been a marked trend towards more openness recently. The regulator may be able to rely upon the provisions for the exclusion of the public in some cases — for example, a contested PCC complaint about the private life of a celebrity.

The need to have an impartial and independent tribunal is also a principle of common law. However, here, as the *Starrs and Chalmers* case has illustrated (see 11.4.2.2 above), Convention law may be stricter. The composition of, and terms of appointment to, some regulatory bodies may require reappraisal to ensure that this requirement is met. These sometimes allow the Secretary of State considerable discretion which may give rise to challenges in particular cases.[4] Regulators will also have to take care not to fall into the trap of prejudging issues that may return before them in the form of a decision as to a person's 'civil rights and obligations', in the way the Gaming Board did in *Kingsley* v *UK* (see 11.4.2.2 above). Where this is unavoidable, provision will have to be made for lawful delegation of the second decision to a body untainted by involvement in the first decision. The seminal common law case on bias was the decision of the House of Lords in *R* v *Gough* [1993] AC 646. Having reviewed the Strasbourg case law, the Court of Appeal said that a 'modest adjustment' of the *Gough* test was needed (*Director-General of Fair Trading* v *The Proprietary Association of Great Britain; sub nom: In Re Medicaments and Related Classes of Goods (No. 2)*, 21 December 2000, (2001) *The Times*, 2 February). Courts would now examine all the circumstances and ask themselves whether a fair-minded and informed observer would conclude that there was a real possibility or real danger that the tribunal was biased.

---

[4] See, for example, regarding the ITC and BSC, Broadcasting Acts 1990 and 1996, Schedule 1, para. 3 and Schedule 3, para. 4 respectively — tenure is in accordance with the 'terms of' the members' appointment by the Secretary of State.

Chapter Twelve

Commercial Speech

12.1 INTRODUCTION

In the United Kingdom, as in most jurisdictions, commercial speech is subject to a large number of restrictions, from the Trade Descriptions Act 1968 regulating misleading advertising to European Directives regulating a number of fields such as tobacco advertising and Codes of Practice which regulate various media such as television and radio. There has been limited consideration, by domestic courts, of the relevance of the right to freedom of expression to commercial speech and advertising.[1] Now that the HRA 1998 is in force, commercial organisations are likely to utilise Article 10 ECHR regularly in seeking to protect their economic interests, and therefore the domestic courts will need to examine the issues raised far more carefully.

Assessing the likely impact of incorporation into domestic law of Article 10 ECHR is difficult because of the paucity of case law in this field, and more particularly the European Court's regular and substantial recourse to the doctrine of the 'margin of appreciation' (see Chapter 2) when deciding cases concerning commercial speech. This lack of guidance may well lead English courts to examine the more evolved jurisprudence of other countries, such as Canada and the USA, both of which provide a substantial degree of protection to truthful and accurate commercial speech (see, e.g., *Central Hudson Gas* v *Public Services Commission* 447 US 557 (1980) and *RJR Macdonald* v *Attorney-General of Canada* (1995) 127 DLR (4th) 1). The distinction between the European and

---

[1] See, e.g., *R* v *Advertising Standards Authority, ex parte City Trading Ltd* [1997] COD 202 where Ognall J, in rejecting an application for judicial review of the ASA's decision to uphold a complaint about advertisements for a 'sex education video', brushed aside arguments which relied upon Article 10 and stated, *obiter*, that censorship of matters that caused widespread offence were likely to be 'necessary in a democratic society'.

Northern American jurisprudence can, at least partially, be explained by the difference in the underlying rationales for the protection of freedom of expression by the two legal systems. The jurisprudence of the US and the United Kingdom, but not the European Court of Human Rights, has accepted that one of the justifications for the protection of expression is the pursuit of truth (including truth as to the quality of various products or services). (See, e.g., Lord Steyn's speech in *R* v *Secretary of State for the Home Department, ex parte Simms*, quoted in Chapter 1, at 1.2.4.)

Before examining the jurisprudence of the European Court and the likely impact on domestic law after October 2000, it is important to address certain preliminary questions, including what constitutes commercial speech and to what extent, if any, it should be protected.

12.1.1   What is commercial speech?

Numerous definitions have been advanced for 'commercial speech' yet none is entirely satisfactory. Perhaps the dominant view is that commercial speech is speech that is designed to promote the economic interests of individuals or enterprises. The most obvious example of commercial speech is advertising, but, as can be seen from the ECHR case law, it extends beyond advertising to include any means of conveying commercial information to the consumer.

12.1.2   Why protect commercial speech?

Commercial speech clearly qualifies as 'speech' or 'expression' on any normal understanding of the words, as it involves the conveying of information and ideas. To exclude commercial speech from protection under Article 10 ECHR would inevitably require courts to draw arbitrary distinctions between it and other kinds of speech. Furthermore, as the US Supreme Court has explained, consumers have an interest in receiving accurate, truthful information about products:

> As to the particular consumer's interest in the free flow of commercial information, that interest may be as keen, if not keener by far, than his interest in the day's most urgent political debate . . . When drug prices vary as strikingly as they do, information as to who is charging what becomes more than a convenience. It could mean the alleviation of physical pain or the enjoyment of basic necessities. (*Virginia State Board of Pharmacy* v *Virginia Citizens Consumer Council* 425 US 748 (1976), at 763–4)

12.1.3   Competing interests

The justifications for restricting commercial speech are generally accepted to be stronger than in the case of political (and possibly artistic) speech. Clearly there is a public interest in forbidding false or misleading claims about products or services. These competing interests of consumer protection and fair competition mean that in every jurisdiction commercial speech is subject to considerable regulation.

12.2   ECHR CASE LAW

12.2.1   Commercial speech: general principles

The leading authority in the ECHR case law on the protection of commercial speech is *Markt Intern Verlag and Klaus Beermann* v *Germany* (1989) 12 EHRR 161. *Markt Intern* grants member states an extremely wide margin of appreciation in regulating and banning commercial speech. The Court was evenly split 9:9, but the President, with his casting vote, concluded that there had been no violation of Article 10 ECHR. The applicants published a bulletin which included an article about the dissatisfaction of a customer who had been unable to obtain the promised reimbursement of a beauty product purchased from a mail-order firm. The bulletin requested further information from its readers as to the commercial practices of the firm. The applicants were restrained by court order from repeating the statements on the grounds that they infringed the German Unfair Competition Act 1909. The German Government again attempted to argue that Article 10 was not engaged because of the commercial nature of the speech (at para. 25). The applicant argued in reply that to restrict the scope of Article 10 to news items of a political or cultural nature would result in depriving a large proportion of the press of any protection.

The Court concluded that the speech, although addressed to tradespeople rather than the public at large, conveyed information of a commercial nature which was within the ambit of Article 10 ECHR (at para. 26). The majority judgment, however, removed virtually all scrutiny of decisions in this field when it concluded that in the area of commercial matters, and in particular unfair competition, states were permitted a wide margin of appreciation, otherwise the Court would have to undertake a re-examination of the facts and all the circumstances of the case (at paras 32–33). The Court confined its review to the question whether the measures taken at the national level were justifiable in principle and proportionate. Applying this very deferential approach the Court concluded that it could not be said that the granting of injunctions went beyond the margin of appreciation left to the national authorities, and therefore there was no breach of Article 10 (at paras 36–38).

This approach was cogently criticised by the various dissenting opinions, which considered the majority's decision as an abdication of the Court's role of supervision and as an unwarranted departure from earlier Article 10 jurisprudence requiring that the necessity of any interference with the right to freedom of expression needed to be 'convincingly established' (at p. 176).[2] The dissenting judgments took a different view of the importance of the expression at issue, stating that:

> It is just as important to guarantee the freedom of expression in relation to the practices of a commercial undertaking as it is in relation to the conduct of a head of government. . . . In order to ensure the openness of business activities it must be possible to disseminate freely information and ideas concerning the products and services proposed to consumers. (at p. 177)

12.2.2 Commercial speech and advertising by professionals

Barthold v *Germany* (1985) 7 EHRR 383, concerned an interview given by a German veterinary surgeon (Mr Barthold) to a local newspaper, in which the vet was critical of the lack of emergency veterinary services at night in Hamburg. He went on to state that his clinic was the only one offering such a service. This interview led to proceedings against Mr Barthold for breaking the rules of professional conduct forbidding advertising and publicity, and for breaching s. 13 of the German Unfair Competition Act 1909. The German courts granted interim and final injunctions requiring him to refrain from repeating the statements on the grounds that the publicity provided exceeded the bounds of objective comment on matters of justified public concern. The Court by a majority found that there had been a violation of Article 10 ECHR. The German Government again sought to argue that Article 10 was not engaged because it did not extend to commercial speech, as this was a matter relating to the right freely to exercise a trade or profession which was a right not protected by the Convention (at para. 40).

The majority judgment rejected this argument on the grounds that the speech in question included the expression of 'opinions' and the imparting of 'information on a topic of general interest' (at paras 41–42). Furthermore, the publication in issue was an article written by a journalist and not a commercial advertisement. The majority, however, explicitly refused to decide whether, as a matter of principle, commercial advertising came within the scope of Article 10 (at para. 42). They went on to find that the restrictions placed on Mr Barthold, while pursing the legitimate aim of 'protecting the rights of others' (at para. 51), were not 'necessary in a democratic society' because they were so strict as not to be proportionate (at paras 52–59). The Court invoked the fear of the chilling effect when it stated that the very strict rules risked discouraging members of liberal professions from contributing to public debate on topics of public interest, as such comment might be treated as entailing (to some degree) an advertising effect (at para. 58). Judge Pettiti's

---

[2] Joint Dissenting Opinion of Judges Golcuklu, Pettit, Russo, Speilmann, De Meyer, Carrillo Salcedo and Valticos.

concurring opinion went further in discussing commercial advertising by the liberal professions, and drew on US jurisprudence to support the general proposition that:

> Freedom of expression in its true dimension is the right to receive and to impart information and ideas. Commercial speech is directly connected with that freedom ... Even if it were to be conceded that the state's power to regulate is capable of being more extensive in relation to commercial advertising, in my view it nevertheless remains the case that 'commercial speech' is included within the sphere of freedom of expression. (at pp. 407–8)[3]

In *Casado Coca* v *Spain* (1994) 18 EHRR 1, the Court had to examine a near absolute ban on lawyers advertising.[4] The applicant placed an advert in a local newspaper containing only neutral factual information, such as name, address and telephone number. There was nothing in the advert that was untrue, offensive or misleading. Neither did the advertisement criticise any fellow members of the Bar. However, contrary to the Commission's opinion, the Court concluded that there was no violation of Article 10 ECHR. The Commission took the view that the near absolute ban on factual advertising was excessive and not necessary in a democratic society. The Commission opined that such a ban infringed not only the rights of the applicant, but also the public's right to receive information. The Court again took refuge in the doctrine of margin of appreciation and concluded by a majority of 7:2 that there was no violation of Article 10. Factors that led the Court to reach this view included the limited nature of the sanction, the lack of consensus on legal advertising throughout Europe and the complexity of the issue (at paras 54–55).

In *Colman* v *United Kingdom* (App. No. 16632/90), the Commission considered the complete ban on advertising by general practitioners which existed, in the UK, prior to the relaxation of rules in May 1990. The Commission concluded that the application was admissible, but before the Court could consider the case it was struck out as a result of a friendly statement, whereby the Government made no admission as to a breach of the Convention but agreed to pay the applicant £12,500.

In *Lindner* v *Germany* (App. No. 32813/96, 9 March 1999) the Court had to consider disciplinary action taken against a German lawyer for advertising contrary to the rules of his profession. In concluding that the application was inadmissible, the Court said:

---

[3] Judge Pettiti cited various US judgments, including *Virginia State Board of Pharmacy* v *Virginia Citizens Consumer Council* 425 US 748 (1976) and *Bates* v *Bar of Arizona* 433 US 350 (1977).

[4] Advertising was permitted in certain, very limited circumstances, namely when a practice was being set up or if there was a change of membership, address or telephone number.

... for the citizen advertising is a means of discovering the characteristics of services and goods offered to him. Nevertheless, it may sometimes be restricted especially to prevent unfair competition and untruthful or misleading advertising. In some contexts, the publication of even objective, truthful advertisements might be restricted in order to ensure respect for the rights of others or owing to special circumstances of particular business activities and professions. Any such restrictions must however be closely scrutinised by the Court, which must weigh the particular requirements of those particular features against the advertising in question. To this end the Court must look at the impugned penalty in the light of the case as a whole.

The Court recognised that the regulation of professional advertising was in a state of flux in the member states of the Council of Europe and that there was a wide range of regulations in member states. However, it saw this as further reason for allowing member states a wider margin of appreciation and, especially in light of the modest penalty imposed on the applicant, did not find the restriction disproportionate in the applicant's case.

12.2.3   Commercial speech critical of competitors or products

In *Jacubowski* v *Germany* (1994) 19 EHRR 64, the applicant had been dismissed as an editor of a news agency which issued a press release questioning the applicant's abilities. The applicant, who was planning to set up on his own, was restrained by injunction from sending a mailing to journalists containing newspaper articles critical of his former employer and a letter offering to meet with them to discuss future developments in the media market. The applicant contended that the injunction violated his right to freedom of expression. The Commission unanimously found a violation of Article 10 ECHR. However, yet again the Court adopted a more deferential approach and concluded, by a majority, that there was no violation having recourse to the margin of appreciation. The Court concluded that the injunction banning the distribution of the circular was not disproportionate because the applicant was still permitted to criticise the news agency. As the applicant's circular merely approved and set out passages of various newspaper articles which were already in the public domain, it is hard to agree with the majority decision. The German Court yet again analysed the matters as unfair competition rather than as relating to the right of freedom of expression, and the European Court refused to criticise such an approach. This conclusion is particularly surprising given the circumstances of the circular, where the applicant had been publicly criticised by the news agency.

In *Hertel* v *Switzerland* (1998) 28 EHRR 534 the Court considered an injunction obtained by the Swiss Association of Manufacturers and Suppliers of Household Electrical Appliances under the Swiss Federal Unfair Competition Act 1986, prohibiting the applicant from stating, *inter alia*, that food prepared in microwave ovens was a danger to human health. The applicant, a scientist, had published a research paper in which he concluded that food prepared in microwave ovens 'may' be damaging to human health. The domestic court concluded that the applicant's article unfairly denigrated goods of others by making 'inaccurate, misleading or unnecessarily wounding statements'. The European Court treated the expression in question as concerning a matter of public interest, namely the effects of microwaves on health, rather than as merely commercial speech. This led the Court to apply a more rigorous test of the necessity of the interference, and it concluded that the injunction violated the applicant's right to freedom of expression because it was disproportionate and therefore not 'necessary in a democratic society'. The fact that the applicant's opinion was a minority one, possibly devoid of merit, was immaterial because the right to freedom of expression is not limited to widely held opinions.

12.2.4 Political advertising

Unfortunately, there is, at present, no substantive case law on this issue. In *Amnesty International (United Kingdom)* v *United Kingdom* (App. No. 38383/97, 18 January 2000), the applicants were prevented by s. 92(2)(a) of the Broadcasting Act 1990 from advertising on the radio in order to raise awareness in the United Kingdom of human rights violations in Rwanda and Burundi. The statutory provision in question provided that licensed radio services must not include 'any advertisement which is inserted by or on behalf of any body whose objects are wholly or mainly of a political nature'. The Radio Authority initially refused to grant an advertising licence. This refusal was unsuccessfully challenged in the domestic courts (*R* v *Radio Authority, ex parte Bull* [1998] QB 294 (CA)) and this lead to an application to the European Court. However, before the Court ruled on the admissibility of the application, the Radio Authority reversed its decision and allowed the applicants to advertise. As a result of this reversal the application was struck out without any consideration of the substantive arguments advanced under Articles 10 and 14 ECHR.

This lack of consideration will be remedied when the Court hears the case of *VgT Vereingegen Tierfabriken* v *Switzerland* (App. No. 24699/94), which concerns the refusal of commercial television companies to broadcast an advertisement from an animal welfare group exhorting the viewers to 'eat less meat, for the sake of your health, the animals and the environment'. The refusal was on the basis that the commercial in question was of a 'clear political character'. The Court, without a detailed examination of the arguments advanced under Articles 10 and 14, concluded that the complaint raises serious issues of law and fact and declared it admissible. If the applicants are successful in their argument either that the prohibition on political advertising on television is contrary to Article 10, or that the present Swiss domestic regime (which permits advertising by the meat industry encouraging meat consumption but does not permit advertising by groups advocating less meat consumption) is discriminatory under Article 10 read with Article 14, this will have a profound impact on UK advertising law. Given that the expression in question concerns matters that are undisputably of public concern, it is likely that the Court will apply the more rigorous scrutiny it adopted in *Hertel* and *Barthold* rather than the very deferential approach typified by *Markt Intern* and *Casado Coca*. However, the existence of bans on political advertising on television in a number of member states (including the United Kingdom) may lead the Court to conclude that the ban is within the state's margin of appreciation.

12.2.5   Speech by commercial organisations on matters of public concern

Although not strictly within the definition of 'commercial speech' set out at the beginning of this chapter, the decision in *Open Door Counselling and Dublin Well Woman* v *Ireland* (1992) 15 EHRR 245 is likely to be of relevance in the commercial expression field, particularly when restrictions on truthful advertising are in issue.[5] Open Door Counselling and Dublin Well Woman were Irish organisations that provided non-directive counselling to pregnant women. This counselling included the provision of information about abortion facilities outside Ireland, including their addresses and telephone numbers. The Society for the Protection of the Unborn Child obtained a permanent injunction preventing staff at the clinics from providing such information to pregnant women.

The Court concluded by a majority of 15:8 that the permanent injunction was a violation of Article 10 ECHR. The majority thought that while the Irish state had a legitimate interest in protecting the right to life of the unborn child,[6] this interest did not grant the state an unfettered and unreviewable power to act to protect this interest. While the Irish state enjoyed a considerable margin of appreciation in relation to this type of expression, this margin was not unlimited and measures were not automatically justified where the right to life of the unborn child is at stake. The Court concluded that the expression in question was subject to protection under Article 10 ECHR and that the absolute nature of the injunction was such that it was disproportionate. The Court stated that although the information in question was likely to offend, shock and disturb a significant proportion of the Irish population, this was not sufficient grounds for restricting it, particularly when the expression in question was limited to factual and truthful statements on services which were lawful in other Convention countries and might be crucial to a woman's health and well-being. The Court, in reaching its

---

[5] See 12.3.3 below in relation to tobacco advertising.

[6] Article 40(3) of the Irish Constitution (the Eighth Amendment), which came into force in 1983, provides: 'The State acknowledges the right to life of the unborn and, with due regard to the equal right to life of the mother, guarantees in its laws to respect, and, as far as practicable, by its laws to defend and vindicate that right.'

decision, further noted that it was not a criminal offence under Irish law for a pregnant woman to travel abroad in order to have an abortion.

12.3 THE LIKELY IMPACT OF THE HRA ON DOMESTIC LAW

12.3.1 Misleading, false and deceptive advertising

Bans or other restrictions on misleading or inaccurate advertising will be unaffected by the HRA 1998. There have already been decisions of the Administrative Court upholding as compatible with Article 10 adjudications of the Advertising Standards Authority that its Code had been violated (see *R v Advertising Standards Authority, ex parte Matthias Rath BV* (2001) *The Times*, 10 January and *Smith Kline Beecham plc* v *Advertising Standards Authority*, 17 January 2001). The Commission has made it clear that such restrictions are permissible to protect the rights of consumers (see *K* v *Federal Republic of Germany* (App. No. 17006/90, 2 July 1991)). This, not unsurprisingly, accords with the position in the USA (see, e.g., *Central Hudson Gas* v *Public Services Commission* 447 US 557 (1980)). Restrictions and prohibitions on advertising of illegal activities, such as the sale of narcotics, will also be unaffected by the 1998 Act. Thus the prohibition of job advertisements that discriminate on the grounds of sex or race will survive challenge (see *Pittsburgh Press Co.* v *The Pittsburgh Commission on Human Relations* 413 US 3376 (1973)).

12.3.2 Truthful advertising

Restrictions on truthful advertising of commercial products are likely at least to raise Convention issues. One of the most controversial areas of product advertising concerns tobacco. In Canada, a challenge to various provisions concerning tobacco advertising and unattributed health warnings was held not to be justifiable since it was an unreasonable restriction on the tobacco company's right to freedom of expression (*RJR Macdonald* v *Attorney-General of Canada* (1995) 127 DLR (4th) 1). The majority of the Canadian Supreme Court took a far more rigorous approach than is usually taken by the European Court of Human Rights and concluded that the state had failed to demonstrate that less restrictive measures would not have achieved the same legitimate aim. Thus, for example, the Government adduced no evidence that a partial ban on advertising would have been less effective than a total ban. A similar approach has been taken by the US Supreme Court in relation to restrictions on advertising of alcohol products (see, e.g., *Rubin* v *Coors Brewing Co.* 115 S Ct 1585 (1995) (Supreme Court declared unconstitutional a federal law that prohibited beer labels from stating the alcohol content of the product) and *44 Liquormart Inc.* v *Rhode Island* 116 S Ct 1495 (1996) (Supreme Court declared unconstitutional a state law that prohibited price advertising of alcoholic beverages), although not advertising of lawful gambling (see *Posadas de Puerto Rico Associates* v *Tourism Company of Puerto Rico* 478 US 328 (1986)).

12.3.3 Tobacco advertising

In Europe, the Council of the EU issued a Directive (98/43/EC) on the approximation of the laws, regulations and administrative provisions relating to the advertising and sponsorship of tobacco products. The Directive prohibited all forms of advertising and sponsorship of tobacco products except at the point of sale. It also prohibited the future use of tobacco product names for non-tobacco goods and, vice versa, the use of non-tobacco product names in connection with tobacco goods. The Council relied on Treaty powers of the EU to take measures for the establishment and functioning of the internal market and the protection of the freedom to provide goods and services. In a challenge to the validity of the Directive, both the Advocate-General and the European Court of Justice found that the Directive could not be justified by the Treaty provisions on which the Council had relied, and the measure was therefore annulled for these reasons (*Germany* v *European Parliament* (Case C-376/98); *R* v *Secretary of State for Health, ex parte Imperial Tobacco Ltd* (Case C-74/99) [2000] All ER (EC) 769 (ECJ)). However, Advocate-General Fennelly gave extensive consideration to an alternative challenge, that the Directive was invalid because it was contrary to Article 10 ECHR (because the European Court of Justice found the Directive invalid on other grounds it did not consider this challenge). His reasoning is very interesting.

The European Court of Justice is guided by general principles of Community law. These include the protection of fundamental rights including freedom of expression (*Elleniki Radiophonia Tileoraissi AE* v *Pliroforissis* (Case C-260/89) [1991] ECR I-2925, at para. 44; *Vereinigte Familiapress Zeitungsverlags-und vertriebs GmbH* v *Heinrich Bauer Verlag* (Case C-368/95) [1997] ECR I-3689, at para. 25), and in determining the range of these rights the ECHR has special significance as a source of inspiration. Freedom of expression includes commercial speech. Although this did not have the same value of enhancing democratic debate as did political speech, it was still to be protected:

> Thus, individuals' freedom to promote commercial activities derives not only from their right to engage in economic activities and the general commitment, in the Community context, to a market economy based upon free competition, but also from their inherent entitlement as human beings freely to express and receive views on any topic, including the merits of the goods or services which they market or purchase. (at para. 154)

Freedom of expression could be curtailed, and one of the permitted aims of restrictions was the protection of health, but because of the fundamental character of freedom of expression, the public interest in the restriction had to be demonstrated by the public authority seeking to impose it.

While restrictions on freedom of expression must normally be justified by showing convincing evidence of a pressing social need, Advocate-General Fennelly saw the Strasbourg Court adopting a different test in relation to restrictions on commercial speech. These would be compatible with Article 10 ECHR if the competent authorities on reasonable grounds considered the restrictions to be necessary (at para. 158, referring to *Markt Intern* and *Groppera Radio*). Thus the Advocate-General applied the same test to the ban on tobacco advertising. It was relevant that the issue was the objective assessment of the likely effects of the ban rather than more nebulous matters such as the protection of morals, but if the Community legislator could show that it acted on the basis of apparently reputable specialist studies, it would not be fatal to the validity of the measure that other reputable studies came to a different conclusion. Here there were studies showing a link between tobacco advertising and the take-up of consumption and which showed the inefficacy of anything other than a total ban on advertising, and the Community did therefore have reasonable grounds to believe that a comprehensive ban on tobacco advertising would result in a significant reduction in consumption and corresponding improvement in public health.

The Advocate-General accepted that a total ban on advertising was a particularly grave intrusion on the exercise of freedom of expression and called for particular scrutiny, but the Community had satisfied this test by its evidence that partial bans were ineffective (at para. 164). The studies showed a potential drop in consumption of about 6.9 per cent. Because of the significant effects of tobacco on health, this meant that the restriction on freedom of expression could not be characterised as disproportionate. The Advocate-General noted that smoking itself was not illegal (and therefore the ban prevented the promotion of a product which could be lawfully sold), but he looked to the *RJR Macdonald* case in the Canadian Supreme Court (see 12.3.2) to take judicial notice of the practical problems of trying to ban smoking itself. He also contrasted the *Open Door Counselling* case, in part because of its 'extremely difficult and sensitive context' (no doubt a reference to the abortion issue) and in part because the case related to the non-directive supply of information rather than to the commercial promotion of abortion (at para. 74, referring to *Open Door* (see 12.2.5 above) at para. 75). Thus the Advocate-General would not have struck down the tobacco advertising ban as disproportionate. He would, though, have taken a different view about the cross-branding prohibitions in the Directive. The justifications for these restrictions were not supported by evidence, and he would have annulled these parts additionally because of their conflict with the freedom of commercial expression (at para. 176).

12.3.4   Advertising directed at vulnerable groups such as children

Restrictions designed to protect vulnerable groups such as children are likely to treated with a degree of deference. The Canadian Supreme Court upheld a Quebec law prohibiting advertising direct to children under the age of 13 (*Irwin Toy* v *Quebec* [1989] 1 SCR 927). The English law regulating such advertising to children merely places limits on the type of advertising rather than a complete ban. As such, English law is likely to be held to be lawful as it is proportionate to the legitimate aim of protecting vulnerable consumers such as children.

12.3.5   Political advertising

Both the Radio Authority's advertising code and the Independent Television Commission's advertising code prohibit political advertisements (except for party political broadcasts).[7] Non-broadcast political advertising, such as billboards, is permitted and is subject to far laxer controls than other forms of advertising. The ban on radio and television advertisements political nature and advertisements which are directed towards a political end. In addition to the ban of Amnesty International discussed at 12.2.4 above, other advertisements that have run into difficulty as a result of their political content include advertisements by Christian Aid and Jubilee 2000. The Index on Censorship has also had advertisements banned. No doubt, the prohibitions on political advertising on radio and televison will be the subject of further challenges in the British courts. The European Court's forthcoming decision in *VgT Vereingegen Tierfabriken* v *Switzerland* (App. No. 24699/94) will provide a strong indication as to the likelihood of success of such challenges.

12.3.6   Public expression of professionals

Many professions place restrictions on what their members can say in public. Such restrictions are likely to be the subject of challenge. One example of restrictions on professionals' speech in the UK is the Bar Code of Conduct, which prohibits barristers from commenting in any news or current affairs media on current matters on which they have been briefed.[8] No such restriction applies to solicitors (including solicitor-advocates). If the restriction were challenged, the Bar Council might well be in difficulty justifying the ban as it is arguably disproportionate. Such a restriction is at risk on the grounds that if solicitor-advocates can comment on matters on which they are briefed, it is not necessary in a democratic society to have a blanket ban on barristers who are performing the same function.

---

[7] See Radio Authority's Advertising Code, r. 9, and the Independent Television Commission's Advertising Code, r. 10.
[8] See Bar Code of Conduct 1998, 'Media Comment', at para. 604.

12.3.7 Advertising by professionals

While the Court's judgment in *Casado Coca* v *Spain* (1994) 18 EHRR 1 (see 12.2.2 above) would appear to indicate that broad restrictions will be immune from challenge this judgment should be treated with caution because the reasoning in the case was based in large part on the fact that bans on advertising by lawyers were imposed by most contracting states. The recent relaxation of the rules on advertising by lawyers throughout the Council of Europe states[9] could mean that the same decision would not be reached today. Furthermore, domestic courts are likely to apply a more rigorous scrutiny because of the inapplicability of the doctrine of 'margin of appreciation'. Support for this view can be gained from the jurisprudence of the Canadian Supreme Court, which has struck down a regulation of the dentists' profession prohibiting dentists from advertising their services, with only minor exceptions such as business cards and exterior signs (*Rocket* v *Royal College of Dental Surgeons* [1990] 1 SCR 232).

---

[9] See Ryssdal, R., (President of the European Court of Human Rights), *The Case Law of the European Court of Human Rights on the Freedom of Expression Guaranteed under the European Convention of Human Rights* (1996).

Chapter Thirteen

Official Secrets, National Security and Public Disorder

13.1 INTRODUCTION

In a wide range of fields, including that of freedom of expression, English courts have refused to scrutinise, in any serious manner, claims by the British government that national security would be imperilled by the exercise of an individual's rights. Thus the House of Lords found in *Council of Civil Service Unions* v *Minister for the Civil Service* [1985] AC 374, that the government's assertion of national security overrode the legitimate expectation which trade unions would otherwise have had, to be consulted. English courts have also exhibited reticence to examine national security issues in immigration cases involving Gulf War detainees (*R* v *Secretary of State for the Home Department, ex parte Cheblak* [1991] 1 WLR 890) and those allegedly involved in international terrorism (*R* v *Secretary of State for the Home Department, ex parte Chahal* [1994] Imm AR 107; the UK Government was later to be found to have acted contrary to the ECHR in *Chahal* v *UK* (1996) 23 EHRR 413). The most notorious example of judicial deference occurred in the *Spycatcher* litigation, where a bitterly divided House of Lords, in a decision defying common sense, upheld interlocutory injunctions against newspapers which had wanted to publish information and extracts from *Spycatcher*, even though, by this time, the book had been published and was widely available in a number of countries including the United States.

This overly deferential approach can be contrasted with that taken by the European Court which, while recognising that states have a margin of appreciation which is relatively broad in the field of national security, has been more willing to scrutinise actions of governments who have invoked the protection of national security. (See, e.g., *Guardian and Observer* v *United Kingdom* (1991) 14 EHRR 153, discussed at 13.2.2 below.)

There are signs that some English judges are losing some of their deference to the government in matters of national security, perhaps as a result of the more robust European jurisprudence. In the recent decision of *R* v *Central Criminal Court, ex parte The Guardian, The Observer and Martin Bright* [2000] UKHRR 796, the Divisional Court allowed, in part, a judicial review against orders requiring newspapers and journalists to disclose certain material relating to communications with former MI5 agent David Shayler. Judge LJ stated:

> Inconvenient or embarrassing revelations whether for the security services of for public authorities, should not be suppressed. Legal proceedings directed towards the seizure of the working papers of individual journalists, or the premises of the newspaper or television programme publishing his or her report, or the threat of such proceedings tends to inhibit discussion. When a genuine investigation into possible corrupt or reprehensible activities by a public authority is being investigated by the media, compelling evidence would normally be needed to demonstrate that the public interest will be served by such proceedings. Otherwise, to the public's disadvantage, legitimate enquiry and discussion and 'the safety valve of effective journalism' would be discouraged, perhaps stifled.

13.2   ECHR CASE LAW

13.2.1   National security: general principle

As in other areas, the Court has taken a broad approach to the existence of an 'interference by the public authority' with the right to freedom of expression. Interferences have included interlocutory injunctions (e.g., *Guardian and Observer* v *United Kingdom* (1991) 14 EHRR 153), arrest and conviction followed by fines and/or imprisonment (e.g., *Hadjianastassiou* v *Greece* (1992) 16 EHRR 219). The Court concluded that the refusal of the military authorities to distribute a particular magazine to their soldiers while distributing other magazines was also an interference (*Vereinigung Demokratischer Soldaten Österreichs and Gubi* v *Austria* (1994) 20 EHRR 56). It has also taken a generous approach to the issue of who benefits from the right to freedom of expression, concluding that it extends to members of the armed forces (e.g., *Engel and others* v *Netherlands* (1976) 1 EHRR 647 and *Hadjianastassiou* v *Greece*) and civil servants (e.g., *Vogt* v *Germany* (1995) 21 EHRR 205). Similarly, 'information and ideas' is also unqualified and extends to military secrets concerning the design and production of a guided missile (*Hadjianastassiou* v *Greece*).

Article 10(2) ECHR, which sets out possible legitimate aims, includes 'the interests of national security', 'territorial integrity' and the 'prevention of disorder'. The Court has not gone behind government assertions as to the legitimate aims. While this approach is not surprising, it is disappointing. For example, in *Observer and Guardian* v *United Kingdom* (1991) 14 EHRR 153, it is hard to see how the interlocutory injunction furthered the interests of national security when the book in question could be read in Australia, the United States, and no doubt the Soviet Union. A rather more searching attitude was taken by a minority of the Court in a case concerning the retention of stale intelligence data by security services. In *Rotaru* v *Romania*, 4 May 2000, seven judges said that they found it hard to see how the collection of data relating to a boy and a student going back more than 50 years (and in one case 63 years), which were demonstrably false, could be said to be justified on grounds of national security. The case concerned a violation of Article 8 ECHR, but, as we have seen, there are clear parallels between the structures of the two provisions.

13.2.2   Publication or disclosure of secret information

The applicants in the companion cases of *Observer and Guardian* v *United Kingdom* (1991) 14 EHRR 153 and *Sunday Times* v *United Kingdom (No. 2)* (1991) 14 EHRR 229, contested interlocutory injunctions preventing further publication of material emanating from Mr Peter Wright's book, *Spycatcher*. Mr Wright's memoirs detailed his time in MI5 and the alleged misdeeds of the security service. After the *Observer* and the *Guardian* had published two short articles detailing the working of the security services, the government alleged, and Millett J inferred, on the balance of probabilities, that the journalists' sources must have come from the offices of the publishers of *Spycatcher* or the solicitors acting for them and the author. On this basis, Millett J granted an interlocutory injunction to restrain any further breaches of confidence, preventing the newspapers from publishing any *Spycatcher* material.

Millett J's judgment was upheld by a majority in the House of Lords. This interlocutory injunction was intended to be temporary, but continued from 11 July 1986 until 13 October 1988 when Scott J, after a trial of the substantive issues, refused to grant a permanent injunction. The newspapers applied to the European Court, alleging that the injunction violated their right to freedom of expression under Article 10 ECHR. Neither the existence of an interference nor the issue of whether the interference was prescribed by law was disputed. The government asserted two legitimate aims: (i) maintaining the authority of the judiciary; and (ii) protecting national security.

The Court accepted both these legitimate aims (at paras 55–57). 'Maintaining the authority of the judiciary' included protecting the rights of litigants. The Court agreed that the purpose of the injunction was to secure the right of the Attorney-General as a litigant.

In relation to the 'interests of national security', the government, before the domestic courts, had contended that disclosure of the information would cause damage to the security services. By the time the case reached the House of Lords, *Spycatcher* had been published in the various countries, including the United States. The government's national security argument underwent what was described by Scott J as a 'curious metamorphosis' (*Attorney-General* v *Guardian Newspapers (No. 2)* [1990] 1 AC 109 at 140 F). From initially seeking to preserve the character of information that ought to be kept secret, the government's national security objective became confined to the promotion of the efficiency and reputation of the security service, notably by: (i) preserving confidence in that service on the part of third parties; (ii) making it clear that the unauthorised publication of memoirs by its former members would not be countenanced; and (iii) deterring others from following in Mr Wright's footsteps ((1991) 14 EHRR 153, at para. 69).

The European Court, disappointingly, accepted that this new aim was within the ambit of protecting the interests of national security. However, the Court unanimously went on to find that the continuation of the injunction from 30 July 1987 to 13 October 1988 was a violation of Article 10 ECHR, because during this period the publication of the book began in the USA, after which it could not be said to be confidential. From that point onwards the interlocutory injunction was disproportionate. The Court rejected the government's argument that the redefined interests of national security were sufficient to justify the continuation of the injunction. The Court decided that the injunction arguably failed to advance the government's stated objectives and, furthermore, the government had other remedies such as an action for an account of profits.[1]

The Court was split as to whether there was a violation of Article 10 ECHR during the period 11 July 1986 to 30 July 1987. A bare majority concluded that there was no violation during this period because, prior to publication in the USA, the injunction was proportionate to the legitimate aim and therefore 'necessary in a democratic society' (at paras 62–64). It was influenced by the fact that the injunction was not a blanket prohibition: while it forbade the publication of information derived from or attributed to Mr Wright in his capacity as a member of the security service, it did not prevent the applicants from campaigning for an independent inquiry into that service. Additionally, the injunction contained provisos excluding certain material from their scope, particularly material that had been previously published by other authors (at para. 64).

Ten judges dissented from this conclusion and thought that there was a violation of Article 10 from the date of Millett J's granting of the interlocutory injunction. The dissenting judges differed in their reasons for this conclusion: some[2] placed

---

[1] The United states Supreme Court has held that such a remedy did not violate the First Amendment, see *Snepp* v *United States* 444 US 507 (1980). This conclusion was reached on the basis that the book in question, *Decent Interval*, by former CIA operative Frank Snepp, contained no classified material.

[2] See partly Dissenting Opinion of Judge Pettiti joined by Judge Pinheiro Farinha, at 200.

emphasis on the public's right to receive information (which the majority did not address) and concluded that an interim injunction, not subsequently lifted after a short period, was 'in effect a disguised means of instituting censure or restraint on the freedom of the press' (at 201); while others objected to the injunction because it was an impermissible prior restraint.[3]

The latter dissent quoted with approval the following statement of Justice Black (joined by Justice Douglas) in the US Supreme Court decision of *New York Times* v *US* and *Washington Post* v *US* 403 US 713 (1971), at 717: 'I firmly believe that "the press must be left free to publish news, whatever the source, without censorship, injunctions, or prior restraint".'

One year later, in *Hadjianastassiou* v *Greece* (1992) 16 EHRR 219, the Court considered an application by an Air Force officer in charge of a project to design and produce a guided missile. The applicant was charged, convicted and sentenced to imprisonment by a military court for disclosing military secrets by selling information from his work on the guided missile project to a private company. While the Court concluded that the court martial was insufficient to provide a fair trial, it unanimously rejected the applicant's claim under Article 10 ECHR. The information was of minor importance and there was a dispute as to whether it was available in unrestricted scientific literature. The state's interest in a particular weapon's system and the state of its progress in manufacture were also legitimate matters to be kept secret. It is important to recognise that the disclosure had been to a private company in return for payment. The applicant's reason for making the disclosure was commercial and, while Article 10 clearly applies to such communications, there was no public interest in disclosure to set against the state's interest.

The third case involving disclosure of secret material concerned a Dutch weekly magazine called *Bluf* (*Vereinging Weekblad Bluf!* v *Netherlands* (1995) 20 EHRR 189). The magazine obtained a report produced by the Dutch security services which showed their interest in the Dutch Communist Party and the anti-nuclear movement. It also gave information about the Polish, Czech and Romanian security services' activities in The Netherlands. The report was six years old and marked 'confidential' (the lowest classification). The magazine proposed to publish the report as a supplement, but before distribution could take place the entire print run was seized by the police. That night the magazine's staff reprinted the issue and sold 2,500 copies on the streets of Amsterdam. Several months later the authorities obtained an order that the issue be withdrawn from circulation. The European Court, adopting a similar approach to that in *Observer and Guardian*, found that the withdrawal order infringed Article 10 ECHR, in part because of the circulation which the reprinted edition had received which meant that the further restrictions were not 'necessary in a democratic society'. While

---

[3] See partly Dissenting Opinion of Judge de Meyer joined by Judges Pettiti, Russo, Foighel and Bigi.

Spycatcher had sold over a million copies as a result of the United states publication, the Court applied the same principles to a far more modest distribution. Not surprisingly, the Dutch government had argued that the distribution had been effected by the magazine itself and it was objectionable to allow the applicant to rely on the publicity achieved by its own wrong. The Court was unmoved by this argument and concluded that it could not make 'necessary' a restriction which had been rendered moot by the *de facto* publicity that the magazine had already received. What was important was the actual state of public knowledge at the time that the restriction was imposed. In this respect the Court followed its approach in *Weber* v *Switzerland* (1990) 12 EHRR 508, discussed at 9.6.9. In the age of the Internet, this feature of the Court's reasoning is likely to be particularly important. States will have considerable practical difficulty in preventing rapid, widespread dissemination of information.

13.2.3 Suppression of speech that threatens public order

In *Arrowsmith* v *United Kingdom* (1978) 3 EHRR 218, an early decision of the Commission, the applicant, a pacifist, failed in her contention that her conviction under ss. 1 and 2 of the Incitement to Disaffection Act 1934, for distributing leaflets to soldiers encouraging them to go absent without leave or refuse to serve in Northern Ireland, was contrary to Article 10 ECHR. The Commission accepted that the interference pursued a legitimate aim, namely the protection of national security (by preventing the weakening of the armed forces) and prevention of disorder in the armed forces. The applicant, relying on US Supreme Court jurisprudence (see Justice Holmes' dissent in *Abrams* v *US* 250 US 616 (1919), at 624), sought to argue that the conviction was disproportionate and unnecessary as there was no 'clear and present danger' that the expression would bring about the substantive evils that Parliament had a right to prevent. The Court rejected this more stringent test and concluded that the conviction and sentence to nine months' imprisonment were proportionate and 'necessary in a democratic society'. The Commission's decision in *Arrowsmith* was disappointing and rightly criticised in two dissenting opinions, because the government failed to adduce any evidence at all of the threat to national security posed by the applicant's unpopular political expression.[4]

The Court adopted an equally weak approach in *Chorherr* v *Austria* (1993) 17 EHRR 358, which concerned the arrest of the applicant for mounting a peaceful demonstration against the purchase of military aircraft during a military ceremony. The police asked the applicant to cease demonstrating, and when he refused he was arrested. The Court, by six votes to three, considered that the arrest was to prevent disorder and that it was proportionate, taking into account the

---

[4] This criticism was repeated in the dissenting judgment of Judge Walsh in *Observer and Guardian* v *UK*.

circumstances of the case and the state's margin of appreciation. The Austrian Government failed to produce evidence that there was a real likelihood of disorder if the applicant had been permitted to carry on peacefully demonstrating, but this absence of evidence again failed to trouble the majority of the Court.

There is a lot to be said for a more rigorous approach when courts are faced with expression that is alleged to be likely to cause disorder.[5] Governments tend to invoke such arguments when faced with expression that is inconvenient and unpopular. The US Supreme Court jurisprudence has progressed beyond the 'clear and present danger' discussed above in relation to *Arrowsmith* v *United Kingdom. Brandenburg* v *Ohio* 395 US 444 (1969) provides a statement of the current test in US law. The court in *Brandenburg* stated:

> ... the constitutional guarantees of free speech and free press do not permit a state to forbid or proscribe advocacy of the use of force or of law violation except where such advocacy is directed to inciting or producing imminent lawless action and is likely to incite or produce such action. (at 447)

This test, which requires evidence from the government that the speech in question is likely to produce lawless action,[6] is in our view preferable to the approach taken by the European Court and Commission. In both *Arrowsmith* and *Chorherr*, the application of this test would have led to a finding that the state's actions violated Article 10 ECHR. It is to be hoped that English courts follow this robust approach rather than the weak and overly deferential approach of the Strasbourg institutions.

13.2.4 Suppression of speech that threatens national security or the territorial integrity of the state

In *Piermont* v *France* (1995) 20 EHRR 301, the applicant, a Member of the European Parliament, was expelled pursuant to an administrative order from French territories in the South Pacific. The Court accepted that France was pursuing the legitimate aims of preventing disorder and maintaining territorial integrity, but concluded that the orders were not necessary in a democratic society.

The Commission has taken a cautious approach in its reviews of the broadcasting bans imposed by the United Kingdom and Irish governments. Both restricted the broadcasting of words spoken by members or supporters of specified

---

[5] This more rigorous test is equally applicable to speech that threatens national security or the territorial integrity of a state; see 13.2.4 below.

[6] The *Brandenburg* test was endorsed by a panel of media and human rights experts in 'The Johannesburg Principles, National Security, Freedom of expression and access to information'. See Coliver, S. et al (eds), *Secrecy and Liberty: National Security, Freedom of Expression and Access to Information* (The Hague, Netherlands, Martinus Nijhoff, 1999).

groups (although the British ban permitted others, such as actors or newscasters, to give voice to the words which the members or supporters could only silently mouth). Furthermore, this restriction did not apply to Sinn Fein candidates during elections. The affected groups included not only terrorist organisations, but also Sinn Fein (which was not a proscribed organisation but an elected political party). None of the United Kingdom broadcasters challenged the ban, but its legality was tested by journalists. They were unsuccessful in the House of Lords (*R* v *Secretary of State for the Home Department, ex parte Brind* [1991] 1 AC 696). The Commission accepted that the measure constituted an interference with the applicant's freedom of expression, although only of a limited kind. The limited nature of the interference was an important factor in the Commission's decision that the ban did not exceed the margin of appreciation which the Convention gave to a state fighting terrorism (*Brind* v *United Kingdom* (App. No. 18714/91) (1994) 77 DR 42; see also *Purcell* v *Ireland* (1991) 70 DR 262).

Recently, the Court handed down a large number of cases against Turkey involving Article 10.[7] These cases arose out of criminal proceedings taken against expression concerning the Kurdish conflict in Eastern Turkey. The convictions of the various applicants were for expression, both written and spoken, held by the Turkish courts to contain separatist propaganda against the Turkish nation and the territorial integrity of the state, or intended to undermine patriotic sentiment and incite hostility and hatred by making distinctions based on ethnic or regional origin or social class. The Court subjected the convictions to close scrutiny. It noted the political situation and tensions in Turkey, but as the speech was political or on matters of public concern there was little scope under Article 10(2). In each case, the European Court analysed the substance and nature of the expression in question, in light of the tense situation in Turkey, when deciding whether the interference was proportionate. Violations of Article 10 were found in 11 out of the 13 cases. The only two cases in which the Court concluded that the conviction was necessary in a democratic society, were *Surek* v *Turkey (No. 1)* and *Surek* v *Turkey (No. 3)*, 8 July 1999. *Surek (No. 1)* concerned the publication of two letters in the applicant's newspaper, while *Surek (No. 3)* concerned an article which called for the use of armed force as a means to achieve national independence for Kurdistan. The Istanbul National Security Court concluded that both the letters and the article contained words which were aimed at the destruction of the territorial integrity of the Turkish state by describing areas of south-east Turkey as an independent state ('Kurdistan') and the PKK as a national liberation movement. The National Security Court further concluded that the letters and article incited violence against an individual, public official and a sector of the

---

[7] The Court handed down 13 cases on 8 July 1999: *Surek* v *Turkey Nos 1, 2, 3 and 4, Tanrikulu* v *Turkey, Cakici* v *Turkey, Karatas* v *Turkey, Polat* v *Turkey, Arslan* v *Turkey, Ceylan* v *Turkey, Okcuoglu* v *Turkey, Gerger* v *Turkey, Erdogdu and Ince* v *Turkey and Baskaya* and *Okcuoglu* v *Turkey.*

population. The majority of the European Court accepted this analysis and granted Turkey a wider margin of appreciation as a result. The majority concluded that the letters and article did incite hatred, and therefore the state's response was proportionate and 'necessary in a democratic society'. The dissenting judges criticised the test applied by the majority in the 13 Turkish cases, namely: 'If the writings published by the applicant supported or instigated the use of violence, then his conviction by the national courts was justifiable in a democratic society.' (*Surek (No. 1)*, at para. 25; *Surek (No. 3)*, at para. 16.) Judge Bonello rejected this yardstick as insufficient and suggested that the test should be similar to the US 'clear and present danger' test (see *Abrams* v *US*, at 13.2.3 above). While a more rigorous test is to be welcomed, we would suggest that the test enunciated in *Brandenburg* v *Ohio* (see 13.2.3), is superior to Justice Holmes' clear and present danger test.[8]

13.3 THE LIKELY IMPACT OF THE HRA ON DOMESTIC LAW

13.3.1 The criminal law

English law protecting national security has improved since the repeal of s. 2 of the Official Secrets Act 1911, although the statute that replaced this enactment, the Official Secrets Act 1989, is not the 'great liberalising measure' it was claimed to be at the time.[9] Section 1 of the Official Secrets Act 1911 is over-broad, and while convictions for espionage are likely to survive scrutiny (see *Hadjianastassiou* v *Greece* (1992) 16 EHRR 219, at 13.2.1 above), prosecutions of journalists and perhaps of former members of the security services who disclose details of incompetence and illegality by government employees may well fall foul of Article 10 because, in reality, the reason for bringing the prosecution is to prevent government embarrassment rather than to protect national security.

Although narrower in scope than s. 2 of the Official Secrets Act 1911, the 1989 Act is liable to be challenged under the HRA 1998. The offences contained in ss. 1–6 are broadly defined. For example, s. 1(1) criminalises unauthorised disclosures by members of the security services. There is no requirement for the Crown to prove any harm or damage. Exposure to liability for this offence can be extended on written notice to others who, though not actually members of the security services, work closely with them (Official Secrets Act 1989, s. 1(1)(b) and (6)). In relation to Crown servants and government contractors who are not members of the security forces and have not been served with written notice, there is a narrower offence of making a *damaging* disclosure of information relating to

---

[8] While Judge Bonello cited *Brandenburg* v *Ohio*, he did not appear to consider it as a development of the 'clear and present danger' test.

[9] Speech by Douglas Hurd, the then Home Secretary, quoted by Shorts, E. and Than, C., *Civil Liberties: Legal Principles of Individual Freedom* (London, Sweet and Maxwell, 1998), at 210.

security or intelligence. 'Damage' is defined as damage to the work of, or any part of, the security and intelligence services (s. 1(4)). It is sufficient that such damage is found to 'be likely to occur' as a result of the disclosure. Further, the prosecution can succeed without proving that the particular information would be likely to cause harm but merely that it is of a class that might have this effect.

Section 5 of the Official Secrets Act 1989 makes it a specific offence for journalists and editors to publish information that they know is protected by the Act, although the prosecution must also prove that they had reason to believe that the publication would be damaging to the security services or to the interests of the United Kingdom. The precise scope of this complex offence is, at present, unclear. For example, it is still not certain whether s. 5 extends to publication of the memoirs of *former* Crown servants. This issue was discussed in the speeches of the House of Lords in *Lord Advocate* v *Scotsman Publications* [1989] 2 All ER 852. Lord Templeman considered that s. 5 did extend to former 'Crown servants', while Lord Jauncey thought that it did not. The HRA 1998 will provide an additional argument in support of Lord Jauncey's restrictive interpretation.

The limited nature of the available defences is also a matter of concern. There is no 'public interest' defence, or a general defence of prior publication. The latter was rejected on the grounds that prior publication would be a factor to be considered in the assessment of whether the disclosure was 'damaging'. It was also contended that further publication could still cause substantial damage, especially if it adds weight to what were originally unsubstantiated rumours.[10] The current prosecution of Mr Shayler a former member of the security services, will provide an early opportunity for the impact of the 1998 Act on the Official Secrets Act 1989 to be explored.

13.3.2 The civil law

The use of injunctions by the state to suppress publication of material that relates to matters of public concern broadly defined, is a further area which may well be affected by the coming into force of the HRA 1998. These prior restraints should be the subject of the most exacting scrutiny because, unlike subsequent punishment for unlawful disclosure, the material in issue never reaches the public. There is much to be said for the US approach in this field, which permits the granting of prior restraints only in the most limited of circumstances. In *Near* v *Minnesota* 283 US 697 (1931), Chief Justice Hughes stated:

> The protection even as to previous restraint is not absolutely unlimited. But the limitation has been recognised only in exceptional cases. No one would question but that a government might prevent actual obstruction to its recruiting service or the publication of the sailing dates of transports or the number and location of troops. (at 716)

---

[10] See *Reform of section 2 of the Official Secrets Act 1911* (Cm 408, 1988), discussed by Shorts and Than, *op. cit.* n. 9, at 216–7.

This approach was further developed in *New York Times* v *US; Washington Post* v *US* 403 US 713 (1971), which is usually known as the *Pentagon Papers* case. The *Pentagon Papers* were a 47-volume secret Pentagon study of the Vietnam War. The study was, according to an affidavit sworn by the general Counsel of the Department of Defense, classified as 'Top Secret-Sensitive'. However, a majority of the Supreme Court held that the government could not restrain the publication of extracts from the work. Justices Black and Douglas thought that prior restraints could never be justified. However, this absolutist view did not command the support of the majority, which held that the Government would have been entitled to injunctions if it could establish that 'disclosure ... will surely result in direct, immediate and irreparable damage to our Nation or its people'.

Such a high burden was not met in relation to the *Pentagon Papers*, which, while containing material highly embarrassing to the United states government and other friendly governments, was largely a historical work and as such did not expose United states troops to danger. This burden recognises the importance of the right to freedom of expression in relation to matters of public concern and requires the courts to scrutinise closely government justifications for seeking an injunction rather than treating such statements at face value. This approach stands in sharp contrast with that of the House of Lords in the *Spycatcher* litigation. Now individuals and media organisations can rely directly on Article 10 ECHR, the courts will not be able to dismiss so lightly arguments in favour of refusing government applications for injunctions.

Appendix One

Human Rights Act 1998

CHAPTER 42

ARRANGEMENT OF SECTIONS

HUMAN RIGHTS ACT 1998

1998 CHAPTER 42

An Act to give further effect to rights and freedoms guaranteed under the European Convention on Human Rights; to make provision with respect to holders of certain judicial offices who become judges of the European Court of Human Rights; and for connected purposes.   [9th November 1998]

BE IT ENACTED by the Queen's most Excellent Majesty, by and with the advice and consent of the Lords Spiritual and Temporal, and Commons, in this present Parliament assembled, and by the authority of the same, as follows:—

Introduction

1.   The Convention Rights

(1)   In this Act 'the Convention rights' means the rights and fundamental freedoms set out in—

(a)   Articles 2 to 12 and 14 of the Convention,

(b)   Articles 1 to 3 of the First Protocol, and

(c)   Articles 1 and 2 of the Sixth Protocol,

as read with Articles 16 to 18 of the Convention.

(2)   Those Articles are to have effect for the purposes of this Act subject to any designated derogation or reservation (as to which see sections 14 and 15).

(3)   The Articles are set out in Schedule 1.

(4)   The Secretary of State may by order make such amendments to this Act as he considers appropriate to reflect the effect, in relation to the United Kingdom, of a protocol.

(5)   In subsection (4) 'protocol' means a protocol to the Convention—

(a)   which the United Kingdom has ratified; or

(b)   which the United Kingdom has signed with a view to ratification.

(6)   No amendment may be made by an order under subsection (4) so as to come into force before the protocol concerned is in force in relation to the United Kingdom.

2.   Interpretation of Convention rights

(1)   A court or tribunal determining a question which has arisen in connection with a Convention right must take into account any—

(a)   judgment, decision, declaration or advisory opinion of the European Court of Human Rights,

(b)   opinion of the Commission given in a report adopted under Article 31 of the Convention,

(c)   decision of the Commission in connection with Article 26 or 27(2) of the Convention, or

(d)   decision of the Committee of Ministers taken under Article 46 of the Convention,

whenever made or given, so far as, in the opinion of the court or tribunal, it is relevant to the proceedings in which that question has arisen.

(2)   Evidence of any judgment, decision, declaration or opinion of which account may have to be taken under this section is to be given in proceedings before any court or tribunal in such manner as may be provided by rules.

(3)   In this section 'rules' means rules of court or, in the case of proceedings before a tribunal, rules made for the purposes of this section—

(a)   by the Lord Chancellor or the Secretary of State, in relation to any proceedings outside Scotland;

(b)   by the Secretary of State, in relation to proceedings in Scotland; or

(c)   by a Northern Ireland department, in relation to proceedings before a tribunal in Northern Ireland—

(i)   which deals with transferred matters; and

(ii)   for which no rules made under paragraph (a) are in force.

Legislation

3.   Interpretation of legislation

(1)   So far as it is possible to do so, primary legislation and subordinate legislation must be read and given effect in a way which is compatible with the Convention rights.

(2)   This section—

(a)   applies to primary legislation and subordinate legislation whenever enacted;

(b)   does not affect the validity, continuing operation or enforcement of any incompatible primary legislation; and

(c)   does not affect the validity, continuing operation or enforcement of any incompatible subordinate legislation if (disregarding any possibility of revocation) primary legislation prevents removal of the incompatibility.

4.   Declaration of incompatibility

(1)   Subsection (2) applies in any proceedings in which a court determines whether a provision of primary legislation is compatible with a Convention right.

(2)   If the court is satisfied that the provision is incompatible with a Convention right, it may make a declaration of that incompatibility.

(3)   Subsection (4) applies in any proceedings in which a court determines whether a provision of subordinate legislation, made in the exercise of a power conferred by primary legislation, is compatible with a Convention right.

(4)   If the court is satisfied—

(a)   that the provision is incompatible with a Convention right, and

(b)   that (disregarding any possibility of revocation) the primary legislation concerned prevents removal of the incompatibility, it may make a declaration of that incompatibility.

(5)   In this section 'court' means—

(a)   the House of Lords;

(b)   the Judicial Committee of the Privy Council;

(c)   the Courts-Martial Appeal Court;

(d)   in Scotland, the High Court of Justiciary sitting otherwise than as a trial court or the Court of Session;

(e)   in England and Wales or Northern Ireland, the High Court or the Court of Appeal.

(6)   A declaration under this section ('a declaration of incompatibility')—

(a)   does not affect the validity, continuing operation or enforcement of the provision in respect of which it is given; and

(b)   is not binding on the parties to the proceedings in which it is made.

5.   Right of Crown to intervene

(1)   Where a court is considering whether to make a declaration of incompatibility, the Crown is entitled to notice in accordance with rules of court.

(2)   In any case to which subsection (1) applies—

(a)   a Minister of the Crown (or a person nominated by him),

(b)   a member of the Scottish Executive,

(c)   a Northern Ireland Minister,

(d)   a Northern Ireland department,

is entitled, on giving notice in accordance with rules of court, to be joined as a party to the proceedings.

(3)   Notice under subsection (2) may be given at any time during the proceedings.

(4)   A person who has been made a party to criminal proceedings (other than in Scotland) as the result of a notice under subsection (2) may, with leave, appeal to the House of Lords against any declaration of incompatibility made in the proceedings.

(5)   In subsection (4)—

'criminal proceedings' includes all proceedings before the Courts-Martial Appeal Court; and

'leave' means leave granted by the court making the declaration of incompatibility or by the House of Lords.

Public authorities

6.   Acts of public authorities

(1)   It is unlawful for a public authority to act in a way which is incompatible with a Convention right.

(2)   Subsection (1) does not apply to an act if—

(a)   as the result of one or more provisions of primary legislation, the authority could not have acted differently; or (b)　in the case of one or more provisions of, or made under, primary legislation which cannot be read or given effect in a way which is compatible with the Convention rights, the authority was acting so as to give effect to or enforce those provisions.

(3)　In this section 'public authority' includes—

(a)　a court or tribunal, and

(b)　any person certain of whose functions are functions of a public nature, but does not include either House of Parliament or a person exercising functions in connection with proceedings in Parliament.

(4)　In subsection (3) 'Parliament' does not include the House of Lords in its judicial capacity.

(5)　In relation to a particular act, a person is not a public authority by virtue only of subsection (3)(b) if the nature of the act is private.

(6)　'An act' includes a failure to act but does not include a failure to—

(a)　introduce in, or lay before, Parliament a proposal for legislation; or

(b)　make any primary legislation or remedial order.

7.　Proceedings

(1)　A person who claims that a public authority has acted (or proposes to act) in a way which is made unlawful by section 6(1) may—

(a)　bring proceedings against the authority under this Act in the appropriate court or tribunal, or

(b)　rely on the Convention right or rights concerned in any legal proceedings,

but only if he is (or would be) a victim of the unlawful act.

(2)　In subsection (1)(a) 'appropriate court or tribunal' means such court or tribunal as may be determined in accordance with rules; and proceedings against an authority include a counterclaim or similar proceeding.

(3)　If the proceedings are brought on an application for judicial review, the applicant is to be taken to have a sufficient interest in relation to the unlawful act only if he is, or would be, a victim of that act.

(4)　If the proceedings are made by way of a petition for judicial review in Scotland, the applicant shall be taken to have title and interest to sue in relation to the unlawful act only if he is, or would be, a victim of that act.

(5)　Proceedings under subsection (1)(a) must be brought before the end of—

(a)　the period of one year beginning with the date on which the act complained of took place; or

(b)　such longer period as the court or tribunal considers equitable having regard to all the circumstances,

but that is subject to any rule imposing a stricter time limit in relation to the procedure in question.

(6)　In subsection (1)(b) 'legal proceedings' includes—

    (a)   proceedings brought by or at the instigation of a public authority; and

    (b)   an appeal against the decision of a court or tribunal.

    (7)   For the purposes of this section, a person is a victim of an unlawful act only if he would be a victim for the purposes of Article 34 of the Convention if proceedings were brought in the European Court of Human Rights in respect of that act.

    (8)   Nothing in this Act creates a criminal offence.

    (9)   In this section 'rules' means—

    (a)   in relation to proceedings before a court or tribunal outside Scotland, rules made by the Lord Chancellor or the Secretary of State for the purposes of this section or rules of court,

    (b)   in relation to proceedings before a court or tribunal in Scotland, rules made by the Secretary of State for those purposes,

    (c)   in relation to proceedings before a tribunal in Northern Ireland—

        (i)   which deals with transferred matters; and

        (ii)   for which no rules made under paragraph (a) are in force,

rules made by a Northern Ireland department for those purposes,

and includes provision made by order under section 1 of the Courts and Legal Services Act 1990.

    (10)   In making rules, regard must be had to section 9.

    (11)   The Minister who has power to make rules in relation to a particular tribunal may, to the extent he considers it necessary to ensure that the tribunal can provide an appropriate remedy in relation to an act (or proposed act) of a public authority which is (or would be) unlawful as a result of section 6(1), by order add to—

    (a)   the relief or remedies which the tribunal may grant; or

    (b)   the grounds on which it may grant any of them.

    (12)   An order made under subsection (11) may contain such incidental, supplemental, consequential or transitional provision as the Minister making it considers appropriate.

    (13)   'The Minister' includes the Northern Ireland department concerned.

8.   Judicial remedies

    (1)   In relation to any act (or proposed act) of a public authority which the court finds is (or would be) unlawful, it may grant such relief or remedy, or make such order, within its powers as it considers just and appropriate.

    (2)   But damages may be awarded only by a court which has power to award damages, or to order the payment of compensation, in civil proceedings.

    (3)   No award of damages is to be made unless, taking account of all the circumstances of the case, including—

    (a)   any other relief or remedy granted, or order made, in relation to the act in question (by that or any other court), and

(b) the consequences of any decision (of that or any other court) in respect of that act,

the court is satisfied that the award is necessary to afford just satisfaction to the person in whose favour it is made.

(4) In determining—

(a) whether to award damages, or

(b) the amount of an award,

the court must take into account the principles applied by the European Court of Human Rights in relation to the award of compensation under Article 41 of the Convention.

(5) A public authority against which damages are awarded is to be treated—

(a) in Scotland, for the purposes of section 3 of the Law Reform (Miscellaneous Provisions) (Scotland) Act 1940 as if the award were made in an action of damages in which the authority has been found liable in respect of loss or damage to the person to whom the award is made;

(b) for the purposes of the Civil Liability (Contribution) Act 1978 as liable in respect of damage suffered by the person to whom the award is made.

(6) In this section—

'court' includes a tribunal;

'damages' means damages for an unlawful act of a public authority; and

'unlawful' means unlawful under section 6(1).

9. Judicial acts

(1) Proceedings under section 7(1)(a) in respect of a judicial act may be brought only—

(a) by exercising a right of appeal;

(b) on an application (in Scotland a petition) for judicial review; or

(c) in such other forum as may be prescribed by rules.

(2) That does not affect any rule of law which prevents a court from being the subject of judicial review.

(3) In proceedings under this Act in respect of a judicial act done in good faith, damages may not be awarded otherwise than to compensate a person to the extent required by Article 5(5) of the Convention.

(4) An award of damages permitted by subsection (3) is to be made against the Crown; but no award may be made unless the appropriate person, if not a party to the proceedings, is joined.

(5) In this section—

'appropriate person' means the Minister responsible for the court concerned, or a person or government department nominated by him;

'court' includes a tribunal;

'judge' includes a member of a tribunal, a justice of the peace and a clerk or other officer entitled to exercise the jurisdiction of a court;

'judicial act' means a judicial act of a court and includes an act done on the instructions, or on behalf, of a judge; and
'rules' has the same meaning as in section 7(9).

Remedial action

10.   Power to take remedial action

(1)   This section applies if—

(a)   a provision of legislation has been declared under section 4 to be incompatible with a Convention right and, if an appeal lies—

(i)   all persons who may appeal have stated in writing that they do not intend to do so;

(ii)   the time for bringing an appeal has expired and no appeal has been brought within that time; or

(iii)   an appeal brought within that time has been determined or abandoned; or

(b)   it appears to a Minister of the Crown or Her Majesty in Council that, having regard to a finding of the European Court of Human Rights made after the coming into force of this section in proceedings against the United Kingdom, a provision of legislation is incompatible with an obligation of the United Kingdom arising from the Convention.

(2)   If a Minister of the Crown considers that there are compelling reasons for proceeding under this section, he may by order make such amendments to the legislation as he considers necessary to remove the incompatibility.

(3)   If, in the case of subordinate legislation, a Minister of the Crown considers—

(a)   that it is necessary to amend the primary legislation under which the subordinate legislation in question was made, in order to enable the incompatibility to be removed, and

(b)   that there are compelling reasons for proceeding under this section, he may by order make such amendments to the primary legislation as he considers necessary.

(4)   This section also applies where the provision in question is in subordinate legislation and has been quashed, or declared invalid, by reason of incompatibility with a Convention right and the Minister proposes to proceed under paragraph 2(b) of Schedule 2.

(5)   If the legislation is an Order in Council, the power conferred by subsection (2) or (3) is exercisable by Her Majesty in Council.

(6)   In this section 'legislation' does not include a Measure of the Church Assembly or of the General Synod of the Church of England.

(7)   Schedule 2 makes further provision about remedial orders.

Other rights and proceedings

11. Safeguard for existing human rights

A person's reliance on a Convention right does not restrict—

(a)   any other right or freedom conferred on him by or under any law having effect in any part of the United Kingdom; or

(b)   his right to make any claim or bring any proceedings which he could make or bring apart from sections 7 to 9.

12. Freedom of expression

(1)   This section applies if a court is considering whether to grant any relief which, if granted, might affect the exercise of the Convention right to freedom of expression.

(2)   If the person against whom the application for relief is made ('the respondent') is neither present nor represented, no such relief is to be granted unless the court is satisfied—

(a)   that the applicant has taken all practicable steps to notify the respondent; or

(b)   that there are compelling reasons why the respondent should not be notified.

(3)   No such relief is to be granted so as to restrain publication before trial unless the court is satisfied that the applicant is likely to establish that publication should not be allowed.

(4)   The court must have particular regard to the importance of the Convention right to freedom of expression and, where the proceedings relate to material which the respondent claims, or which appears to the court, to be journalistic, literary or artistic material (or to conduct connected with such material), to—

(a)   the extent to which—

(i)   the material has, or is about to, become available to the public; or

(ii)   it is, or would be, in the public interest for the material to be published;

(b)   any relevant privacy code.

(5)   In this section—

'court' includes a tribunal; and

'relief' includes any remedy or order (other than in criminal proceedings).

13. Freedom of thought, conscience and religion

(1)   If a court's determination of any question arising under this Act might affect the exercise by a religious organisation (itself or its members collectively) of the Convention right to freedom of thought, conscience and religion, it must have particular regard to the importance of that right.

(2)   In this section 'court' includes a tribunal.

Derogations and reservations

14. Derogations

(1)   In this Act 'designated derogation' means—

(a)   the United Kingdom's derogation from Article 5(3) of the Convention; and

(b)   any derogation by the United Kingdom from an Article of the Convention, or of any protocol to the Convention, which is designated for the purposes of this Act in an order made by the Secretary of State.

(2)   The derogation referred to in subsection (1)(a) is set out in Part I of Schedule 3.

(3)   If a designated derogation is amended or replaced it ceases to be a designated derogation.

(4)   But subsection (3) does not prevent the Secretary of State from exercising his power under subsection (1)(b) to make a fresh designation order in respect of the Article concerned.

(5)   The Secretary of State must by order make such amendments to Schedule 3 as he considers appropriate to reflect—

(a)   any designation order; or

(b)   the effect of subsection (3).

(6)   A designation order may be made in anticipation of the making by the United Kingdom of a proposed derogation.

15. Reservations

(1)   In this Act 'designated reservation' means—

(a)   the United Kingdom's reservation to Article 2 of the First Protocol to the Convention; and

(b)   any other reservation by the United Kingdom to an Article of the Convention, or of any protocol to the Convention, which is designated for the purposes of this Act in an order made by the Secretary of State.

(2)   The text of the reservation referred to in subsection (1)(a) is set out in Part 11 of Schedule 3.

(3)   If a designated reservation is withdrawn wholly or in part it ceases to be a designated reservation.

(4)   But subsection (3) does not prevent the Secretary of State from exercising his power under subsection (1)(b) to make a fresh designation order in respect of the Article concerned.

(5)   The Secretary of State must by order make such amendments to this Act as he considers appropriate to reflect—

(a)   any designation order; or

(b)   the effect of subsection (3).

16. Period for which designated derogations have effect

(1)   If it has not already been withdrawn by the United Kingdom, a designated derogation ceases to have effect for the purposes of this Act—

(a)   in the case of the derogation referred to in section 14(1)(a), at the end of the period of five years beginning with the date on which section 1(2) came into force;

(b)   in the case of any other derogation, at the end of the period of five years beginning with the date on which the order designating it was made.

(2)   At any time before the period—

(a)   fixed by subsection (1)(a) or (b), or

(b)   extended by an order under this subsection,

comes to an end, the Secretary of State may by order extend it by a further period of five years.

(3)   An order under section 14(1)(b) ceases to have effect at the end of the period for consideration, unless a resolution has been passed by each House approving the order.

(4)   Subsection (3) does not affect—

(a)   anything done in reliance on the order; or

(b)   the power to make a fresh order under section 14(1)(b).

(5)   In subsection (3) 'period for consideration' means the period of forty days beginning with the day on which the order was made.

(6)   In calculating the period for consideration, no account is to be taken of any time during which—

(a)   Parliament is dissolved or prorogued; or

(b)   both Houses are adjourned for more than four days.

(7)   If a designated derogation is withdrawn by the United Kingdom, the Secretary of State must by order make such amendments to this Act as he considers are required to reflect that withdrawal.

17. Periodic review of designated reservations

(1)   The appropriate Minister must review the designated reservation referred to in section 15(1)(a)—

(a)   before the end of the period of five years beginning with the date on which section 1(2) came into force; and

(b)   if that designation is still in force, before the end of the period of five years beginning with the date on which the last report relating to it was laid under subsection (3).

(2)   The appropriate Minister must review each of the other designated reservations (if any)—

(a)   before the end of the period of five years beginning with the date on which the order designating the reservation first came into force; and

(b)   if the designation is still in force, before the end of the period of five years beginning with the date on which the last report relating to it was laid under subsection (3).

(3)   The Minister conducting a review under this section must prepare a report on the result of the review and lay a copy of it before each House of Parliament.

Judges of the European Court of Human Rights

18.   Appointment to European Court of Human Rights

(1)   In this section 'judicial office' means the office of—

(a)   Lord Justice of Appeal, Justice of the High Court or Circuit judge, in England and Wales;

(b)   judge of the Court of Session or sheriff, in Scotland;

(c)   Lord Justice of Appeal, judge of the High Court or county court judge, in Northern Ireland.

(2)   The holder of a judicial office may become a judge of the European Court of Human Rights ('the Court') without being required to relinquish his office.

(3)   But he is not required to perform the duties of his judicial office while he is a judge of the Court.

(4)   In respect of any period during which he is a judge of the Court—

(a)   a Lord Justice of Appeal or Justice of the High Court is not to count as a judge of the relevant court for the purposes of section 2(1) or 4(1) of the Supreme Court Act 1981 (maximum number of judges) nor as a judge of the Supreme Court for the purposes of section 12(1) to (6) of that Act (salaries etc.);

(b)   a judge of the Court of Session is not to count as a judge of that court for the purposes of section 1(1) of the Court of Session Act 1988 (maximum number of judges) or of section 9(1)(c) of the Administration of Justice Act 1973 ('the 1973 Act') (salaries etc.);

(c)   a Lord Justice of Appeal or judge of the High Court in Northern Ireland is not to count as a judge of the relevant court for the purposes of section 2(1) or 3(1) of the Judicature (Northern Ireland) Act 1978 (maximum number of judges) nor as a judge of the Supreme Court of Northern Ireland for the purposes of section 9(1)(d) of the 1973 Act (salaries etc.);

(d)   a Circuit judge is not to count as such for the purposes of section 18 of the Courts Act 1971 (salaries etc.);

(e)   a sheriff is not to count as such for the purposes of section 14 of the Sheriff Courts (Scotland) Act 1907 (salaries etc.);

(f)   a county court judge of Northern Ireland is not to count as such for the purposes of section 106 of the County Courts Act (Northern Ireland) 1959 (salaries etc.).

(5) If a sheriff principal is appointed a judge of the Court, section 11(1) of the Sheriff Courts (Scotland) Act 1971 (temporary appointment of sheriff principal) applies, while he holds that appointment, as if his office is vacant.

(6) Schedule 4 makes provision about judicial pensions in relation to the holder of a judicial office who serves as a judge of the Court.

(7) The Lord Chancellor or the Secretary of State may by order make such transitional provision (including, in particular, provision for a temporary increase in the maximum number of judges) as he considers appropriate in relation to any holder of a judicial office who has completed his service as a judge of the Court.

Parliamentary procedure

19.   Statements of compatibility

(1) A Minister of the Crown in charge of a Bill in either House of Parliament must, before Second Reading of the Bill—

(a) make a statement to the effect that in his view the provisions of the Bill are compatible with the Convention rights ('a statement of compatibility'); or

(b) make a statement to the effect that although he is unable to make a statement of compatibility the government nevertheless wishes the House to proceed with the Bill.

(2) The statement must be in writing and be published in such manner as the Minister making it considers appropriate.

Supplemental

20.   Orders etc. under this Act

(1) Any power of a Minister of the Crown to make an order under this Act is exercisable by statutory instrument.

(2) The power of the Lord Chancellor or the Secretary of State to make rules (other than rules of court) under section 2(3) or 7(9) is exercisable by statutory instrument.

(3) Any statutory instrument made under section 14, 15 or 16(7) must be laid before Parliament.

(4) No order may be made by the Lord Chancellor or the Secretary of State under section 1(4), 7(11) or 16(2) unless a draft of the order has been laid before, and approved by, each House of Parliament.

(5) Any statutory instrument made under section 18(7) or Schedule 4, or to which subsection (2) applies, shall be subject to annulment in pursuance of a resolution of either House of Parliament.

(6) The power of a Northern Ireland department to make—

(a) rules under section 2(3)(c) or 7(9)(c), or

(b) an order under section 7(11),

is exercisable by statutory rule for the purposes of the Statutory Rules (Northern Ireland) Order 1979.

(7)   Any rules made under section 2(3)(c) or 7(9)(c) shall be subject to negative resolution; and section 41(6) of the Interpretation Act (Northern Ireland) 1954 (meaning of 'subject to negative resolution') shall apply as if the power to make the rules were conferred by an Act of the Northern Ireland Assembly.

(8)   No order may be made by a Northern Ireland department under section 7(11) unless a draft of the order has been laid before, and approved by, the Northern Ireland Assembly.

21.   Interpretation etc.

(1)   In this Act—

'amend' includes repeal and apply (with or without modifications);

'the appropriate Minister' means the Minister of the Crown having charge of the appropriate authorised government department (within the meaning of the Crown Proceedings Act 1947);

'the Commission' means the European Commission of Human Rights;

'the Convention' means the Convention for the Protection of Human Rights and Fundamental Freedoms, agreed by the Council of Europe at Rome on 4th November 1950 as it has effect for the time being in relation to the United Kingdom;

'declaration of incompatibility' means a declaration under section 4;

'Minister of the Crown' has the same meaning as in the Ministers of the Crown Act 1975;

'Northern Ireland Minister' includes the First Minister and the deputy First Minister in Northern Ireland;

'primary legislation' means any—

(a)   public general Act;

(b)   local and personal Act;

(c)   private Act;

(d)   Measure of the Church Assembly;

(e)   Measure of the General Synod of the Church of England;

(f)   Order in Council—

(i)   made in exercise of Her Majesty's Royal Prerogative;

(ii)   made under section 38(1)(a) of the Northern Ireland Constitution Act 1973 or the corresponding provision of the Northern Ireland Act 1998; or

(iii)   amending an Act of a kind mentioned in paragraph (a), (b) or (c);

and includes an order or other instrument made under primary legislation (otherwise than by the National Assembly for Wales, a member of the Scottish Executive, a Northern Ireland Minister or a Northern Ireland department) to the extent to which it operates to bring one or more provisions of that legislation into force or amends any primary legislation;

'the First Protocol' means the protocol to the Convention agreed at Paris on 20th March 1952;

'the Sixth Protocol' means the protocol to the Convention agreed at Strasbourg on 28th April 1983;

'the Eleventh Protocol' means the protocol to the Convention (restructuring the control machinery established by the Convention) agreed at Strasbourg on 11th May 1994;

'remedial order' means an order under section 10;

'subordinate legislation' means any—

(a)   Order in Council other than one—

(i)   made in exercise of Her Majesty's Royal Prerogative;

(ii)   made under section 38(1)(a) of the Northern Ireland Constitution Act 1973 or the corresponding provision of the Northern Ireland Act 1998; or

(iii)   amending an Act of a kind mentioned in the definition of primary legislation;

(b)   Act of the Scottish Parliament;

(c)   Act of the Parliament of Northern Ireland;

(d)   Measure of the Assembly established under section 1 of the Northern Ireland Assembly Act 1973;

(e)   Act of the Northern Ireland Assembly;

(f)   order, rules, regulations, scheme, warrant, byelaw or other instrument made under primary legislation (except to the extent to which it operates to bring one or more provisions of that legislation into force or amends any primary legislation);

(g)   order, rules, regulations, scheme, warrant, byelaw or other instrument made under legislation mentioned in paragraph (b), (c), (d) or (e) or made under an Order in Council applying only to Northern Ireland;

(h)   order, rules, regulations, scheme, warrant, byelaw or other instrument made by a member of the Scottish Executive, a Northern Ireland Minister or a Northern Ireland department in exercise of prerogative or other executive functions of Her Majesty which are exercisable by such a person on behalf of Her Majesty;

'transferred matters' has the same meaning as in the Northern Ireland Act 1998; and

'tribunal' means any tribunal in which legal proceedings may be brought.

(2)   The references in paragraphs (b) and (c) of section 2(1) to Articles are to Articles of the Convention as they had effect immediately before the coming into force of the Eleventh Protocol.

(3)   The reference in paragraph (d) of section 2(1) to Article 46 includes a reference to Articles 32 and 54 of the Convention as they had effect immediately before the coming into force of the Eleventh Protocol.

(4)   The references in section 2(1) to a report or decision of the Commission or a decision of the Committee of Ministers include references to a report or

decision made as provided by paragraphs 3, 4 and 6 of Article 5 of the Eleventh Protocol (transitional provisions).

(5)   Any liability under the Army Act 1955, the Air Force Act 1955 or the Naval Discipline Act 1957 to suffer death for an offence is replaced by a liability to imprisonment for life or any less punishment authorised by those Acts; and those Acts shall accordingly have effect with the necessary modifications.

22.   Short title, commencement, application and extent

(1)   This Act may be cited as the Human Rights Act 1998.

(2)   Sections 18, 20 and 21(5) and this section come into force on the passing of this Act.

(3)   The other provisions of this Act come into force on such day as the Secretary of State may by order appoint; and different days may be appointed for different purposes.

(4)   Paragraph (b) of subsection (1) of section 7 applies to proceedings brought by or at the instigation of a public authority whenever the act in question took place; but otherwise that subsection does not apply to an act taking place before the coming into force of that section.

(5)   This Act binds the Crown.

(6)   This Act extends to Northern Ireland.

(7)   Section 21(5), so far as it relates to any provision contained in the Army Act 1955, the Air Force Act 1955 or the Naval Discipline Act 1957, extends to any place to which that provision extends.

SCHEDULES

Section 1(3)

SCHEDULE 1
THE ARTICLES

PART I
THE CONVENTION

RIGHTS AND FREEDOMS

Article 2
Right to life

1.   Everyone's right to life shall be protected by law. No one shall be deprived of his life intentionally save in the execution of a sentence of a court following his conviction of a crime for which this penalty is provided by law.

2.   Deprivation of life shall not be regarded as inflicted in contravention of this Article when it results from the use of force which is no more than absolutely necessary:

(a)   in defence of any person from unlawful violence;

(b)   in order to effect a lawful arrest or to prevent the escape of a person lawfully detained;

(c)   in action lawfully taken for the purpose of quelling a riot or insurrection.

Article 3
Prohibition of torture

No one shall be subjected to torture or to inhuman or degrading treatment or punishment.

Article 4
Prohibition of slavery and forced labour

1.   No one shall be held in slavery or servitude.

2.   No one shall be required to perform forced or compulsory labour.

3.   For the purpose of this Article the term 'forced or compulsory labour' shall not include:

(a)   any work required to be done in the ordinary course of detention imposed according to the provisions of Article 5 of this Convention or during conditional release from such detention;

(b)   any service of a military character or, in case of conscientious objectors in countries where they are recognised, service exacted instead of compulsory military service;

(c)   any service exacted in case of an emergency or calamity threatening the life or well-being of the community;

(d)   any work or service which forms part of normal civic obligations.

Article 5
Right to liberty and security

1.   Everyone has the right to liberty and security of person. No one shall be deprived of his liberty save in the following cases and in accordance with a procedure prescribed by law:

(a)   the lawful detention of a person after conviction by a competent court;

(b)   the lawful arrest or detention of a person for non-compliance with the lawful order of a court or in order to secure the fulfilment of any obligation prescribed by law;

(c)   the lawful arrest or detention of a person effected for the purpose of bringing him before the competent legal authority on reasonable suspicion of having committed an offence or when it is reasonably considered necessary to prevent his committing an offence or fleeing after having done so;

(d)   the detention of a minor by lawful order for the purpose of educational supervision or his lawful detention for the purpose of bringing him before the competent legal authority;

(e)   the lawful detention of persons for the prevention of the spreading of infectious diseases, of persons of unsound mind, alcoholics or drug addicts or vagrants;

(f)   the lawful arrest or detention of a person to prevent his effecting an unauthorised entry into the country or of a person against whom action is being taken with a view to deportation or extradition.

2.   Everyone who is arrested shall be informed promptly, in a language which he understands, of the reasons for his arrest and of any charge against him.

3.   Everyone arrested or detained in accordance with the provisions of paragraph 1(c) of this Article shall be brought promptly before a judge or other officer authorised by law to exercise judicial power and shall be entitled to trial within a reasonable time or to release pending trial. Release may be conditioned by guarantees to appear for trial.

4.   Everyone who is deprived of his liberty by arrest or detention shall be entitled to take proceedings by which the lawfulness of his detention shall be decided speedily by a court and his release ordered if the detention is not lawful.

5.   Everyone who has been the victim of arrest or detention in contravention of the provisions of this Article shall have an enforceable right to compensation.

Article 6
Right to a fair trial

1.   In the determination of his civil rights and obligations or of any criminal charge against him, everyone is entitled to a fair and public hearing within a reasonable time by an independent and impartial tribunal established by law. Judgment shall be pronounced publicly but the press and public may be excluded from all or part of the trial in the interest of morals, public order or national security in a democratic society, where the interests of juveniles or the protection of the private life of the parties so require, or to the extent strictly necessary in the opinion of the court in special circumstances where publicity would prejudice the interests of justice.

2.   Everyone charged with a criminal offence shall be presumed innocent until proved guilty according to law.

3.   Everyone charged with a criminal offence has the following minimum rights:

(a)   to be informed promptly, in a language which he understands and in detail, of the nature and cause of the accusation against him;

(b)   to have adequate time and facilities for the preparation of his defence;

(c)   to defend himself in person or through legal assistance of his own choosing or, if he has not sufficient means to pay for legal assistance, to be given it free when the interests of justice so require;

(d)   to examine or have examined witnesses against him and to obtain the attendance and examination of witnesses on his behalf under the same conditions as witnesses against him;

(e)   to have the free assistance of an interpreter if he cannot understand or speak the language used in court.

Article 7
No punishment without law

1.   No one shall be held guilty of any criminal offence on account of any act or omission which did not constitute a criminal offence under national or international law at the time when it was committed. Nor shall a heavier penalty be imposed than the one that was applicable at the time the criminal offence was committed.

2.   This Article shall not prejudice the trial and punishment of any person for any act or omission which, at the time when it was committed, was criminal according to the general principles of law recognised by civilised nations.

Article 8
Right to respect for private and family life

1.   Everyone has the right to respect for his private and family life, his home and his correspondence.

2.   There shall be no interference by a public authority with the exercise of this right except such as is in accordance with the law and is necessary in a democratic society in the interests of national security, public safety or the economic well being of the country, for the prevention of disorder or crime, for the protection of health or morals, or for the protection of the rights and freedoms of others.

Article 9
Freedom of thought, conscience and religion

1.   Everyone has the right to freedom of thought, conscience and religion; this right includes freedom to change his religion or belief and freedom, either alone or in community with others and in public or private, to manifest his religion or belief, in worship, teaching, practice and observance.

2.   Freedom to manifest one's religion or beliefs shall be subject only to such limitations as are prescribed by law and are necessary in a democratic society in the interests of public safety, for the protection of public order, health or morals, or for the protection of the rights and freedoms of others.

Article 10
Freedom of expression

1.   Everyone has the right to freedom of expression. This right shall include freedom to hold opinions and to receive and impart information and ideas without interference by public authority and regardless of frontiers. This Article shall not prevent States from requiring the licensing of broadcasting, television or cinema enterprises.

2. The exercise of these freedoms, since it carries with it duties and responsibilities, may be subject to such formalities, conditions, restrictions or penalties as are prescribed by law and are necessary in a democratic society, in the interests of national security, territorial integrity or public safety, for the prevention of disorder or crime, for the protection of health or morals, for the protection of the reputation or rights of others, for preventing the disclosure of information received in confidence, or for maintaining the authority and impartiality of the judiciary.

Article 11
Freedom of assembly and association

1. Everyone has the right to freedom of peaceful assembly and to freedom of association with others, including the right to form and to join trade unions for the protection of his interests.

2. No restrictions shall be placed on the exercise of these rights other than such as are prescribed by law and are necessary in a democratic society in the interests of national security or public safety, for the prevention of disorder or crime, for the protection of health or morals or for the protection of the rights and freedoms of others. This Article shall not prevent the imposition of lawful restrictions on the exercise of these rights by members of the armed forces, of the police or of the administration of the State.

Article 12
Right to marry

Men and women of marriageable age have the right to marry and to found a family, according to the national laws governing the exercise of this right.

Article 14
Prohibition of discrimination

The enjoyment of the rights and freedoms set forth in this Convention shall be secured without discrimination on any ground such as sex, race, colour, language, religion, political or other opinion, national or social origin, association with a national minority, property, birth or other status.

Article 16
Restrictions on political activity of aliens

Nothing in Articles 10, 11 and 14 shall be regarded as preventing the High Contracting Parties from imposing restrictions on the political activity of aliens.

Article 17
Prohibition of abuse of rights

Nothing in this Convention may be interpreted as implying for any State, group or person any right to engage in any activity or perform any act aimed at the destruction of any of the rights and freedoms set forth herein or at their limitation to a greater extent than is provided for in the Convention.

Article 18
Limitation on use of restrictions on rights

The restrictions permitted under this Convention to the said rights and freedoms shall not be applied for any purpose other than those for which they have been prescribed.

PART II
THE FIRST PROTOCOL

Article 1
Protection of property

Every natural or legal person is entitled to the peaceful enjoyment of his possessions. No one shall be deprived of his possessions except in the public interest and subject to the conditions provided for by law and by the general principles of international law.

The preceding provisions shall not, however, in any way impair the right of a State to enforce such laws as it deems necessary to control the use of property in accordance with the general interest or to secure the payment of taxes or other contributions or penalties.

Article 2
Right to education

No person shall be denied the right to education. In the exercise of any functions which it assumes in relation to education and to teaching, the State shall respect the right of parents to ensure such education and teaching in conformity with their own religious and philosophical convictions.

Article 3
Right to free elections

The High Contracting Parties undertake to hold free elections at reasonable intervals by secret ballot, under conditions which will ensure the free expression of the opinion of the people in the choice of the legislature.

PART III
THE SIXTH PROTOCOL

Article 1
Abolition of the death penalty

The death penalty shall be abolished. No one shall be condemned to such penalty or executed.

Article 2
Death penalty in time of war

A State may make provision in its law for the death penalty in respect of acts committed in time of war or of imminent threat of war; such penalty shall be applied only in the instances laid down in the law and in accordance with its provisions. The State shall communicate to the Secretary General of the Council of Europe the relevant provisions of that law.

SCHEDULE 2
REMEDIAL ORDERS

Orders

1.—(1)   A remedial order may—

(a)   contain such incidental, supplemental, consequential or transitional provision as the person making it considers appropriate;

(b)   be made so as to have effect from a date earlier than that on which it is made;

(c)   make provision for the delegation of specific functions;

(d)   make different provision for different cases.

(2)   The power conferred by sub-paragraph (1)(a) includes—

(a)   power to amend primary legislation (including primary legislation other than that which contains the incompatible provision); and

(b)   power to amend or revoke subordinate legislation (including subordinate legislation other than that which contains the incompatible provision).

(3)   A remedial order may be made so as to have the same extent as the legislation which it affects.

(4)   No person is to be guilty of an offence solely as a result of the retrospective effect of a remedial order.

Procedure

2.   No remedial order may be made unless—

(a)   a draft of the order has been approved by a resolution of each House of Parliament made after the end of the period of 60 days beginning with the day on which the draft was laid; or

(b)   it is declared in the order that it appears to the person making it that, because of the urgency of the matter, it is necessary to make the order without a draft being so approved.

Orders laid in draft

3.—(1)   No draft may be laid under paragraph 2(a) unless—

(a)   the person proposing to make the order has laid before Parliament a document which contains a draft of the proposed order and the required information; and

(b)   the period of 60 days, beginning with the day on which the document required by this sub-paragraph was laid, has ended.

(2)   If representations have been made during that period, the draft laid under paragraph 2(a) must be accompanied by a statement containing—

(a)   a summary of the representations; and

(b)   if, as a result of the representations, the proposed order has been changed, details of the changes.

Urgent cases

4.—(1)   If a remedial order ('the original order') is made without being approved in draft, the person making it must lay it before Parliament, accompanied by the required information, after it is made.

(2)   If representations have been made during the period of 60 days beginning with the day on which the original order was made, the person making it must (after the end of that period) lay before Parliament a statement containing—

(a)   a summary of the representations; and

(b)   if, as a result of the representations, he considers it appropriate to make changes to the original order, details of the changes.

(3)   If sub-paragraph (2)(b) applies, the person making the statement must—

(a)   make a further remedial order replacing the original order; and

(b)   lay the replacement order before Parliament.

(4)   If, at the end of the period of 120 days beginning with the day on which the original order was made, a resolution has not been passed by each House approving the original or replacement order, the order ceases to have effect (but without that affecting anything previously done under either order or the power to make a fresh remedial order).

Definitions

5.   In this Schedule—

'representations' means representations about a remedial order (or proposed remedial order) made to the person making (or proposing to make) it and includes any relevant Parliamentary report or resolution; and

'required information' means—

(a)   an explanation of the incompatibility which the order (or proposed order) seeks to remove, including particulars of the relevant declaration, finding or order; and

(b)   a statement of the reasons for proceeding under section 10 and for making an order in those terms.

Calculating periods

6.   In calculating any period for the purposes of this Schedule, no account is to be taken of any time during which—

(a)   Parliament is dissolved or prorogued; or

(b)   both Houses are adjourned for more than four days.

SCHEDULE 3
DEROGATION AND RESERVATION

PART I
DEROGATION

The 1988 notification

The United Kingdom Permanent Representative to the Council of Europe presents his compliments to the Secretary General of the Council, and has the honour to convey the following information in order to ensure compliance with the obligations of Her Majesty's Government in the United Kingdom under Article 15(3) of the Convention for the Protection of Human Rights and Fundamental Freedoms signed at Rome on 4 November 1950.

There have been in the United Kingdom in recent years campaigns of organised terrorism connected with the affairs of Northern Ireland which have manifested themselves in activities which have included repeated murder, attempted murder, maiming, intimidation and violent civil disturbance and in bombing and fire raising which have resulted in death, injury and widespread destruction of property. As a result, a public emergency within the meaning of Article 15(1) of the Convention exists in the United Kingdom.

The Government found it necessary in 1974 to introduce and since then, in cases concerning persons reasonably suspected of involvement in terrorism connected with the affairs of Northern Ireland, or of certain offences under the legislation, who have been detained for 48 hours, to exercise powers enabling further detention without charge, for periods of up to five days, on the authority of the Secretary of State. These powers are at present to be found in Section 12 of the Prevention of Terrorism (Temporary Provisions) Act 1984, Article 9 of the Prevention of Terrorism (Supplemental Temporary Provisions) Order 1984 and Article 10 of the Prevention of Terrorism (Supplemental Temporary Provisions) (Northern Ireland) Order 1984.

Section 12 of the Prevention of Terrorism (Temporary Provisions) Act 1984 provides for a person whom a constable has arrested on reasonable grounds of suspecting him to be guilty of an offence under Section 1, 9 or 10 of the Act, or to be or to have been involved in terrorism connected with the affairs of Northern Ireland, to be detained in right of the arrest for up to 48 hours and thereafter, where the Secretary of State extends the detention period, for up to a further five days. Section 12 substantially re-enacted Section 12 of the Prevention of Terrorism (Temporary Provisions) Act 1976 which, in turn, substantially re-enacted Section 7 of the Prevention of Terrorism (Temporary Provisions) Act 1974.

Article 10 of the Prevention of Terrorism (Supplemental Temporary Provisions) (Northern Ireland) Order 1984 (SI 1984/417) and Article 9 of the Prevention of Terrorism (Supplemental Temporary Provisions) Order 1984 (SI 1984/418) were both made under Sections 13 and 14 of and Schedule 3 to the 1984 Act and substantially re-enacted powers of detention in Orders made under the 1974 and 1976 Acts. A person who is being examined under Article 4 of either Order on his arrival in, or on seeking to leave, Northern Ireland or Great Britain for the purpose of determining whether he is or has been involved in terrorism connected with the affairs of Northern Ireland, or whether there are grounds for suspecting that he has committed an offence under Section 9 of the 1984 Act, may be detained under Article 9 or 10, as appropriate, pending the conclusion of his examination. The period of this examination may exceed 12 hours if an examining officer has reasonable grounds for suspecting him to be or to have been involved in acts of terrorism connected with the affairs of Northern Ireland.

Where such a person is detained under the said Article 9 or 10 he may be detained for up to 48 hours on the authority of an examining officer and thereafter, where the Secretary of State extends the detention period, for up to a further five days.

In its judgment of 29 November 1988 in the Case of *Brogan and Others*, the European Court of Human Rights held that there had been a violation of Article 5(3) in respect of each of the applicants, all of whom had been detained under Section 12 of the 1984 Act. The Court held that even the shortest of the four periods of detention concerned, namely four days and six hours, fell outside the constraints as to time permitted by the first part of Article 5(3). In addition, the Court held that there had been a violation of Article 5(5) in the case of each applicant.

Following this judgment, the Secretary of State for the Home Department informed Parliament on 6 December 1988 that, against the background of the terrorist campaign, and the over-riding need to bring terrorists to justice, the Government did not believe that the maximum period of detention should be reduced. He informed Parliament that the Government were examining the matter with a view to responding to the judgment. On 22 December 1988, the Secretary of State further informed Parliament that it remained the Government's wish, if it could be achieved, to find a judicial process under which extended detention might be reviewed and where appropriate authorised by a judge or other judicial officer. But a further period of reflection and consultation was necessary before the Government could bring forward a firm and final view.

Since the judgment of 29 November 1988 as well as previously, the Government have found it necessary to continue to exercise, in relation to terrorism connected with the affairs of Northern Ireland, the powers described above enabling further detention without charge for periods of up to 5 days, on the authority of the Secretary of State, to the extent strictly required by the exigencies of the situation to enable necessary enquiries and investigations properly to be completed in order to decide whether criminal proceedings should be instituted. To the extent that the exercise of these powers may be inconsistent with the obligations imposed by the Convention the Government has availed itself of the right of derogation conferred by Article 15(1) of the Convention and will continue to do so until further notice.

Dated 23 December 1988.

The 1989 notification

The United Kingdom Permanent Representative to the Council of Europe presents his compliments to the Secretary General of the Council, and has the honour to convey the following information.

In his communication to the Secretary General of 23 December 1988, reference was made to the introduction and exercise of certain powers under section 12 of the Prevention of Terrorism (Temporary Provisions) Act 1984, Article 9 of the Prevention of Terrorism (Supplemental Temporary Provisions) Order 1984 and Article 10 of the Prevention of Terrorism (Supplemental Temporary Provisions) (Northern Ireland) Order 1984.

These provisions have been replaced by section 14 of and paragraph 6 of Schedule 5 to the Prevention of Terrorism (Temporary Provisions) Act 1989, which make comparable provision. They came into force on 22 March 1989. A copy of these provisions is enclosed.

The United Kingdom Permanent Representative avails himself of this opportunity to renew to the Secretary General the assurance of his highest consideration.

23 March 1989.

PART II
RESERVATION

At the time of signing the present (First) Protocol, I declare that, in view of certain provisions of the Education Acts in the United Kingdom, the principle affirmed in the second sentence of Article 2 is accepted by the United Kingdom only so far as it is compatible with the provision of efficient instruction and training, and the avoidance of unreasonable public expenditure.

Dated 20 March 1952. Made by the United Kingdom Permanent Representative to the Council of Europe.

SCHEDULE 4
JUDICIAL PENSIONS

Duty to make orders about pensions

1.—(1)   The appropriate Minister must by order make provision with respect to pensions payable to or in respect of any holder of a judicial office who serves as an ECHR judge.

(2)   A pensions order must include such provision as the Minister making it considers is necessary to secure that—

(a)   an ECHR judge who was, immediately before his appointment as an ECHR judge, a member of a judicial pension scheme is entitled to remain as a member of that scheme;

(b)   the terms on which he remains a member of the scheme are those which would have been applicable had he not been appointed as an ECHR judge; and

(c)   entitlement to benefits payable in accordance with the scheme continues to be determined as if, while serving as an ECHR judge, his salary was that which would (but for section 18(4)) have been payable to him in respect of his continuing service as the holder of his judicial office.

Contributions

2.   A pensions order may, in particular, make provision—

(a)   for any contributions which are payable by a person who remains a member of a scheme as a result of the order, and which would otherwise be payable by deduction from his salary, to be made otherwise than by deduction from his salary as an ECHR judge; and

(b)   for such contributions to be collected in such manner as may be determined by the administrators of the scheme.

Amendments of other enactments

3.   A pensions order may amend any provision of, or made under, a pensions Act in such manner and to such extent as the Minister making the order considers necessary or expedient to ensure the proper administration of any scheme to which it relates.

Definitions

4.   In this Schedule—

'appropriate Minister' means—

(a)   in relation to any judicial office whose jurisdiction is exercisable exclusively in relation to Scotland, the Secretary of State; and

(b)   otherwise, the Lord Chancellor;

'ECHR judge' means the holder of a judicial office who is serving as a judge of the Court;

'judicial pension scheme' means a scheme established by and in accordance with a pensions Act;

'pensions Act means—

(a)   the County Courts Act (Northern Ireland) 1959;

(b)   the Sheriffs' Pensions (Scotland) Act 1961;

(c)   the Judicial Pensions Act 1981; or

(d)   the Judicial Pensions and Retirement Act 1993; and

'pensions order' means an order made under paragraph 1.

Appendix Two

European Convention on Human Rights

CONVENTION FOR THE PROTECTION OF HUMAN RIGHTS AND
FUNDAMENTAL FREEDOMS AS AMENDED BY PROTOCOL NO. 11
(Date of entry into force 1 November 1998)

The governments signatory hereto, being members of the Council of Europe,

Considering the Universal Declaration of Human Rights proclaimed by the General Assembly of the United Nations on 10th December 1948;

Considering that this Declaration aims at securing the universal and effective recognition and observance of the Rights therein declared;

Considering that the aim of the Council of Europe is the achievement of greater unity between its members and that one of the methods by which that aim is to be pursued is the maintenance and further realisation of human rights and fundamental freedoms;

Reaffirming their profound belief in those fundamental freedoms which are the foundation of justice and peace in the world and are best maintained on the one hand by an effective political democracy and on the other by a common understanding and observance of the human rights upon which they depend;

Being resolved, as the governments of European countries which a re like-minded and have a common heritage of political traditions, ideals, freedom and the rule of law, to take the first steps for the collective enforcement of certain of the rights stated in the Universal Declaration,

Have agreed as follows:

Article 1
Obligation to respect human rights

The High Contracting Parties shall secure to everyone within their jurisdiction the rights and freedoms defined in Section I of this Convention.

Section I — Rights and freedoms

Article 2
Right to life

1   Everyone's right to life shall be protected by law. No one shall be deprived of his life intentionally save in the execution of a sentence of a court following his conviction of a crime for which this penalty is provided by law.

2   Deprivation of life shall not be regarded as inflicted in contravention of this article when it results from the use of force which is no more than absolutely necessary:

 a   in defence of any person from unlawful violence;

 b   in order to effect a lawful arrest or to prevent the escape of a person lawfully detained;

 c   in action lawfully taken for the purpose of quelling a riot or insurrection.

Article 3
Prohibition of torture

No one shall be subjected to torture or to inhuman or degrading treatment or punishment.

Article 4
Prohibition of slavery and forced labour

1   No one shall be held in slavery or servitude.

2   No one shall be required to perform forced or compulsory labour.

3   For the purpose of this article the term 'forced or compulsory labour' shall not include:

 a   any work required to be done in the ordinary course of detention imposed according to the provisions of Article 5 of this Convention or during conditional release from such detention;

 b   any service of a military character or, in case of conscientious objectors in countries where they are recognised, service exacted instead of compulsory military service;

 c   any service exacted in case of an emergency or calamity threatening the life or well-being of the community;

 d   any work or service which forms part of normal civic obligations.

Article 5
Right to liberty and security

1   Everyone has the right to liberty and security of person. No one shall be deprived of his liberty save in the following cases and in accordance with a procedure prescribed by law:

 a   the lawful detention of a person after conviction by a competent court;

    b   the lawful arrest or detention of a person for non-compliance with the lawful order of a court or in order to secure the fulfilment of any obligation prescribed by law;

    c   the lawful arrest or detention of a person effected for the purpose of bringing him before the competent legal authority on reasonable suspicion of having committed an offence or when it is reasonably considered necessary to prevent his committing an offence or fleeing after having done so;

    d   the detention of a minor by lawful order for the purpose of educational supervision or his lawful detention for the purpose of bringing him before the competent legal authority;

    e   the lawful detention of persons for the prevention of the spreading of infectious diseases, of persons of unsound mind, alcoholics or drug addicts or vagrants;

    f   the lawful arrest or detention of a person to prevent his effecting an unauthorised entry into the country or of a person against whom action is being taken with a view to deportation or extradition.

2   Everyone who is arrested shall be informed promptly, in a language which he understands, of the reasons for his arrest and of any charge against him.

3   Everyone arrested or detained in accordance with the provisions of paragraph 1.c of this article shall be brought promptly before a judge or other officer authorised by law to exercise judicial power and shall be entitled to trial within a reasonable time or to release pending trial. Release may be conditioned by guarantees to appear for trial.

4   Everyone who is deprived of his liberty by arrest or detention shall be entitled to take proceedings by which the lawfulness of his detention shall be decided speedily by a court and his release ordered if the detention is not lawful.

5   Everyone who has been the victim of arrest or detention in contravention of the provisions of this article shall have an enforceable right to compensation.

Article 6
Right to a fair trial

1   In the determination of his civil rights and obligations or of any criminal charge against him, everyone is entitled to a fair and public hearing within a reasonable time by an independent and impartial tribunal established by law. Judgment shall be pronounced publicly but the press and public may be excluded from all or part of the trial in the interests of morals, public order or national security in a democratic society, where the interests of juveniles or the protection of the private life of the parties so require, or to the extent strictly necessary in the opinion of the court in special circumstances where publicity would prejudice the interests of justice.

2   Everyone charged with a criminal offence shall be presumed innocent until proved guilty according to law.

3   Everyone charged with a criminal offence has the following minimum rights:

   a   to be informed promptly, in a language which he understands and in detail, of the nature and cause of the accusation against him;

   b   to have adequate time and facilities for the preparation of his defence;

   c   to defend himself in person or through legal assistance of his own choosing or, if he has not sufficient means to pay for legal assistance, to be given it free when the interests of justice so require;

   d   to examine or have examined witnesses against him and to obtain the attendance and examination of witnesses on his behalf under the same conditions as witnesses against him;

   e   to have the free assistance of an interpreter if he cannot understand or speak the language used in court.

Article 7
No punishment without law

1   No one shall be held guilty of any criminal offence on account of any act or omission which did not constitute a criminal offence under national or international law at the time when it was committed. Nor shall a heavier penalty be imposed than the one that was applicable at the time the criminal offence was committed.

2   This article shall not prejudice the trial and punishment of any person for any act or omission which, at the time when it was committed, was criminal according to the general principles of law recognised by civilised nations.

Article 8
Right to respect for private and family life

1   Everyone has the right to respect for his private and family life, his home and his correspondence.

2   There shall be no interference by a public authority with the exercise of this right except such as is in accordance with the law and is necessary in a democratic society in the interests of national security, public safety or the economic well-being of the country, for the prevention of disorder or crime, for the protection of health or morals, or for the protection of the rights and freedoms of others.

Article 9
Freedom of thought, conscience and religion

1   Everyone has the right to freedom of thought, conscience and religion; this right includes freedom to change his religion or belief and freedom, either alone or in community with others and in public or private, to manifest his religion or belief, in worship, teaching, practice and observance.

2   Freedom to manifest one's religion or beliefs shall be subject only to such limitations as are prescribed by law and are necessary in a democratic society in the interests of public safety, for the protection of public order, health or morals, or for the protection of the rights and freedoms of others.

Article 10
Freedom of expression

1   Everyone has the right to freedom of expression. This right shall include freedom to hold opinions and to receive and impart information and ideas without interference by public authority and regardless of frontiers. This article shall not prevent States from requiring the licensing of broadcasting, television or cinema enterprises.

2   The exercise of these freedoms, since it carries with it dudes and responsibilities, may be subject to such formalities, conditions, restrictions or penalties as are prescribed by law and are necessary in a democratic society, in the interests of national security, territorial integrity or public safety, for the prevention of disorder or crime, for the protection of health or morals, for the protection of the reputation or rights of others, for preventing the disclosure of information received in confidence, or for maintaining the authority and impartiality of the judiciary.

Article 11
Freedom of assembly and association

1   Everyone has the right to freedom of peaceful assembly and to freedom of association with others, including the right to form and to join trade unions for the protection of his interests.

2   No restrictions shall be placed on the exercise of these rights other than such as are prescribed by law and are necessary in a democratic society in the interests of national security or public safety, for the prevention of disorder or crime, for the protection of health or morals or for the protection of the rights and freedoms of others. This article shall not prevent the imposition of lawful restrictions on the exercise of these rights by members of the armed forces, of the police or of the administration of the State.

Article 12
Right to marry

Men and women of marriageable age have the right to marry and to found a family, according to the national laws governing the exercise of this right.

Article 13
Right to an effective remedy

Everyone whose rights and freedoms as set forth in this Convention are violated shall have an effective remedy before a national authority notwithstanding that the violation has been committed by persons acting in an official capacity.

Article 14
Prohibition of discrimination

The enjoyment of the rights and freedoms set forth in this Convention shall be secured without discrimination on any ground such as sex, race, colour, language, religion, political or other opinion, national or social origin, association with a national minority, property, birth or other status.

Article 15
Derogation in time of emergency

1   In time of war or other public emergency threatening the life of the nation any High Contracting Party may take measures derogating from its obligations under this Convention to the extent strictly required by the exigencies of the situation, provided that such measures are not inconsistent with its other obligations under international law.

2   No derogation from Article 2, except in respect of deaths resulting from lawful acts of war, or from Articles 3, 4 (paragraph 1) and 7 shall be made under this provision.

3   Any High Contracting Party availing itself of this right of derogation shall keep the Secretary General of the Council of Europe fully informed of the measures which it has taken and the reasons therefor. It shall also inform the Secretary General of the Council of Europe when such measures have ceased to operate and the provisions of the Convention are again being fully executed.

Article 16
Restrictions on political activity of aliens

Nothing in Articles 10, 11 and 14 shall be regarded as preventing the High Contracting Parties from imposing restrictions on the political activity of aliens.

Article 17
Prohibition of abuse of rights

Nothing in this Convention may be interpreted as implying for any State, group or person any right to engage in any activity or perform any act aimed at the destruction of any of the rights and freedoms set forth herein or at their limitation to a greater extent than is provided for in the Convention.

Article 18
Limitation on use of restrictions on rights

The restrictions permitted under this Convention to the said rights and freedoms shall not be applied for any purpose other than those for which they have been prescribed.

Section II — European Court of Human Rights

Article 19
Establishment of the Court

To ensure the observance of the engagements undertaken by the High Contracting Parties in the Convention and the Protocols thereto, there shall be set up a European Court of Human Rights, hereinafter referred to as 'the Court'. It shall function on a permanent basis.

Article 20
Number of judges

The Court shall consist of a number of judges equal to that of the High Contracting Parties.

Article 21
Criteria for office

1   The judges shall be of high moral character and must either possess the qualifications required for appointment to high judicial office or be jurisconsults of recognised competence.

2   The judges shall sit on the Court in their individual capacity.

3   During their term of office the judges shall not engage in any activity which is incompatible with their independence, impartiality or with the demands of a full-time office; all questions arising from the application of this paragraph shall be decided by the Court.

Article 22
Election of judges

1   The judges shall be elected by the Parliamentary Assembly with respect to each High Contracting Party by a majority of votes cast from a list of three candidates nominated by the High Contracting Party.

2   The same procedure shall be followed to complete the Court in the event of the accession of new High Contracting Parties and in filling casual vacancies.

Article 23
Terms of office

1   The judges shall be elected for a period of six years. They may be re-elected. However, the terms of office of one-half of the judges elected at the first election shall expire at the end of three years.

2   The judges whose terms of office are to expire at the end of the initial period of three years shall be chosen by lot by the Secretary General of the Council of Europe immediately after their election.

3   In order to ensure that, as far as possible, the terms of office of one-half of the judges are renewed every three years, the Parliamentary Assembly may decide, before proceeding to any subsequent election, that the term or terms of office of one or more judges to be elected shall be for a period other than six years but not more than nine and not less than three years.

4   In cases where more than one term of office is involved and where the Parliamentary Assembly applies the preceding paragraph, the allocation of the terms of office shall be effected by a drawing of lots by the Secretary General of the Council of Europe immediately after the election.

5   A judge elected to replace a judge whose term of office has not expired shall hold office for the remainder of his predecessor's term.

6   The terms of office of judges shall expire when they reach the age of 70.

7   The judges shall hold office until replaced. They shall, however, continue to deal with such cases as they already have under consideration.

Article 24
Dismissal

No judge may be dismissed from his office unless the other judges decide by a majority of two-thirds that he has ceased to fulfil the required conditions.

Article 25
Registry and legal secretaries

The Court shall have a registry, the functions and organisation of which shall be laid down in the rules of the Court. The Court shall be assisted by legal secretaries.

Article 26
Plenary Court

The plenary Court shall

    a   elect its President and one or two Vice-Presidents for a period of three years; they may be re-elected;

    b   set up Chambers, constituted for a fixed period of time;

    c   elect the Presidents of the Chambers of the Court; they may be re-elected;

    d   adopt the rules of the Court, and

    e   elect the Registrar and one or more Deputy Registrars.

Article 27
Committees, Chambers and Grand Chamber

1   To consider cases brought before it, the Court shall sit in committees of three judges, in Chambers of seven judges and in a Grand Chamber of seventeen judges. The Court's Chambers shall set up committees for a fixed period of time.

2   There shall sit as an *ex officio* member of the Chamber and the Grand Chamber the judge elected in respect of the State Party concerned or, if there is none or if he is unable to sit, a person of its choice who shall sit in the capacity of judge.

3   The Grand Chamber shall also include the President of the Court, the Vice-Presidents, the Presidents of the Chambers and other judges chosen in accordance with the rules of the Court. When a case is referred to the Grand Chamber under Article 43, no judge from the Chamber which rendered the judgment shall sit in the Grand Chamber, with the exception of the President of the Chamber and the judge who sat in respect of the State Party concerned.

Article 28
Declarations of inadmissibility by committees

A committee may, by a unanimous vote, declare inadmissible or strike out of its list of cases an application submitted under Article 34 where such a decision can be taken without further examination. The decision shall be final.

Article 29
Decisions by Chambers on admissibility and merits

1   If no decision is taken under Article 28, a Chamber shall decide on the admissibility and merits of individual applications submitted under Article 34.

2   A Chamber shall decide on the admissibility and merits of inter-State applications submitted under Article 33.

3   The decision on admissibility shall be taken separately unless the Court, in exceptional cases, decides otherwise.

Article 30
Relinquishment of jurisdiction to the Grand Chamber

Where a case pending before a Chamber raises a serious question affecting the interpretation of the Convention or the protocols thereto, or where the resolution of a question before the Chamber might have a result inconsistent with a judgment previously delivered by the Court, the Chamber may, at any time before it has rendered its judgment, relinquish jurisdiction in favour of the Grand Chamber, unless one of the parties to the case objects.

Article 31
Powers of the Grand Chamber

The Grand Chamber shall

    a   determine applications submitted either under Article 33 or Article 34 when a Chamber has relinquished jurisdiction under Article 30 or when the case has been referred to it under Article 43; and

    b   consider requests for advisory opinions submitted under Article 47.

Article 32
Jurisdiction of the Court

    1   The jurisdiction of the Court shall extend to all matters concerning the interpretation and application of the Convention and the protocols thereto which are referred to it as provided in Articles 33, 34 and 47.

    2   In the event of dispute as to whether the Court has jurisdiction, the Court shall decide.

Article 33
Inter-State cases

Any High Contracting Party may refer to the Court any alleged breach of the provisions of the Convention and the protocols thereto by another High Contracting Party

Article 34
Individual applications

The Court may receive applications from any person, non-governmental organisation or group of individuals claiming to be the victim of a violation by one of the High Contracting Parties of the rights set forth in the Convention or the protocols thereto. The High Contracting Parties undertake not to hinder in any way the effective exercise of this right.

Article 35
Admissibility criteria

    1   The Court may only deal with the matter after all domestic remedies have been exhausted, according to the generally recognised rules of international law, and within a period of six months from the date on which the final decision was taken.

    2   The Court shall not deal with any application submitted under Article 34 that

    a   is anonymous; or

    b   is substantially the same as a matter that has already been examined by the Court or has already been submitted to another procedure of international investigation or settlement and contains no relevant new information.

3   The Court shall declare inadmissible any individual application submitted under Article 34 which it considers incompatible with the provisions of the Convention or the protocols thereto, manifestly ill-founded, or an abuse of the right of application.

4   The Court shall reject any application which it considers inadmissible under this Article. It may do so at any stage of the proceedings.

Article 36
Third party intervention

1   In all cases before a Chamber of the Grand Chamber, a High Contracting Party one of whose nationals is an applicant shall have the right to submit written comments and to take part in hearings.

2   The President of the Court may, in the interest of the proper administration of justice, invite any High Contracting Party which is not a party to the proceedings or any person concerned who is not the applicant to submit written comments or take part in hearings.

Article 37
Striking out applications

1   The Court may at any stage of the proceedings decide to strike an application out of its list of cases where the circumstances lead to the conclusion that

   a   the applicant does not intend to pursue his application; or

   b   the matter has been resolved; or

   c   for any other reason established by the Court, it is no longer justified to continue the examination of the application.

However, the Court shall continue the examination of the application if respect for human rights as defined in the Convention and the protocols thereto so requires.

2   The Court may decide to restore an application to its list of cases if it considers that the circumstances justify such a course.

Article 38
Examination of the case and friendly settlement proceedings

1   If the Court declares the application admissible, it shall

   a   pursue the examination of the case, together with the representatives of the parties, and if need be, undertake an investigation, for the effective conduct of which the States concerned shall furnish all necessary facilities;

   b   place itself at the disposal of the parties concerned with a view to securing a friendly settlement of the matter on the basis of respect for human rights as defined in the Convention and the protocols thereto.

2   Proceedings conducted under paragraph 1.b shall be confidential.

Article 39
Finding of a friendly settlement

If a friendly settlement is effected, the Court shall strike the case out of its list by means of a decision which shall be confined to a brief statement of the facts and of the solution reached.

Article 40
Public hearings and access to documents

1   Hearings shall be in public unless the Court in exceptional circumstances decides otherwise.

2   Documents deposited with the Registrar shall be accessible to the public unless the President of the Court decides otherwise.

Article 41
Just satisfaction

If the Court finds that there has been a violation of the Convention or the protocols thereto, and if the internal law of the High Contracting Party concerned allows only partial reparation to be made, the Court shall, if necessary afford just satisfaction to the injured party.

Article 42
Judgments of Chambers

Judgments of Chambers shall become final in accordance with the provisions of Article 44, paragraph 2.

Article 43
Referral to the Grand Chamber

1   Within a period of three months from the date of the judgment of the Chamber, any party to the case may, in exceptional cases, request that the case be referred to the Grand Chamber.

2   A panel of five judges of the Grand Chamber shall accept the request if the case raises a serious question affecting the interpretation or application of the Convention or the protocols thereto, or a serious issue of general importance.

3   If the panel accepts the request, the Grand Chamber shall decide the case by means of a judgment.

Article 44
Final judgments

1   The judgment of the Grand Chamber shall be final.

2   The judgment of a Chamber shall become final

a   when the parties declare that they will not request that the case be referred to the Grand Chamber; or b   three months after the date of the judgment, if reference of the case to the Grand Chamber has not been requested; or

c   when the panel of the Grand Chamber rejects the request to refer under Article 43.

3   The final judgment shall be published.

Article 45
Reasons for judgments and decisions

1   Reasons shall be given for judgments as well as for decisions declaring applications admissible or inadmissible.

2   If a judgment does not represent, in whole or in part, the unanimous opinion of the judges, any judge shall be entitled to deliver a separate opinion.

Article 46
Binding force and execution of judgments

1   The High Contracting Parties undertake to abide by the final judgment of the Court in any case to which they are parties.

2   The final judgment of the Court shall be transmitted to the Committee of Ministers, which shall supervise its execution.

Article 47
Advisory opinions

1   The Court may, at the request of the Committee of Ministers, give advisory opinions on legal questions concerning the interpretation of the Convention and the protocols thereto.

2   Such opinions shall not deal with any question relating to the content or scope of the rights or freedoms defined in Section I of the Convention and the protocols thereto, or with any other question which the Court or the Committee of Ministers might have to consider in consequence of any such proceedings as could be instituted in accordance with the Convention.

3   Decisions of the Committee of Ministers to request an advisory opinion of the Court shall require a majority vote of the representatives entitled to sit on the Committee.

Article 48
Advisory jurisdiction of the Court

The Court shall decide whether a request for an advisory opinion submitted by the Committee of Ministers is within its competence as defined in Article 47.

Article 49
Reasons for advisory opinions

1   Reasons shall be given for advisory opinions of the Court.

2   If the advisory opinion does not represent, in whole or in part, the unanimous opinion of the judges, any judge shall be entitled to deliver a separate opinion.

3   Advisory opinions of the Court shall be communicated to the Committee of Ministers.

Article 50
Expenditure on the Court

The expenditure on the Court shall be borne by the Council of Europe.

Article 51
Privileges and immunities of judges

The judges shall be entitled, during the exercise of their functions, to the privileges and immunities provided for in Article 40 of the Statute of the Council of Europe and in the agreements made thereunder.

Section III — Miscellaneous provisions

Article 52
Inquiries by the Secretary General

On receipt of a request from the Secretary General of the Council of Europe any High Contracting Party shall furnish an explanation of the manner in which its internal law ensures the effective implementation of any of the provisions of the Convention.

Article 53
Safeguard for existing human rights

Nothing in this Convention shall be construed as limiting or derogating from any of the human rights and fundamental freedoms which may be ensured under the laws of any High Contracting Party or under any other agreement to which it is a Party.

Article 54
Powers of the Committee of Ministers

Nothing in this Convention shall prejudice the powers conferred on the Committee of Ministers by the Statute of the Council of Europe.

Article 55
Exclusion of other means of dispute settlement

The High Contracting Parties agree that, except by special agreement, they will not avail themselves of treaties, conventions or declarations in force between them for the purpose of submitting, by way of petition, a dispute arising out of the interpretation or application of this Convention to a means of settlement other than those provided for in this Convention.

Article 56
Territorial application

1   Any State may at the time of its ratification or at any time thereafter declare by notification addressed to the Secretary General of the Council of Europe that the present Convention shall, subject to paragraph 4 of this Article, extend to all or any of the territories for whose international relations it is responsible.

2   The Convention shall extend to the territory or territories named in the notification as from the thirtieth day after the receipt of this notification by the Secretary General of the Council of Europe.

3   The provisions of this Convention shall be applied in such territories with due regard, however, to local requirements.

4   Any State which has made a declaration in accordance with paragraph 1 of this article may at any time thereafter declare on behalf of one or more of the territories to which the declaration relates that it accepts the competence of the Court to receive applications from individuals, non-governmental organisations or groups of individuals as provided by Article 34 of the Convention.

Article 57
Reservations

1   Any State may, when signing this Convention or when depositing its instrument of ratification, make a reservation in respect of any particular provision of the Convention to the extent that any law then in force in its territory is not in conformity with the provision. Reservations of a general character shall not be permitted under this article.

2   Any reservation made under this article shall contain a brief statement of the law concerned.

Article 58
Denunciation

1   A High Contracting Party may denounce the present Convention only after the expiry of five years from the date on which it became a party to it and after six months' notice contained in a notification addressed to the Secretary General of the Council of Europe, who shall inform the other High Contracting Parties.

2   Such a denunciation shall not have the effect of releasing the High Contracting Party concerned from its obligations under this Convention in respect of any act which, being capable of constituting a violation of such obligations, may have been performed by it before the date at which the denunciation became effective.

3   Any High Contracting Party which shall cease to be a member of the Council of Europe shall cease to be a Party to this Convention under the same conditions.

4   The Convention may be denounced in accordance with the provisions of the preceding paragraphs in respect of any territory to which it has been declared to extend under the terms of Article 56.

Article 59
Signature and ratification

1   This Convention shall be open to the signature of the members of the Council of Europe. It shall be ratified. Ratifications shall be deposited with the Secretary General of the Council of Europe.

2   The present Convention shall come into force after the deposit of ten instruments of ratification.

3   As regards any signatory ratifying subsequently, the Convention shall come into force at the date of the deposit of its instrument of ratification.

4   The Secretary General of the Council of Europe shall notify all the members of the Council of Europe of the entry into force of the Convention, the names of the High Contracting Parties who have ratified it, and the deposit of all instruments of ratification which may be effected subsequently.

Done at Rome this 4th day of November 1950, in English and French, both texts being equally authentic, in a single copy which shall remain deposited in the archives of the Council of Europe.

The Secretary General shall transmit certified copies to each of the signatories.

PROTOCOL [NO. 1] TO THE CONVENTION FOR THE PROTECTION OF HUMAN RIGHTS AND FUNDAMENTAL FREEDOMS, AS AMENDED BY PROTOCOL NO. 11

The governments signatory hereto, being members of the Council of Europe,

Being resolved to take steps to ensure the collective enforcement of certain rights and freedoms other than those already included in Section I of the Convention for the Protection of Human Rights and Fundamental Freedoms signed at Rome on 4 November 1950 (hereinafter referred to as 'the Convention'),

Have agreed as follows:

Article 1
Protection of property

Every natural or legal person is entitled to the peaceful enjoyment of his possessions. No one shall be deprived of his possessions except in the public interest and subject to the conditions provided for by law and by the general principles of international law.

The preceding provisions shall not, however, in any way impair the right of a State to enforce such laws as it deems necessary to control the use of property in accordance with the general interest or to secure the payment of taxes or other contributions or penalties.

Article 2
Right to education

No person shall be denied the right to education. In the exercise of any functions which it assumes in relation to education and to teaching, the State shall respect the right of parents to ensure such education and teaching in conformity with their own religious and philosophical convictions.

Article 3
Right to free elections

The High Contracting Parties undertake to hold free elections at reasonable intervals by secret ballot, under conditions which will ensure the free expression of the opinion of the people in the choice of the legislature.

Article 4
Territorial application

Any High Contracting Party may at the time of signature or ratification or at any time thereafter communicate to the Secretary General of the Council of Europe a declaration stating the extent to which it undertakes that the provisions of the present Protocol shall apply to such of the territories for the international relations of which it is responsible as are named therein.

Any High Contracting Party which has communicated a declaration in virtue of the preceding paragraph may from time to time communicate a further declaration modifying the terms of any former declaration or terminating the application of the provisions of this Protocol in respect of any territory.

A declaration made in accordance with this article shall be deemed to have been made in accordance with paragraph 1 of Article 56 of the Convention.

Article 5
Relationship to the Convention

As between the High Contracting Parties the provisions of Articles 1, 2, 3 and 4 of this Protocol shall be regarded as additional articles to the Convention and all the provisions of the Convention shall apply accordingly.

Article 6
Signature and ratification

This Protocol shall be open for signature by the members of the Council of Europe, who are the signatories of the Convention; it shall be ratified at the same time as or after the ratification of the Convention. It shall enter into force after the deposit of ten instruments of ratification. As regards any signatory ratifying subsequently, the Protocol shall enter into force at the date of the deposit of its instrument of ratification.

The instruments of ratification shall be deposited with the Secretary General of the Council of Europe, who will notify all members of the names of those who have ratified.

Done at Paris on the 20th day of March 1952, in English and French, both texts being equally authentic, in a single copy which shall remain deposited in the archives of the Council of Europe. The Secretary General shall transmit certified copies to each of the signatory governments.

PROTOCOL NO. 4 TO THE CONVENTION FOR THE PROTECTION OF HUMAN RIGHTS AND FUNDAMENTAL FREEDOMS, SECURING CERTAIN RIGHTS AND FREEDOMS OTHER THAN THOSE ALREADY INCLUDED IN THE CONVENTION AND IN THE FIRST PROTOCOL THERETO, AS AMENDED BY PROTOCOL NO. 11

The governments signatory hereto, being members of the Council of Europe,

Being resolved to take steps to ensure the collective enforcement of certain rights and freedoms other than those already included in Section 1 of the Convention for the Protection of Human Rights and Fundamental Freedoms signed at Rome on 4th November 1950 (hereinafter referred to as the 'Convention') and in Articles 1 to 3 of the First Protocol to the Convention, signed at Paris on 20th March 1952,

Have agreed as follows:

Article 1
Prohibition of imprisonment for debt

No one shall be deprived of his liberty merely on the ground of inability to fulfil a contractual obligation.

Article 2
Freedom of movement

1   Everyone lawfully within the territory of a State shall, within that territory, have the right to liberty of movement and freedom to choose his residence.

2   Everyone shall be free to leave any country, including his own.

3   No restrictions shall be placed on the exercise of these rights other than such as are in accordance with law and are necessary in a democratic society in the interests of national security or public safety, for the maintenance of *ordre public*, for the prevention of crime, for the protection of health or morals, or for the protection of the rights and freedoms of others.

4   The rights set forth in paragraph 1 may also be subject, in particular areas, to restrictions imposed in accordance with law and justified by the public interest in a democratic society.

Article 3
Prohibition of expulsion of nationals

1   No one shall be expelled, by means either of an individual or of a collective measure, from the territory of the State of which he is a national.

2   No one shall be deprived of the right to enter the territory of the state of which he is a national.

Article 4
Prohibition of collective expulsion of aliens

Collective expulsion of aliens is prohibited.

Article 5
Territorial application

1   Any High Contracting Party may, at the time of signature or ratification of this Protocol, or at any time thereafter, communicate to the Secretary General of the Council of Europe a declaration stating the extent to which it undertakes that the provisions of this Protocol shall apply to such of the territories for the international relations of which it is responsible as are named therein.

2   Any High Contracting Party which has communicated a declaration in virtue of the preceding paragraph may, from time to time, communicate a further declaration modifying the terms of any former declaration or terminating the application of the provisions of this Protocol in respect of any territory.

3   A declaration made in accordance with this article shall be deemed to have been made in accordance with paragraph 1 of Article 56 of the Convention.

4   The territory of any State to which this Protocol applies by virtue of ratification or acceptance by that State, and each territory to which this Protocol is applied by virtue of a declaration by that State under this article, shall be treated as separate territories for the purpose of the references in Articles 2 and 3 to the territory of a State.

5   Any State which has made a declaration in accordance with paragraph 1 or 2 of this Article may at any time thereafter declare on behalf of one or more of the territories to which the declaration relates that it accepts the competence of the Court to receive applications from individuals, non-governmental organisations or groups of individuals as provided in Article 34 of the Convention in respect of all or any of Articles 1 to 4 of this Protocol.

Article 6
Relationship to the Convention

As between the High Contracting Parties the provisions of Articles 1 to 5 of this Protocol shall be regarded as additional Articles to the Convention, and all the provisions of the Convention shall apply accordingly.

Article 7
Signature and ratification

1   This Protocol shall be open for signature by the members of the Council of Europe who are the signatories of the Convention; it shall be ratified at the same time as or after the ratification of the Convention. It shall enter into force after the deposit of five instruments of ratification. As regards any signatory ratifying subsequently, the Protocol shall enter into force at the date of the deposit of its instrument of ratification.

2   The instruments of ratification shall be deposited with the Secretary General of the Council of Europe, who will notify all members of the names of those who have ratified.

In witness whereof the undersigned, being duly authorised thereto, have signed this Protocol.

Done at Strasbourg, this 16th day of September 1963, in English and in French, both texts being equally authoritative, in a single copy which shall remain deposited in the archives of the Council of Europe. The Secretary General shall transmit certified copies to each of the signatory states.

PROTOCOL NO. 6 TO THE CONVENTION FOR THE PROTECTION OF HUMAN RIGHTS AND FUNDAMENTAL FREEDOMS CONCERNING THE ABOLITION OF THE DEATH PENALTY, AS AMENDED BY PROTOCOL NO. 11

The member States of the Council of Europe, signatory to this Protocol to the Convention for the Protection of Human Rights and Fundamental Freedoms, signed at Rome on 4 November 1950 (hereinafter referred to as 'the Convention'),

Considering that the evolution that has occurred in several member States of the Council of Europe expresses a general tendency in favour of abolition of the death penalty;

Have agreed as follows:

Article 1
Abolition of the death penalty

The death penalty shall be abolished. No-one shall be condemned to such penalty or executed.

Article 2
Death penalty in time of war

A State may make provision in its law for the death penalty in respect of acts committed in time of war or of imminent threat of war; such penalty shall be applied only in the instances laid down in the law and in accordance with its provisions. The State shall communicate to the Secretary General of the Council of Europe the relevant provisions of that law.

Article 3
Prohibition of derogations

No derogation from the provisions of this Protocol shall be made under Article 15 of the Convention.

Article 4
Prohibition of reservations

No reservation may be made under Article 57 of the Convention in respect of the provisions of this Protocol.

Article 5
Territorial application

1   Any State may at the time of signature or when depositing its instrument of ratification, acceptance or approval, specify the territory or territories to which this Protocol shall apply.

2   Any State may at any later date, by a declaration addressed to the Secretary General of the Council of Europe, extend the application of this Protocol to any other territory specified in the declaration. In respect of such territory the Protocol shall enter into force on the first day of the month following the date of receipt of such declaration by the Secretary General.

3   Any declaration made under the two preceding paragraphs may, in respect of any territory specified in such declaration, be withdrawn by a notification addressed to the Secretary General. The withdrawal shall become effective on the first day of the month following the date of receipt of such notification by the Secretary General.

Article 6
Relationship to the Convention

As between the States Parties the provisions of Articles 1 to 5 of this Protocol shall be regarded as additional articles to the Convention and all the provisions of the Convention shall apply accordingly.

Article 7
Signature and ratification

The Protocol shall be open for signature by the member States of the Council of Europe, signatories to the Convention. It shall be subject to ratification, acceptance or approval. A member State of the Council of Europe may not ratify, accept or approve this Protocol unless it has, simultaneously or previously, ratified the Convention. Instruments of ratification, acceptance or approval shall be deposited with the Secretary General of the Council of Europe.

Article 8
Entry into force

1   This Protocol shall enter into force on the first day of the month following the date on which five member States of the Council of Europe have expressed their consent to be bound by the Protocol in accordance with the provisions of Article 7.

2   In respect of any member State which subsequently expresses its consent to be bound by it, the Protocol shall enter into force on the first day of the month following the date of the deposit of the instrument of ratification, acceptance or approval.

Article 9
Depositary functions

The Secretary General of the Council of Europe shall notify the member States of the Council of:

a   any signature;

b   the deposit of any instrument of ratification, acceptance or approval;

c   any date of entry into force of this Protocol in accordance with Articles 5 and 8;

d   any other act, notification or communication relating to this Protocol.

In witness whereof the undersigned, being duly authorised thereto, have signed this Protocol.

Done at Strasbourg, this 28th day of April 1983, in English and in French, both texts being equally authentic, in a single copy which shall be deposited in the archives of the Council of Europe. The Secretary General of the Council of Europe shall transmit certified copies to each member State of the Council of Europe.

PROTOCOL NO. 7 TO THE CONVENTION FOR THE PROTECTION OF HUMAN RIGHTS AND FUNDAMENTAL FREEDOMS, AS AMENDED BY PROTOCOL NO. 11

The member States of the Council of Europe signatory hereto,

Being resolved to take further steps to ensure the collective enforcement of certain rights and freedoms by means of the Convention for the Protection of Human Rights and Fundamental Freedoms signed at Rome on 4 November 1950 (hereinafter referred to as 'the Convention'),

Have agreed as follows

Article 1
Procedural safeguards relating to expulsion of aliens

1   An alien lawfully resident in the territory of a State shall not be expelled therefrom except in pursuance of a decision reached in accordance with law and shall be allowed:

a   to submit reasons against his expulsion,

b   to have his case reviewed, and

c   to be represented for these purposes before the competent authority or a person or persons designated by that authority.

2   An alien may be expelled before the exercise of his rights under paragraph 1.a, b and c of this Article, when such expulsion is necessary in the interests of public order or is grounded on reasons of national security.

Article 2
Right of appeal in criminal matters

1   Everyone convicted of a criminal offence by a tribunal shall have the right to have his conviction or sentence reviewed by a higher tribunal. The exercise of this right, including the grounds on which it may be exercised, shall be governed by law.

2   This right may be subject to exceptions in regard to offences of a minor character, as prescribed by law, or in cases in which the person concerned was tried in the first instance by the highest tribunal or was convicted following an appeal against acquittal.

Article 3
Compensation for wrongful conviction

When a person has by a final decision been convicted of a criminal offence and when subsequently his conviction has been reversed, or he has been pardoned, on the ground that a new or newly discovered fact shows conclusively that there has been a miscarriage of justice, the person who has suffered punishment as a result of such conviction shall be compensated according to the law or the practice of the State concerned, unless it is proved that the non-disclosure of the unknown fact in time is wholly or partly attributable to him.

Article 4
Right not to be tried or punished twice

1   No one shall be liable to be tried or punished again in criminal proceedings under the jurisdiction of the same State for an offence for which he has already been finally acquitted or convicted in accordance with the law and penal procedure of that State.

2   The provisions of the preceding paragraph shall not prevent the reopening of the case in accordance with the law and penal procedure of the State concerned, if there is evidence of new or newly discovered facts, or if there has been a fundamental defect in the previous proceedings, which could affect the outcome of the case.

3   No derogation from this Article shall be made under Article 15 of the Convention.

Article 5
Equality between spouses

Spouses shall enjoy equality of rights and responsibilities of a private law character between them, and in their relations with their children, as to marriage, during marriage and in the event of its dissolution. This Article shall not prevent States from taking such measures as are necessary in the interests of the children.

Article 6
Territorial application

1   Any State may at the time of signature or when depositing its instrument of ratification, acceptance or approval, specify the territory or territories to which the Protocol shall apply and state the extent to which it undertakes that the provisions of this Protocol shall apply to such territory or territories.

2   Any State may at any later date, by a declaration addressed to the Secretary General of the Council of Europe, extend the application of this Protocol to any other territory specified in the declaration. In respect of such territory the Protocol shall enter into force on the first day of the month following the expiration of a period of two months after the date of receipt by the Secretary General of such declaration.

3   Any declaration made under the two preceding paragraphs may, in respect of any territory specified in such declaration, be withdrawn or modified by a notification addressed to the Secretary General. The withdrawal or modification shall become effective on the first day of the month following the expiration of a period of two months after the date of receipt of such notification by the Secretary General.

4   A declaration made in accordance with this Article shall be deemed to have been made in accordance with paragraph 1 of Article 56 of the Convention.

5   The territory of any State to which this Protocol applies by virtue of ratification, acceptance or approval by that State, and each territory to which this Protocol is applied by virtue of a declaration by that State under this Article, may be treated as separate territories for the purpose of the reference in Article 1 to the territory of a State.

6   Any State which has made a declaration in accordance with paragraph 1 or 2 of this Article may at any time thereafter declare on behalf of one or more of the territories to which the declaration relates that it accepts the competence of the Court to receive applications from individuals, non-governmental organisations or groups of individuals as provided in Article 34 of the Convention in respect of Articles 1 to 5 of this Protocol.

Article 7
Relationship to the Convention

As between the States Parties, the provisions of Article 1 to 6 of this Protocol shall be regarded as additional Articles to the Convention, and all the provisions of the Convention shall apply accordingly.

Article 8
Signature and ratification

This Protocol shall be open for signature by member States of the Council of Europe which have signed the Convention. It is subject to ratification, acceptance or approval. A member State of the Council of Europe may not ratify, accept or approve this Protocol without previously or simultaneously ratifying the Convention. Instruments of ratification, acceptance or approval shall be deposited with the Secretary General of the Council of Europe.

Article 9
Entry into force

1   This Protocol shall enter into force on the first day of the month following the expiration of a period of two months after the date on which seven member States of the Council of Europe have expressed their consent to be bound by the Protocol in accordance with the provisions of Article 8.

2   In respect of any member State which subsequently expresses its consent to be bound by it, the Protocol shall enter into force on the first day of the month following the expiration of a period of two months after the date of the deposit of the instrument of ratification, acceptance or approval.

Article 10
Depositary functions

The Secretary General of the Council of Europe shall notify all the member States of the Council of Europe of:

a   any signature;

b   the deposit of any instrument of ratification, acceptance or approval;

c   any date of entry into force of this Protocol in accordance with Articles 6 and 9;

d   any other act, notification or declaration relating to this Protocol.

In witness whereof the undersigned, being duly authorised thereto, have signed this Protocol.

Done at Strasbourg, this 22nd day of November 1984, in English and French, both texts being equally authentic, in a single copy which shall be deposited in the archives of the Council of Europe. The Secretary General of the Council of Europe shall transmit certified copies to each member State of the Council of Europe.

PROTOCOL NO. 12 TO THE CONVENTION FOR THE PROTECTION OF HUMAN RIGHTS AND FUNDAMENTAL FREEDOMS

The member states of the Council of Europe signatory hereto,

Having regard to the fundamental principle according to which all persons are equal before the law and are entitled to the equal protection of the law;

Being resolved to take further steps to promote the equality of all persons through the collective enforcement of a general prohibition of discrimination by means of the Convention for the Protection of Human Rights and Fundamental Freedoms signed at Rome on 4 November 1950 (hereinafter referred to as 'the Convention');

Reaffirming that the principle of non-discrimination does not prevent States Parties from taking measures in order to promote full and effective equality, provided that there is an objective and reasonable justification for those measures,

Have agreed as follows:

Article 1
General prohibition of discrimination

1   The enjoyment of any right set forth by law shall be secured without discrimination on any ground such as sex, race, colour, language, religion, political or other opinion, national or social origin, association with a national minority, property, birth or other status.

2   No one shall be discriminated against by any public authority on any ground such as those mentioned in paragraph 1.

Article 2
Territorial application

1   Any state may, at the time of signature or when depositing its instrument of ratification, acceptance or approval, specify the territory or territories to which this Protocol shall apply.

2   Any state may at any later date, by a declaration addressed to the Secretary General of the Council of Europe, extend the application of this Protocol to any other territory specified in the declaration, in respect of such territory the Protocol shall enter into force on the first day of the month following the expiration of a period of three months after the date of receipt by the Secretary General of such declaration.

3   Any declaration made under the two preceding paragraphs may, in respect of any territory specified in such declaration, be withdrawn or modified by a notification addressed to the Secretary General. The withdrawal or modification shall become effective on the first day of the month following the expiration of a period of three months after the date of receipt of such notification by the Secretary General.

4   A declaration made in accordance with this article shall be deemed to have been made in accordance with paragraph 1 of Article 56 of the Convention.

5   Any state which has made a declaration in accordance with paragraph 1 or 2 of this article may at any time thereafter declare on behalf of one or more of the territories to which the declaration relates that it accepts the competence of the Court to receive applications from individuals, non-governmental organisations or groups of individuals as provided by Article 34 of the Convention in respect of Article 1 of this Protocol.

Article 3
Relationship to the Convention

As between the States Parties, the provisions of Articles 1 and 2 of this Protocol shall be regarded as additional articles to the Convention, and all the provisions of the Convention shall apply accordingly.

Article 4
Signature and ratification

This Protocol shall be open for signature by member states of the Council of Europe which have signed the Convention. It is subject to ratification, acceptance or approval. A member state of the Council of Europe may not ratify, accept or approve this Protocol without previously or simultaneously ratifying the Convention. Instruments of ratification, acceptance or approval shall be deposited with the Secretary General of the Council of Europe.

Article 5
Entry into force

1   This Protocol shall enter into force on the first day of the month following the expiration of a period of three months after the date on which ten member states of the Council of Europe have expressed their consent to be bound by the Protocol in accordance with the provisions of Article 4.

2   In respect of any member state which subsequently expresses its consent to be bound by it, the Protocol shall enter into force on the first day of the month following the expiration of a period of three months after the date of the deposit of the instrument of ratification, acceptance or approval.

Article 6
Depositary functions

The Secretary General of the Council of Europe shall notify all the member states of the Council of Europe of:

a   any signature;

b   the deposit of any instrument of ratification, acceptance or approval;

c   any date of entry into force of this Protocol in accordance with Articles 2 and 5;

d   any other act, notification or communication relating to this Protocol.

In witness whereof the undersigned, being duly authorised thereto, have signed this Protocol.

Done at ...., this .... day of .... 2000, in English and French, both texts being equally authentic, in a single copy which shall be deposited in the archives of the Council of Europe. The Secretary General of the Council of Europe shall transmit certified copies to each member state of the Council of Europe.

Index